TV C[illegible]
The Ultimate Guide to 70s and 80s Pop Culture

Edited by Graham Kibble-White

Visit the TV Cream popular nostalgia website at
www.tv.cream.org

First published in 2005 by
Virgin Books
Thames Wharf Studios
Rainville Rd
London W6 9HA

ISBN 0 7535 1080 4

Design and typesetting by Phoenix Photosetting, Chatham, Kent

Printed and bound by Bookmarque

Contents

Cover image: logos on badges are reproduced by kind permission of the following licence holders:

Ask Aspel, Radio 1, Grange Hill, Beeb, Jigsaw – BBC
Grange Hill – Mersey Television
Ladybird – Ladybird logo copyright © Ladybird Books Ltd, reproduced by permission of Ladybird Books Ltd
Quatro – 'Quatro' is a registered trade mark of The Coca-Cola Company and is reproduced with kind permission from The Coca-Cola Company
Milk's gotta lotta bottle – The Dairy Council
Rod Hull – International Artistes/Toby Hull
ATV logo – London Features International Ltd
Look-In – IPC Media
Bros – The Press Association
Weetabix – Weetabix Ltd
Tomorrow People and Magpie – FremantleMedia Enterprises Ltd

ABOUT THE AUTHORS

Graham Kibble-White is a journalist and creator of www.offthetelly.co.uk. He's currently deputy TV editor at the Press Association and has written freelance for various television-related magazines and www.bbc.co.uk. In 2002, he penned *Twenty Years of Brookside* for Carlton Books and has since contributed a chapter to the *BFI Television Handbook 2005*. He's been involved with *TV Cream* since about 1999 (he thinks).

Chris Hughes is a journalist who has been writing for *TV Cream* since 1998. He was the author of *Four Four Two: Great Footballers* for Virgin Books, and has contributed to several volumes in the *Rough Guide* series for Penguin. He has appeared as an interviewee on assorted nostalgia programmes for Channel Four and Five, and written for innumerable magazines, some of which are still going.

Ian Jones began writing for *TV Cream* in 2000. He edits the site's weekly email guide to digital TV and radio, and has participated in numerous programmes about television history. He's also contributed telly-related articles to www.bbc.co.uk and various magazines, and his first book, *Morning Glory: A History of British Breakfast Television*, was published by Kelly Books in 2004.

Jack Kibble-White has written for *ScriptWriter* magazine, www.bbc.co.uk, and – since 1999 – *TV Cream*. He has acted as programme consultant on a number of Channel Four entertainment documentaries and contributed to BBC4's *Time Shift* series, as well as making occasional appearances on Five Live and Channel Five, usually to talk about old telly.

Phil Norman is the one to blame, having founded *TV Cream* in the summer of 1997. In the years since, it has grown from a tiny repository of Fred Harris anecdotes into a very large repository of Fred Harris anecdotes. In the meantime, he has contributed to numerous nostalgia-related magazine articles and TV programmes.

Steve Williams is a writer and researcher who, since 2000, has compiled *TV Cream*'s weekly email guide to terrestrial television, a service which has been described as both 'excellent' and 'perilously obsessive'. He has also supplied research for a number of books and TV programmes and written for *Radio Times*.

ACKNOWLEDGEMENTS

Thanks go out to Andrew Collins for that quote, general support and just for being a thoroughly decent bloke. Get in there! Plus, a nod of appreciation to Gary Gillatt, for making the necessary introductions. He's the nicest man in *Doctor Who* fandom, apparently.

Extra special appreciation and respect goes to everyone at www.tv.cream.org. You're all great, but in particular we're tipping our hats to: Steve Berry, Chris Diamond, Nick Dimmock, Nick Mailer, Jane Redfern, Ian Tomkinson, Simon Tyers and TJ Worthington. Purveyors of The Right Kind of Nostalgia, all.

Hello There!

It's the mid-1970s. From out of the TV set comes a bass guitar sounding a crunching, urgent riff as a red Jag pulls into the BBC's Birmingham studios. A kettledrum boings and the brass section kicks into life. A man in a sheepskin jacket throws himself off the top of an office block and a roller-skating nutter clad in a white boiler suit careers into a brown settee.

Oh yes. ***Pebble Mill at One*** is just starting and you've managed to secure the day off school having successfully persuaded your mother of the debilitating nature of that stomach ache.

'You all right?' she asks. 'Still feeling a bit sick', you reply, shovelling down another triangle of Marmite on toast. But, of course, in reality everything's ace.

While the rest of the world are dreading an afternoon of ***Music and Movement*** and praying that – just for some excitement – someone might find a dead bat on the roof of the bicycle shed and use it as a football, you're enjoying some private time with your parent and, even more importantly, the fantastically dazzling world of light chat, cooking ecclesiastics, musical intermissions and motorcycle display teams that precedes this afternoon's visit to *Camberwick Green*.

It's this sort of memory, specific to one but common to many, that is the impetus for this book.

If you grew up in the 1970s and 1980s, it's impossible to recollect your childhood without recourse to contemporary pop culture. A birthday party enlivened by the presentation of a long lusted-after ***Big Trak***; a tall tale from an uncle that was so funny you blew ***Top Deck*** out your nose; a car journey enlivened by a family singalong to Fiddler's Dram; a summer holiday morning blighted by the non-arrival of your ***Krazy*** comic and – oh no! – the Belfast gang on *Why Don't You . . . ?* These toys, fizzy drinks, songs, comics and telly programmes were perhaps made to be thrown away, but they've become the beacons for a generation's youth.

TV Cream's aim is to relight a few of these torches. We've trawled through the two decades in question buffing up memories of over 300 pop-cultural products. Some you'll recall with little help from us (the ***Cabbage Patch Kids***!), others you'll have clean forgotten about until you chance upon them in our demented grab bag (surely no one's even uttered the phrase ***'Captain Zep Space Detective'*** since 1984?). But if we've done our job right, most should get whatever part of you it is that's supposed to pang, panging like mad.

WHAT IS TV CREAM?

Well, that's a good question – and we're afraid the answer is: we're off of the Internet. *TV Cream* (that's www.tv.cream.org) is the much fancied online destination for anyone who wants to dig up information on British pop culture from – yep – the 1970s and 1980s.

Created in 1997, which in web terms is dead long ago, the site is a crazy conglomeration of hard fact, hazy memories and mild profanity. ***Look-In*** with swearing, basically.

WHAT IS IN THIS BOOK?

Within these pages you'll find all-new material that builds on the irreverent but fact-based ethos we've been plying online. Set sail for laffs and hardcore infotainment!

Everything – no matter how arcane or transient – from the worlds of TV, radio, comics, annuals, books, magazines, pop, sweets, food and drink, toys, school and fashion that we consider crucial in defining the era is included. Naturally, there's a huge emphasis on TV here, reflecting its dominant position in the world of pop culture, but we hope other stuff also gets a fair shake of the stick.

So, what was our criteria for deciding which items merited inclusion? Well, the grand plan was to write about those things that, while encapsulating the time in which they came to prominence, failed to really transcend it (and, weirdly, that includes something like ***Commando*** comic which is somehow still running today). With that in mind, programmes like *Doctor Who* didn't make the cut. A fine specimen of British telly, it's still so ubiquitous and celebrated that an image of Tom Baker shooting the breeze with Davros could just as easily evoke last week's repeat on UKTV Gold, rather than a 1975 adventure in time, space and Surrey.

Somewhat perversely, though, the range of ***Doctor Who* annuals** which accompanied most of the show's original run do merit inclusion. With their daffy stories, curiously drawn comic strips and blatant page-filling fact features they could only have been a product of their time. You see, it's the everyday, uncelebrated stuff from the age that we're interested in here.

Therefore, if you're disappointed to find your favourite bit of pop-cultural tat hasn't been included, that's probably because we reckon it was built to last, and has never really gone away. That, or we've forgotten all about it. Contact us via our website and we'll be happy to confirm either way.

HOW THIS BOOK WORKS

To allow you to interrogate *TV Cream*'s contents with the utmost efficiency (who knows when you're next going to need information on how Hartley Hare broke the news ***Pipkins*** was ending, like, fast?) the entries in the book have been arranged into alphabetical order and assigned a nifty little icon which gives you an immediate idea of what each thing actually is.

Here's what to look for:

– Adverts from off the telly

– Annuals, of the like you'd receive every Christmas from an aunt or uncle

– A mixture of items and ephemera that we couldn't categorise (including one that's just a font)

– Novels, autobiographies and the like

– Comic books

– Continuity, or the bits that happen between TV programmes that aren't the ads

– Food and drink

– Magazines

– Popular music

– Radio programmes and other related stuff

– School gubbins

– Essential pieces of technological kit

– Toys

– TV programmes (you'll be seeing a lot of this one)

Throughout, you'll notice that every item has been assigned a 'peak year', which will tell you when it was at its zenith of popularity or ubiquity. We've also given everything a handy 'retrometer' rating out of ten.

Now, what on Earth is a retrometer? It's a fiendishly complicated device which rates the overall warm glow-inducing quotient of the object up for discussion. We can assure you it's based on hardcore scientific fact – a bit like a clapometer if truth be told – and is in no way just an arbitrary score tagged onto the bottom of each entry. So please don't go quibbling with its results, because there are people in labs who'll get very upset.

AND FINALLY . . .

So that's about it. It now falls upon us to wave you off into a morass of top 1970s and 1980s memories. But before we leave you to the tender mercies of Cuddly Ken, **Nimble Bread**, the shavers of Class 5C and Shaky who's still trying to work out just what is going on behind that green door, a quick word on nostalgia.

It's great, isn't it? But don't get us wrong: although we're here to celebrate the past we're all for present-day stuff – and even the future – too. While we may bang on about all things retro, we wouldn't want you to think of us as a bunch of fogies yah-booing the current scene. It's *TV Cream*'s opinion that British pop culture is, and always will be, great. So long as there are kids willing to wag school for lunch on their lap and whatever follows the midday news, then it'll stay that way. And in twenty or thirty years' time, maybe they'll be here talking to their peers about all the stuff they enjoyed back in their day.

Only they'll probably be doing it all on luminous Etch-a-Sketches – or something.

A–C: 3-2-1 to The Custard Stops at Hatfield

3-2-1

Riddle-me-ree television

Peak year: 1982, as half the nation stuck with it every Saturday

Pitching up in 1978 as a blatant spoiler for ***The Generation Game***, *3-2-1* didn't come close to matching that show in ratings until the early 1980s.

It did outscore its rival, however, in dementedness, asking viewers to sit through – never mind understand – a sequence of dazzling bemusement: three heterosexual couples answering 'list' questions against the clock, the winning pair leaving to come back and do it again next week, the other two going on to a physical challenge, then the winners of that watching six sketches and songs and earning a number of clues, one of which related to a huge prize.

'Fortune and fame' were promised if you unscrambled these notoriously impenetrable teasers, which in turn were linked to that week's 'theme', usually a half-arsed variation on music hall, involving B-list celebrities doing a turn in between a novelty act and the chance to win a hostess trolley.

The whole thing always felt about to tumble off air, such was its scale – mammoth sets, tons of 'characters', from hostesses The Gentle Secs to resident gagsters – and the fact Ted Rogers struggled to hold it all together. Kids and grannies, however, were enchanted with his dexterous digit-work and Dusty Bin, and *3-2-1* survived until 1988.

It lasted so long because Yorkshire Television threw loads at it, correctly figuring everybody had to be interested in at least one thing, even if it was just the flying YTV chevron at the start.

RETROMETER: 7/10

2000AD

'Splundig vur Thrigg!'

Peak year: 1982, as Dredd's writers decide Mega City One has become too big, and promptly blow half of it up in a nuclear war

Simply put, there had never been a comic like *2000AD*.

Rising from the ashes of IPC's abortive ***Action***, the brainchild of freelance editor Pat Mills and John Wagner began as the means to carry on that paper's violently subversive work, this time under the Mary Whitehouse-bypassing guise of science fiction.

Under the aegis of pompous, apefaced alien editor Tharg, who spoke a language made of typographical errors and annoyed the hell out of all readers over eleven, the 'Galaxy's Greatest Comic' went into orbit on 26 February 1977, with a tempting blend of Dan Dare, dinosaurs, *Six Million Dollar Man* rip-offs, and a free 'space spinner'. By the second issue, fascist future cop Judge Dredd turned up. Guess which one of those heralded a new era in British comics?

Dredd exemplified Mills and Wagner's approach to the quality stories in *2000AD*: lots of exciting and scenic futuristic adventure as per, shifting the emphasis away from boring heroic stiff upper lips and onto flat-out psychotic bastardry. The initial premise for the character was of a totalitarian police officer who doled out summary executions for anything more serious than littering – a concept which mellowed with age, though not that much.

Elsewhere, dispossessed characters like Strontium Dog and Nemesis the Warlock – mutant bounty hunter and alien terrorist respectively – fought no-holds-barred guerrilla wars against oppressive human regimes. Slaine was an axe-wielding pagan warrior prone to hideous spasms of violence, while Northamptonian magus Alan Moore created Halo Jones, a sarcastic female anti-hero stuck in the world of future mass unemployment. Something, as they say, for everyone.

Another first was the freedom given to the artists. While the likes of *Battle* had sterling artwork, it was all very much made to conform to a realistic house style, and the old letterpress printing method rendered them in a heavy black and grimy white that often gave a rather drab feel. In contrast, *2000AD* employed a range of weird and wonderful artists whose names became legends to rival their US counterparts. There was the mighty Brian Bolland, a Michelangelo for the average thirteen-year-old; Mike McMahon, whose flea-bitten, big-footed characters turned Mega City One into a giant Elephant and Castle shopping centre; Carlos Ezquerra, who designed the original Judge Dredd; and, perhaps best of all, Kevin O'Neill, who created for Pat Mills' 'Nemesis' easily the most grotesque, fetishistic, sinewy and gore-strewn artwork ever seen in a children's picture weekly.

As the 1980s drew to a close, the 'graphic novel' fad led *2000AD* to try its hand at po-mo tricksiness. 'Zenith', a rare incursion into superhero territory, featured a feckless pop-star-cum-hero and a few swipes at Thatcher and Richard Branson; war saga 'Bad Company' went all *Apocalypse Now* on the narrative experimentation front; and subterranean limbo weirdness 'The Dead' was *Logan's Run* rewritten by Samuel Beckett. We were firmly in 'grown-up comics' territory by now – you could tell, because characters' thoughts appeared in sombre square caption boxes rather than frivolous 'thinks' clouds – but there was nothing particularly juvenile about the first ten years of *2000AD* anyway. That buffoonish alien editor had every reason to look insufferably smug.

RETROMETER: 10/10

'Absolute Beginners' by David Bowie

Dave shimmies on oversized office equipment

Peak year: 1986

There's meandering around LA with orange hair or wailing underneath the Berlin Wall, but there's also hoofing with Mick Jagger on a piece of urban scaffolding and, in this instance, pirouetting gracefully on a giant typewriter.

1980s-vintage Bowie albums were shoddy affairs, but on 7" was where he always delivered the goods, and throughout the decade the man rustled up a string of danceable, hummable discs. Pick of the bunch was 'Absolute Beginners', written for the appalling eponymous 1950s-based fantasy flick, but itself a piece of near-peerless penmanship.

Over thundering drums and shimmering strings, Dave cleared his throat with the odd 'ba ba ba-oooh' before a twinkling piano welcomed him to the mic for a few plaintive facts. 'I've nothing much to offer,' he explained, 'there's nothing much to take.' A woman turned up to duet 'as long as we're together, the rest can go to hell,' then the piano soared upwards and the listener was tipped into a classic Bowie warblathon.

'As long as you're still smiling,' reassured Dave, a dazzling sax solo hit the highest note imaginable, and there was no choice but to croon along at the top of your voice.

The entire affair was utterly date-stamped as mid-1980s, but then that was precisely the point. 'It's absolutely true!'

RETROMETER: 9/10

Ace of Wands

'Tarot cards, Tarot the diamond man'

Peak year: 1972, the year Brian 'Mr Barrowclough' Wilde turned super-villain

With its prog-rock theme ('iron roads, asphalt sky/windows made from water'), flamboyant leading man ('a twentieth-century Robin Hood – with a pinch of Merlin and a dash of Houdini') and a splendidly 1970s obsession with the nouveau riche ('I'll have the avocado vinaigrette and the moules marinière'), *Ace of Wands* was rich stuff for a kids' show.

The programme starred Michael Mackenzie as the loved-up, long-haired stage conjurer Tarot, who fought crime in his spare time, assisted by Malayan fishing owl Ozymandias (real name:

Fred Owl) and human friends – glamorous assistant Lulli (Judy *'General Hospital'* Loe), cockney rough Sam (Tony *'Get Some In!'* Selby) and elderly bookseller Mr Sweet (Donald Layne-Smith).

First airing in July 1970, the series boasted a legion of genuinely scary nasties, including oriental art thief Tun-Ju, wheelchair-bound chessmaster Ceribraun and the mind-bending Henry T Peacock, played with icy conviction by Brian Wilde.

However, the stand-out baddy had to be Mr Stabs (Russell 'Lonely' Hunter) who'd unleash his evil powers on unfortunates via a rhyme that began: 'Hand of Stabs . . .'

By the time *Ace of Wands* reached its third series, Tarot had acquired two new sidekicks, Mikki (Petra Markham) and Chas (Roy Holder). Thankfully the conjuring content remained the same due to the continued presence of magic advisor Ali Bongo. That said, the painful jump-cuts which accompanied some of the tricks proved the show wasn't averse to relying on a little camera jiggery-pokery, alongside the sleight of hand.

In 1972 the whole thing came to a close as Chas blew-up an evil supercomputer, 'fate reached out a hand' and the powers-that-be at Thames Television threw their lot in with ***The Tomorrow People*** instead.

RETROMETER: 9/10

Action 

'The sevenpenny nightmare'

Peak year: 1976, the original, glorious incarnation

Boys' comics were drab affairs in 1976, still clinging to the template of the (recently deceased) original version of ***Eagle***. Spotting a gap in the market between the Alf Tuppers and 'Achtung Fritz's, IPC launched *Action* on 14 February, designed by Pat Mills to be more relevant to modern kids.

How did they do it? Well, by ripping off films and TV, mostly. *Dirty Harry* met *The Sweeney* to become hard-nosed secret agent 'Dredger'. *Rollerball* mutated into 'Death Game 1999'. *Jaws* was given a spin and retold from the shark's point of view in 'Hookjaw'. In a similar vein, 'Hellman' gave war comics a heroic Nazi officer.

They weren't all brilliantly written, but it was a breath of fresh air (and indeed gore) for your average excitement-starved teen. Sales hit 250,000.

Two strips started causing adult concern. 'Kids Rule OK!' depicted a plague killing off everyone over eighteen, leaving the kids to reinvent society – with bike chains and clubs if necessary. Football story 'Play Till You Drop' earned reprobation from FA members for its use of terrace violence as a plot device.

Mary Whitehouse and The Responsible Society were alerted. The *Sun* and the *Daily Mail* ran sensationalist, damning spreads. Supervising editor John Sanders was dragged over the coals by Frank Bough on ***Nationwide***, leading WH Smith and co to suggest they were no longer interested in stocking this comic any more. Panicking, IPC pulled the plug, and the issue of 23 October vanished from the shops, to howls of protest.

When it returned, something wasn't quite right. The gore and the violence had been toned down, and the stories tended to have neater, cosier, less gritty endings. Readers deserted the new-look *Action* in droves. On 11 December 1977 came that sure sign of comic death, 'exciting news inside!' and the publication was engulfed by venerable IPC war title *Battle* the following week.

RETROMETER: 9/10

Action Man 

Palitoy's shoebox soldier of fortune

Peak year: 1976, and the introduction of Eagle Eyes

Not only did he fight them on the beaches, Action Man fought them in the bedrooms, he fought them in the coal bunkers and he even fought them in the bath. If it was a *coup d'état* on the adventure playground or a peacekeeping mission underneath the stairs, Action Man was there.

From unpromising beginnings as a rather stiff, lifeless figure, Action Man underwent a series of refinements throughout the 1970s, introducing features such as lifelike hair, 'hands that really grip!' and Eagle Eyes, operated by a lever on his neck which made his pupils dart from left to right in a rather shifty fashion. There was even a Talking Commander ('Action Man patrol, fall in!') and an impressively bearded Adventurer in a polo-neck jumper.

It all made Action Man irresistible to a generation of future Andy McNabs keen to re-enact the Iranian embassy siege, and Palitoy capitalised on this appeal by marketing an impressive arsenal of uniforms, artillery and equipment, including Red Devil parachutes, scuba kit and a 'roto-copter', along with a fleet of jeeps, tanks and snowmobiles.

If most of this military hardware remained out of reach of most kids' pocket money, there was always Lesley Judd on *Blue Peter* demonstrating how to make an armoured car for your 'action figure' from an old cereal packet.

RETROMETER: 7/10

Adrian Juste

Segueing from the Jesus and Mary Chain to a skit about supermarket chains – now that's professionalism!

Peak year: 1985: Adrian staged a publicity shot in which he gets thrown out of

Radio One's Egton House – little does he know that nine years later etc. etc.

To any self-respecting eight-year-old, Juste's Saturday lunchtime mix of pop music and archive comedy was anarchic and hilarious, creating a happy aural world that everyone wanted to be a part of. However, that quasi-helium laugh, compressed Smashy-Nicey DJ pronunciation and all round thumbs-aloftness would apparently soon come to signify everything that was wrong with 'our' Radio One.

Spearheading a style of broadcasting that, from 1977 to 1994, involved adopting a faux Kenny Everett voice and pretending to have conversations with pre-recorded performers, Juste believed that even the most finely honed piece of Victoria Wood observational humour could be enhanced with the odd, 'oh really?' or, 'so what did you do?' thrown in by his nibs.

Definitely one of the old guard at fab Radio One, our fella was swept from power in 1994 by incoming new boss Matthew Bannister. Juste has since tried to put the record straight about those 'glory years', claiming that most of what has been written is a distortion put about by media studies twerps, *Guardian* readers and members of the Groucho Club. If that's the case, you can now add this book to that honourable list.

RETROMETER: 7/10

The Adventure Game 

Rumoured to involve talking aspidistra
Peak year: 1984, when Noel Edmonds himself dared to cross the vortex

For a dirt-cheap BBC2 alternative to the evening news, *The Adventure Game* was a matchless creation. To the tune of – depending on your age – a frantic military march by Grieg or delightful guitar noodlings by Carulli, a trio of 'time-travellers' would stray upon Arg, 'small planet of little consequence'.

Blankety Blank-style selection rules generally guaranteed one actor/star (Sue Nicholls, Paul Darrow), one boffin (James Burke, Heinz Wolff) and one kids' favourite (Derek Griffiths, Sarah Greene).

To return to Earth, our heroes had to overcome a kerfuffled butler, a backwards-talking Australian, a logic-stepping-stone floorplan, the retrieval of plastic currency from Argonic acid paddling pools and some business with a BBC Acorn, before arriving at the vortex: a rickety gantry strung over a bit of open galaxy, across which the celebs tiptoed, alternating moves with an unpleasant blob of computer wizardry only we could see. Contact with it meant immediate evaporation (and the humiliation of having to 'walk' back to Earth).

As for the celebrated conversational houseplant, His Highness the Rangdo didn't so much talk as unleash alien sweary-sounds if not met with a forelock-tugging 'gronda gronda' from all and sundry. By the end he'd turned into a teapot. Meanwhile, Moira Stuart played a shape-changing dragon and Lesley Judd a double agent.

Only 22 episodes of *The Adventure Game* were made, but everyone who watched never forgot.

RETROMETER: 10/10

'Ain't No Pleasing You' by Chas and Dave

Inexplicably successful pub rock duo come up with a genuine classic

Peak year: 1982

What Chas and Dave were doing bothering the upper reaches of the UK pop chart in the early 1980s is anybody's guess. Granted, this was the age of Joe Dolce and Rene and Renato, but novelty pop acts could usually only expect one decent crack at the Top 10 before kindly being shown the door marked 'anonymity beckons'. Yet this pair of love-a-ducks stormed the charts first of all in 1980 with 'Rabbit' (as catchy as myxomatosis), and then again with 'Ozzie's Dream'.

A number one hit seemed within their grasp, and in order to achieve it they released a song that, contrary to much of their oeuvre, was entirely brilliant without having to rely on cheeky cockney mannerisms.

From the compressed drum-roll intro to the orchestral swoops and chugging piano and bass, here was a tune that – while not wholly earnest – was no novelty record either. A soaring, rollicking tale of disenchantment with the 'trouble and strife', it demanded to be bellowed to the rafters while holding aloft a tankard of foaming ale.

A storming ***Top of the Pops*** performance in front of a dutifully swaying crowd suggested the top slot was at last in their grasp, but criminally Chas and Dave were to be denied by Bucks Fizz's 'My Camera Never Lies' – a song whose main hook went, 'ahhh – click – click!'

RETROMETER: 9/10

Airfix

Male models

Peak year: 1976, when the Lynx helicopter landed in 1:72 form

For a generation, the heady aroma of polystyrene cement and Humbrol paint is all that is needed to recapture endless Sunday afternoons diligently constructing HMS Belfast or the F14-A Tomcat.

The male population can be divided into two camps: those who did everything by the instruction book and carefully removed the components from their plastic chassis with a knife and sandpaper before meticulously assembling them under laboratory conditions, and the rest of us who just flung everything together as hurriedly as possible in order to get to the fun bit of painting it and applying the decals. Inevitably, the process of soaking the miniaturised RAF roundels or Luftwaffe insignia in a bowl of warm water and ceremonially applying them to the fuselage was liable to end in rage and frustration as they folded, crumpled or split before they could be fixed in place.

Perhaps the most curious element of the entire phenomenon was the Airfix Club Page in ***Buster*** comic, edited by club president Dick Emery – although disappointingly his dispatches never contained any 'ooh, you are awful' bits of business, but merely featured letters, tips and news of the forthcoming Messerschmitt BF109.

RETROMETER: 5/10

Alcohol Ads 

'Campari and lemonade, how can you possibly?'

Peak Year: 1981, and the 'just drink it'-style ad for 'CAAAR-LING!! Carling Black Label!'

Alcohol and telly have never been a comfortable fit – with advertisers wary of extolling the virtues of popping back a ring-pull to a family audience. As a result, the best booze ads have been those that diluted their strength with humour.

So, while Lorraine Chase simultaneously repulsed and beguiled a well-to-do gent by sloshing lemonade in her Campari and chirping: 'Nice 'ere, innit?', Leonard Rossiter slung Cinzano Bianco all over Joan Collins's top, and Pru off of *C.A.T.S Eyes* let a bullshit merchant patter her up with promises of a film shoot in Malibu while she sloshed back the drink of the same name.

But, if low-concept sitcom wasn't quite the right match for the product, then you could always have a crack at selling it in song. Courage Best really did 'beat all the rest' when they employed Chas 'n' Dave to hammer out its good points on the old 'Joanna', although, in 1988, McEwans got the jump on everyone with their 'chin-head' band of lager drinkers crooning about 'something so real'. However, special mention must go to the 'bottle of Guinness supporters' club' – a memorable ditty in its own right.

Despite these two tried and tested routes, some brands just couldn't contain themselves. Stuff the comedy, stuff the songs, stuff the Babycham deer! (What demographic was that appealing to?) Booze is for boozing – and that's best done by men! Hooray, then, for Carling Black Label's lads' night-in with the fellas descending upon a table stacked full of cans and declaring: 'We've got it right, no frills, no fuss – it's OK by us.' Get it down you!

RETROMETER: 7/10

All Creatures Great and Small

Farmland fantasia par excellence

Peak year: 1980, just before James and Siegfried joined the RAF

Nobody could, or will ever, wade through a meadow of slurry in his best suit and emerge looking as dignified as Christopher Timothy. Fact.

All Creatures Great and Small's sepia if sodden universe was Darrowby village and its reassuringly well-staffed veterinary practice run by bluff cove Siegfried Farnon (an ace Robert Hardy), boisterous younger brother and aspirant campanologist Tristan (Peter Davison), and James Herriott (Timothy), real-life scribe of original novels and dispenser of soft words to posh daughters bereaved of their tabby and grizzled agriculturalists blubbing at the loss of a pensionable heifer.

Their stern fare was forever offset by ancient toff Mrs Pumphrey and her queasy canine Tricki-Woo, plus comical cumbersome 1930s gadgetry typified by Siegfried's giant wireless dispensing topical updates on 'the crisis in Europe'.

The title sequence summed it all up exquisitely: Hardy and Timothy sharing a joke motoring through picturesque lanes while the eternally hummable theme settled the nerves like the obligatory pot of Yorkshire tea.

RETROMETER: 9/10

Also-ran Crisps

They didn't want to be Smith's crisps

Peak year: 1973, year of the Tudor Crisps Soccer Fans League giveaway – 20 plastic rosettes of teams from Hull to Glentoran

Leicester may dominate the potato-chipping landscape of modern Britain, but not so long ago there were numerous rivals to its crown.

Take the infamous hedgehog-flavour crisps, launched as a marketing stunt by Welsh pub chain Philip Lewis in 1981, causing a profit-soaring outcry from animal rights groups and a profit-halting investigation from the Office of Fair Trading when it was revealed they were actually flavoured with pork rather than spiny garden companions.

Newcastle provided the north and Scotland with both the pioneering Hogget's crisps and the full-flavoured Tudor crisps, illustrated with a smug-looking Henry VIII stuffing his face, and immortalised in a regional advert set in an imposing tower block (the 'Dunston

Rocket' in Gateshead), wherein a paperboy made an offer his mate couldn't refuse. 'Deliver this lot an' I'll give ya a canny bag o' Tudor!' 'Why man, for Tudor I'd climb a mountain!' Then the killer punchline: 'Pity that lift's oot of order!'

Pickled onion, gammon, kipper and chocolate flavour were the order of the day until the early 1990s, when Walkers devoured the Peterlee factory and various ex-board members initiated the Phileas Fogg range.

RETROMETER: 7/10

Angel Delight

Milking it

Peak year: 1976, the peak of that ice-skating commercial

A nation long reconciled to spending just as many hours in the kitchen preparing pudding as the main course (it's Thursday, so it must be jam roly-poly) was always going to need something immediately comprehensible to shake it out of its sweetmeat servitude.

Bird's Angel Delight was just the thing, and moreover offered an additional boon by using up those half-bottles of milk left over from breakfast. It debuted in supermarkets in 1967 promising the taste of strawberries and cream from colourful pouches of micro-dust. The fact this luminous powder had to be vigorously whipped together with milk was the cue for dad to 'take a turn' with the mixing bowl, thereby proving that no one could ever say he didn't 'do his bit around here'.

While a panoply of flavours and spin-offs, including birthday-party favourite the milkshake and the sadly over-ambitious home-made ice lolly, ensured the brand lined your 'afters' cupboard through the 1970s, its ultra-functionalism lost favour in the fussy **Ice Magic**-ed 1980s.

RETROMETER: 9/10

Angels

Pre-*Casualty* hospital drama with issues and stuff

Peak year: 1979: *Angels* went twice-weekly and a teatime habit was formed

Has any soap opera ever had as arresting an opening sequence as *Angels*? If you listen to the tune itself (a thumping guitar riff accompanied by someone rubbing their plimsoll against a gymnasium floor) you can't help but picture a Ford Anglia piling out of a shop window.

Angels' actual title sequence is not quite as high-octane: an ambulance creeping into a parking space and a nurse helping a lad with gym shorts up onto a bed is quite a contrast, but still – it makes for an intriguing, if slightly jarring whole.

Initially dubbed 'Z-Beds' (because it was a bit like *Z-Cars* but about nursing), *Angels* ran successfully from 1975–79 as a 50-minute drama. But then the decision was made to change it to two half-hour episodes a week, effectively giving it the look and smell of a common-or-garden soap. Its supposed gritty approach (it featured extramarital affairs, characters on the pill and hard drinking) meant the BBC could pretend the series was a 'continuing drama' rather then something as working class as – say – *Crossroads*, but given that half the cast and the production team went on to work on *EastEnders* after *Angels* finished in 1983 then we reckon soap it is.

Oh, and if you'd ever wondered what Fiona Fullerton had done to make her famous then *Angels* is your answer.

RETROMETER: 8/10

Annie Nightingale 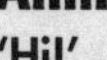

'Hi!'

Peak year: 1984, when Sunday evenings meant The Mighty Wah! and last-minute essays

Radio One's resident big-sister figure provided the soundtrack to those panicky last-gasp Sunday-night homework sessions with a loosely alternative playlist, i.e. 'The Love Cats' by The Cure, that Fish Heads song and something by the Frank Chickens.

For anyone managing to get a request played, the refectory bar kudos was infinite, but it was a feat of ingenuity that involved an enormous amount of resourcefulness. 'I've had bits of loo paper, silver pen on black paper, and a sock the other week. The strangest was a kind of knitted flag which asked for "A Rose Has to Die" by The Dooleys.'

RETROMETER: 8/10

As It Happens by Jimmy Savile 

Mr Cigar fixes it for the entire planet

Peak year: 1974

Fittingly enough for a book that's just as oddly compulsive as its subject, *As It Happens* reads exactly the same way its author talks. Page after page resounds to the clunk-clicking of lunatic phraseology ('Attacks of fright in plenty did I have'), though Jim'll, typically, is quick to dispel any suggestion he spoke the whole thing onto tape by including a photo of his manuscripts ('Longhand words and knocked-off books keep down the expense!').

From the off it's clear he knows everybody in the whole world and everybody in the whole world likes to ring him up to do a personal appearance, which he'll only agree to if he can spend the preceding night in a tent on a deserted hill with six girls as 'bodyguards'.

A succession of outrageous revelations – Jim teaches himself advanced physics down a mine; Jim 'invents' the disco; Jim becomes the world's first ever DJ – culminates in a grisly finale as Sir Savile recounts his 'introduction to the sex act'.

A tome to be sampled once only.

RETROMETER: 7/10

Ask Aspel

The suave proto-VCR

Peak year: 1978: Kate Bush was on!

Way back when, the only way to see your favourite telly again was if it was repeated, or, if you were a kid, when Michael Aspel read out your request on his chummy clip show.

In between behind-the-scenes features and relaxed chats with singers, gymnasts and the like, the Most Likeable Man on Telly cued up Michael Crawford stunts and *Doctor Who* regenerations for the assembled masses. Even the titles were fun, with Mike comically buried in viewers' letters to a jaunty tune while a gang of kids shouted the programme title. You didn't get that with a Ferguson Videostar.

RETROMETER: 7/10

Asterix the Gaul

Big-nosed Gallic wit that gained in translation

Peak year: 1971, year of urbanisation satire 'The Mansions of the Gods'

Quite possibly the most erudite comic ever published, Rene Goscinny and Albert Uderzo's *Asterix* books were combining slapstick fun with satirical wit when Matt Groening was still in short trousers.

On one level, the books told the story of a small rebel village in ancient Gaul holding out against the Roman occupation via a strength-giving magic potion. But that wasn't the half of it.

Over twenty-odd adventures, Asterix and Obelix encountered just about every European nationality, and came up against phoney soothsayers, pretentious architects, duplicitous civil servants, ruthless capitalists and trade unions – 'slaves work better since they started paying them, and think of the saving on whips!' At their best, they were undeniably smart, full of classical allusions, often very moral, but never, ever preachy, aloof or dull.

Much of the credit for the English editions had to go to translators Anthea Bell (Martin's sister) and Derek Hockridge who, faced with reams of French puns and cultural in-references, had no choice but to rewrite most of the books from their own perspective, making them co-authors rather than mere translators. Most of the verbal gags and all the punning names (Fulliautomatix, Marcus Ginantonicus, Anticlimax, Squareonthehypotenus) were their work, but it all blended seamlessly with Goscinny's fiendishly clever plots.

After Goscinny died in 1977, Uderzo wrote and drew subsequent entries in the canon which remained faithful to the spirit of the series but never really worked as satisfactorily as the classics. Film versions, both cartoon and live action, also singularly failed to capture the sharpness and joy of the original books which, thank Toutatis, remain in print to this day.

RETROMETER: 9/10

Audio Taping

It's killing music, but it's saving your favourite Sid Snot sketches

Peak year: 1982, the year everyone's party tapes had Tony Blackburn on them

Nowadays your recordable DVDs and iPods allow you to store your favourite music and TV in whatever format you want. However, in the pre-VHS era, if you wanted to enjoy your favourite show again, you either had to invest in a bulky, expensive reel-to-reel video recorder or, rather easier, hold the microphone from your tape deck to the telly speaker and make an audio copy. Inevitably you'd hear your sister shrieking in the background, but given the theme to *Windmill* was unlikely to make it onto seven inch, this was as good as it got.

Similarly, if you couldn't afford to buy your favourite current singles, Sunday teatimes would see you crouched over the radio, taping what you wanted off ***The Top 40*** on Radio One. Inevitably this meant keeping your finger over the stop button, desperate to avoid getting any of the DJ's voice on the tape – adding that extra sheen of professionalism.

As any Musicians Union member would tell you, recording such copyrighted material was illegal, and clearly not to be encouraged. However, in later years, the BBC managed to retrieve a substantial amount of stuff no longer in the archives, thanks to a home-taping amnesty.

Sadly there was no call for low-quality copies of Adam Ant singles drowned out by your mum shouting you down for your tea.

RETROMETER: 8/10

Aztec Bars

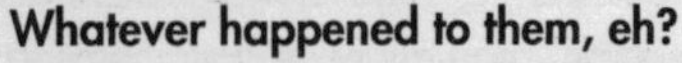

Whatever happened to them, eh?

Peak year: 1970: chocolate-bar-meets-World Cup-meets-extinct-Mexican civilisation

The quintessential 'forgotten' sweet, quick to be eulogised over whenever anyone's jockeying for a bit of old confectionery-related badinage, the Aztec bar was Cadbury's ill-fated attempt to unseat Britain's best-selling slab of brown – the mighty Mars Bar.

Created in 1968, this raisin-addled concoction was promoted by an ambitious and expensive TV advert depicting a fully-feathered Aztec warrior legging it up the side of a pyramid to the sound of ritualistic drums and pan pipes. Once atop the construction he made straight for that chocolate bar, peeling back the dark-blue foil before chomping away happily.

The sweet hit its stride in 1970, with the arrival of the World Cup finals in Mexico and a Cadbury-sponsored spot-the-ball competition which landed the winner an all-expenses-paid trip to the tournament. The second prize? A slightly less impressive crisp Bank of England fiver.

Alas, just ten years after its creation, the Aztec – true to form, when you think about it – died out, alongside other Cadbury stablemates Nunch ('the nunchiest bar ever!'), Whistler (with its 'extra crunchy formula') and, best of all, the stupidly named Hazel in Sweet Disguises (what we'd all been waiting for: a confectionery-based parody of John Fred and the Playboy Band's 1968 number three hit!).

RETROMETER: 8/10

Barclaycard

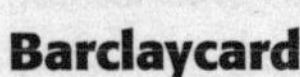

Whicker's world of credit

Peak year: 1984: the last days of the jet set

Credit cards used to evoke an exotically luxuriant lifestyle. What orgies of epicurean excess, for example, carried on behind the doubtlessly imposing doors of the mysterious Diner's Club?

Cardholders were a breed apart, living a non-stop, well-groomed life of club class jet-setting in open-necked shirts, or storming into lush hotel lobbies and demanding 'I've GOT to get back to Bahrain!'

During the 1980s, Barclaycard – after some relatively down-to-Earth ads featuring a punked-up Dudley Moore buying records – stepped up a social gear by drafting in the jet-setter's jet-setter, Alan Whicker. He personified the trans-Atlantic lifestyle, his swooping tones firmly associated in the public mind with the moneyed world of film stars, monarchs, shahs and sheikhs. If a safari suit could talk, it'd talk like Whicker.

The premise was simple: in a variety of

exotic locations, Whicker extolled the globetrotting virtues of what he called 'Bu-harclaycard' by interrogating hapless fellow travellers over the worth of their inferior plastic in a series of awkward prose poems: 'Will it let you sample the vintage vino?/will it help you look like Al Pacino?' Local tradesmen answered with a curt 'non!' leaving the Whickster to swoop languidly in and purloin the goods with ease using his superior door-jemmying rectangle, which he claimed, with gentlemanly discretion, was 'accepted in more places than . . . CERTAIN charge cards I could mention.'

Despite Whicker's best efforts, most future credit-card ads took their cue from Access's classless, chummy 'flexible friend', heralding the modern era of APR rates and debt consolidation, where anyone with a fixed address and a clean shirt can acquire a brace of wallet stiffeners with ease. A triumph for financial democracy maybe, but with those lounge suits gone, the world's that bit less glamorous.

RETROMETER: 7/10

Barratt Homes

Airborne luxury housing announcements

Peak year: 1979: suburban Year Zero

Building firms don't tend to make memorable adverts, but Barratt's long-lived 1970s campaign, in which a helicopter zoomed over the majestic expanses of link-detached residences on Orchard Mews and Fairview Drive struck a chord. This was down to the none-more-actorly voice of the chopper's passenger, Patrick Allen.

His rich tones (even his voice seemed to wear a cravat) somehow imbued the mundane talk of double garages and double glazing with the stamp of fruity authority.

Point of confusion: Allen also voiced the infamous *Protect and Survive* nuclear fallout films – did that mean a Barratt home could survive a ten megaton attack?

RETROMETER: 6/10

Bazooka

Yankee chew-dle dandy

Peak year: 1978, when everyone coveted Joe's secret compartment ring

It brought a touch of rootin' tootin' glamour to drab provincial newsagent counters, but perhaps Bazooka bubblegum's greatest legacy was introducing the evocative phrase 'zip code' to a generation of impressionable British schoolkids.

A tuppence bought you a hunk of shocking pink gloop to annoy your mum with by blowing colossal bubbles and treading it into the Axminster. But that wasn't the main attraction, as inside every red, white and blue wrapper there was a free comic depicting the escapades of Bazooka Joe, a wise-cracking 1950s all-American kid in baseball cap and eyepatch, and his buddies Pesty, Hungry Herman, Mort and co. Comic might be a bit of an exaggeration; the thing was so small you needed some sort of James Bond-style microfilm device to read it, and it was printed on impossibly thin waxy paper. Yet everyone collected them (even if references to 'drugstores' and 'recess' went over heads) as it all possessed a sort of irresistible Big Apple mystique.

Bazooka Joe also held the promise of access to an Aladdin's cave of booty. If you chomped your way through half a ton and sent off hundreds of comics to an address in St Paul, Minnesota, in return you could obtain anything from a Telescope ('Get a close-up view of distant planes, buildings etc.') to the Amazing Two-Way Aluminium Space Phones ('For secret talks with friends in other rooms or houses. No one can listen in'). For British kids, however, that meticulous instruction to 'include your zip code' meant the prospect of owning a Magic Magnet Set or Sea Shell Kit ('Twenty valuable shells from the seven seas. No two alike') was destined to remain but a tantalising dream.

RETROMETER: 9/10

BBC Christmas Idents

Beeb engineers get the tinsel out to brighten up the announcements

Peak year: 1977, when the revolving pudding was just as much a part of the festive season as Morecambe and Wise

For 362 days of the year, you knew where you were with the BBC1 globe – inoffensively spinning around between programmes. For the festive season, though, things were different, as to go with the glitter and sparkle of the *Mike Yarwood* special was a specially customised ident. Different every year, you'd wait with baited breath come Christmas Eve for the grand unveiling.

Whatever the festive scene, there was always one constant – a revolving bit. Until 1985 the idents were mechanical, and we like to imagine bearded boffins at TV Centre sweating for weeks, making sure that plum pudding was rotating on its precise mathematical axis. Such effort perhaps seemed unnecessary as, on 27 December, the thing was flung in a cupboard and never used again, like so many other Christmas toys.

Memorable efforts over the years included 1977's simple but effective (revolving) Christmas pudding, 1978's terrifying (revolving) Santa's head, which promptly broke down, and 1984's (revolving) snow-people, including a snow-woman on Michael Grade's insistence.

The last mechanical ident in 1985

saw two tweeting (revolving) robins and was much mocked for its low-tech nature. Come January it was blown up by Noel Edmonds on *The Late Late Breakfast Show*. We've nursed a small grudge ever since.

RETROMETER: 9/10

BBC Computer
The doughty, and weighty, *ordinateur de l'école*

Peak year: 1981, when the first wave hit schools, hand in hand with *The Computer Programme*

It was marketed as a home computer, but the machine's price (a whopping four hundred quid for the 32K version) and user milieu (bearded, ale-quaffing ex-Cantabrians, by and large) made it a no-go for your average family.

Schools, though, welcomed the cream-coloured breezeblock. It was built for hefty collegiate use – a proper keyboard, a programming language you could actually program in, and a very polite vocabulary: cock-ups were greeted not with the usual curt 'error!' but a more genteel 'mistake'. It even made the digital equivalent of a polite clearing of the throat when switched on. Schools without a proper computer room compounded this stolid appearance by purchasing a sturdy trolley to wheel it about on, in the manner of the school **telly cabinet**.

Above all, it was EDUCATIONAL. You wouldn't find Everyone's a Wally on the Beeb. 'Games' deemed suitable by computer masters often took the form of text-based 'mathemagical adventures' that laboriously led the child from one mathematical problem to another: ***The Adventure Game*** with the fun let out. That, or old favourite the 'turtle', a pen-holding buggy you could instruct to draw patterns in the manner of a hideously overpriced Spirograph.

Still, a lesson sitting in front of a micro was a lesson not sitting in front of a blackboard, so no one really minded the imagination-crushing seriousness of it all. Besides, it could well inspire a future Bill Gates. Or so the headmaster fervently hoped, on perusing the massive invoice for computer, desk, disk drive, turtle . . .

RETROMETER: 6/10

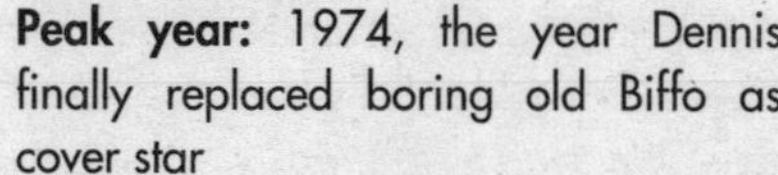

The Beano Book
Stocking-filling stalwart

Peak year: 1974, the year Dennis finally replaced boring old Biffo as cover star

A pivotal Christmas present for millions of youngsters, the *Beano Book* had been a tradition since 1939, but the 1970s brought a Golden Age as the wordy adventure strips were shorn away for non-stop merriment.

A cover depicting a riotous (often snowball-filled) stunt, with the calamitous consequences revealed on the back, enclosed large-panelled stories from the regulars, each page headed with a pithy, rhyming summary of its contents ('A five-mile run doesn't look much fun!') interspersed with puzzles and pun-based features. That it only took about twenty minutes to read didn't matter, it was just great to have the Holy Trinity of Dennis, Minnie and the Bash Street Kids enshrined between boards.

Other strips of the time included the bizarrely coiffured sporty duo of 'Ball Boy' and 'Billy Whizz', the buckshot-riddled 'Three Bears', cantankerous bird 'Jacky Daw (with Maw and Paw)', McHaggis-shooting loons the 'McTickles' ('McBang!'), and 'Tom, Dick and Sally', which surfed the zeitgeist like no other Beano strip, devoting whole stories to deely-boppers, the 'Prince Charming' dance and Joan Armatrading.

RETROMETER: 9/10

Beasts

Almost Pauline Quirke's scariest work

Peak year: 1976, six episodes of classic Nigel Kneale telly

Variously labelled as a horror anthology, a sci-fi series or simply a collection of plays all about animals, from its roll-call of 'I've seen that actor somewhere before' performers, to its classic videotape-with-lens-flare-whenever-a-match-is-lit aesthetic, *Beasts* is a prime example of mid-1970s evocative, low-budget ITV drama.

Written by Nigel '*Quatermass*' Kneale, each of the six stories featured animals as the spooky protagonists, ranging from intelligent rats to the ghost of an intelligent dolphin (Kneale was always a great fan of 'intelligence'). But *Beasts* was no flight of fancy. The writer's unceasing desire to rationalise the irrational made for some horribly plausible denouements, such as the discovery of a poltergeist in a supermarket ('Special Offer') and the demise of a couple at the claws of the aforementioned super rats ('During Barty's Party').

This latter episode is especially well remembered with the threat being conveyed to the viewer through sound alone (the noise of the rats' unceasing scratching growing ever louder as the play continued).

Beasts was just one of a number of scary anthologies littering the ITV schedules in the late 1970s, but unlike *Shadows* or *Tales of the Unexpected*, it never treated its audience as children, or fools incapable of spotting an obviously telegraphed twist ending (usually involving Timothy West turning into a giant bee).

RETROMETER: 8/10

Beeb  

'The BBC Junior Television Magazine'

Peak year: 1985, when Ro-laaand dined with Gary Glitter on the cover

ITV had ***Look-In***, with its intoxicating cocktail of *Mind Your Language*, Flintlock and Westward TV listings, but the men in cravats at the BBC had nothing to rival the 'junior ***TV Times***' until the launch of *Beeb* in 1985.

The biggest weapon in *Beeb*'s armoury was 'Grange Hill', featuring Bronson-era comprehensive escapades ('Eating in the corridors, McGuire?') in cartoon form. Less enthralling were the exploits of bearded 'zoo vet' Donald Turner from *One by One*, usually involving giraffes with toothache. Tedious BBC sci-fi saga *The Tripods* got its own full-colour strip, and *Bananaman*, *The Family Ness* and *Automan* all appeared too.

Features included a regular *Saturday Superstore* page, devoted one week to the shooting of the video to Mike, Cheggers and Saz's non-hit 'Two Left Feet', plus lyrics.

Blue Peter's contribution was typified by a two-page article by Michael Sundin (it's got his signature at the end, he must have written it) about a bike ride to Kilimanjaro, while John Craven investigated editing suites ('You've no doubt seen the electronic jiggery-pokery in programmes like *The Kenny Everett Show* . . . ').

Other highlights included David Icke's 'Sports Desk', Mark Curry's '10nis Tips' (complete with daffy picture of Curry, glasses askew), and the staple of all 1980s teen mags – 'Budget Fashion Special – Looking Good for Less than £25'.

But the highlight of *Beeb*'s brief life has to be the issue with cover stars Gary Glitter and Ro-laaand Browning off of *Grange Hill*, chuckling over an intimate dinner for two ('What's Eating Roland?'). How Janet St Clair must have seethed with envy.

RETROMETER: 5/10

Bendy Pencils 

Back-to-school craziness

Peak year: 1982: School kids everywhere go on a bender

Toying dangerously with our grip on the laws of physics, the bendable pencil looked like your average HB, even wrote like one (well, after a fashion) and yet it could . . . bend?!

These pliable instruments shared space in the (*Star Wars*/Rainbow Brite/*A-Team*-themed) pencil case with a whole array of wacky writing fare, most of it sporting a culinary theme, for some reason.

Generally imbued with a whiff of fruit, it was every boy's duty to try eating at least one smelly eraser every term. Then, there was the egg-pen. Looks like an egg, but actually it's a pen! And the pencil-sharpener fashioned like a Coca-Cola can. Looks like a Coke can . . . well, you get the idea. Alongside all this came a swathe of writing equipment fashioned to look like slices of pizza, because – hey – kids love pizza!

However, kicking all this consumable-related stuff into a cocked hat – and even eclipsing the ruler which presented a rudimentary animated scene when tilted – was the Magic Pen set. You could marvel as the colours changed in front of your eyes, or sketch out a bitingly satirical Chad in invisible ink whose message could only be revealed when your mate ran their 'de-coding' pen over the page ('Wot? No homework!').

RETROMETER: 6/10

Betamax

The bridesmaid of home entertainment

Peak Year: 1978, and Britons embraced the future with the Sony SL-8000.

Of course, the picture's better on Betamax – so claimed home hi-fi nutters in the mid-1980s unwilling to admit the entertainment system they'd spent hundreds on was minutes away from becoming obsolete.

Sony's also-ran of the video age was launched in the UK in 1978, but had been plugging away in the US since 1975. A year later JVC had joined the fray with its VHS format and while Sony was slow to bring other manufacturers on board, the newcomer quickly jumped into bed with various Japanese electronic firms. Soon VHS was everywhere.

Even though Beta led the way in innovations (it's the system that brought us fast-forward and rewind!), VHS's ubiquity and the tapes' greater recording capacity swayed the public. By 1988, Sony threw in the towel, and got ready to launch their own VHS recorders.

So, it was goodbye to those stubby one-wheeled tapes – but at least laser disk was now on the horizon. Ooo, get that picture quality!

RETROMETER: 5/10

Big Deal

A rarity – a BBC drama set on a run-down estate in London that doesn't star that woman who always plays prostitutes in *The Bill*

Peak year: 1984, before Robbie's wings were clipped by his missus

Ray 'and as if by magic . . . ' Brooks played the saggy-faced, grotty-jumper-wearing gambling addict Robbie Box. His down-at-heel escapades were small time, usually ending with Robbie neither ahead nor behind the game. However the various wrangles, scuffles and indignities heaped upon him in the course of an episode somehow made for cheering viewing.

Inevitably there had to be a long-suffering partner and Jan Oliver (played by Sharon Duce) was it. She spent most of the series trying to get Robbie on the straight and narrow, and then – as is the way of these things – almost fell for the posh, slightly smarmy bloke at her work (leading to the predictable scene in which Robbie finally realises that his family means more to him than gambling).

But despite the soap opera, *Big Deal* is best remembered for those tense smoky card games where Rob antagonises the local hard man (who has to be restrained from hitting him, natch) before losing all his wonga on the turn of the final card. After that it was the ritualistic, bittersweet, bottle-of-milk-glugging-early-morning walk home, signifying it was time for Bobby 'Bucks Fizz' Gee's definitely of-its-moment theme tune to kick in. 'Ah well, big deal!'

RETROMETER: 7/10

Big D Nuts on Cards in Pubs

About as close as you got to a woman in some establishments

Peak year: 1978, the height of Benny Hill's fame

With the rise of the gastropub, it's now possible to enjoy fantastic-quality food with your beer, but this certainly wasn't the case a few decades ago. In the 1970s there were only about three foodstuffs served in a pub, and if it didn't come in a packet then you were out of luck.

The most obvious accompaniment to a pint of Best was a packet of Big D peanuts, plucked off a bit of cardboard on the back wall that, as every comedy sketch had it, was graced with a shot of a dollybird. Cue much excitement when the bar was down to the last few packs, like an X-rated version of the bonus round in *Catchphrase*.

If you fancied something different, virtually the only other foodstuff that was sold in the pub – and seemingly nowhere else – was Scampi Fries, or as the pack had it, 'Scampi (Flavour) Fries'. A cut above your average crisp, these added a touch of class to the alcohol experience, possibly because scampi seems an incredibly bizarre flavour for a crisp. Or fry.

RETROMETER: 6/10

Big Glasses

Such a shame Timmy Mallett never got in the pages of *Vogue*

Peak year: 1986, when they were a condition of employment in local radio

Some television personalities have a problem in that they don't actually possess much in the way of a personality. Here, something's required to ensure people remember who you are. Hence the popularity in the mid-1980s of big glasses.

One reason why big glasses were so commonplace at the time was that there were a lot more aesthetically challenged people on television. Whereas now TV presenters are chosen for their looks as much as their talents, in the past it was possible to get on air if you were short-sighted, possessed ginger hair or talked in an annoying regional accent. This was even the case if all three applied – fortunately for Mark Curry.

Of course the daddy of them all was Timmy Mallett, who could often be found telling ***Look-In*** just how many pairs of oversized spectacles he owned to prove what a crazy kind of guy he was. Indeed Timmy often sported the whole 'I'm mad, me' uniform, favouring massive bright-coloured bermuda shorts and baseball caps with giant hands wielding mallets sticking out of the top – the latter clearly invented for his patronage alone.

As a breakfast television presenter, we're sure many people must have been put off their Weetabix.

RETROMETER: 7/10

Big Trak

'Goes forward and reverse, spins, turns, fires and more!'

Peak year: 1982, Big Trak makes it in the movies – well, it can be seen in the background in a scene in *ET*

Back at the cusp of the home computer revolution, kids were desperate to get their hands on anything vaguely computery and toy manufacturers were only too happy to comply. MB Electronics' Big Trak was one of the best of the bunch. It (as the name suggests) was a futuristic tank that looked like a strange Gerry Anderson land vehicle. But aesthetics were the least of its appeal. Dubbed as 'fully programmable', it was possible to configure Big Trak to perform up to sixteen different commands (each one basically consisting of a direction and a duration), meaning that you could theoretically get it to go to the kitchen and bring back a can of Coke.

But that wasn't all – Big Trak also had flashy lights that could be programmed to emit a laser gun sound to imply that it was actually shooting at you. This led to multiple incidents of dads having to pretend to be slain in a Big Trak ambush while they were trying to watch ***World of Sport***.

Of course, you never actually owned Big Trak yourself (it was far too expensive), but it was one of the major factors as to why you maintained that uneasy friendship with the rich kid up the road.

RETROMETER: 9/10

The Big Yellow Teapot

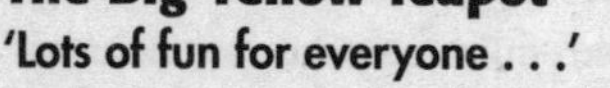

'Lots of fun for everyone . . .'

Peak year: 1980, the Bluebird toy company is founded

The Big Yellow Teapot, like its arch-rival Palitoy's Family Treehouse, was plastic manna for the nation's young girls.

This was in no small part thanks to the – at one time ubiquitous – television commercial that consisted of a lot of annoying noisy kids having far too much fun playing with the rather anonymous-looking inhabitants of the titular urn on the superfluous merry-go-round that was hidden beneath the lid.

Indeed, why we needed a doll's house in the form of a giant teapot – and a yellow one at that – remains something of a mystery; at least the aforementioned Treehouse was based on a real-world premise. The teapot's two-room layout and odd furniture (such as a little red box which had the word 'tea' written on it) baffled anyone who tried to work out what its charm actually was.

And yet, the fact you couldn't even properly revolve the two rooms inside without opening the drawbridge at the front somehow only added to the thing's idiosyncratic appeal.

RETROMETER: 7/10

Birdseye Steakhouse Grills

What will you give your old man with his Steakhouse Grill?

Peak year: 1983, when everyone joined in with the 'fried onion rings' bit

You remember the one. It featured a load of hungry builders in the back of a van, singing the immortal lines, to the tune of 'Que Sera Sera', 'will it be chips or jacket spuds/will it be salad or frozen peas/will it be mushrooms/fried onion rings/you'll have to wait and see/hope it's chips it's chips/we hope it's chips.'

Yes, what a great advert for McCain Oven Chips that was. Except, in a baffling case of mass delusion, everyone's now forgotten that the commercial was, in fact, for Steakhouse Grills, presumably on the basis that seeing as they were singing about chips, they must have been advertising chips.

RETROMETER: 7/10

Blankety Blank

The self-loathing word game

Peak year: 1981, the year audiences reached 15 million(!)

Everyone knows about this, so we'll take the mechanics of the game – Supermatches, Head-to-Heads etc. – as read if we may. More important things were afoot in this mockery of a sham of a quiz.

The two-tier celebrity seating plan, for instance: a handy gazetteer of British showbiz types. Top row: bluff male eccentric (Patrick Moore/Barry Cryer); bluff female eccentric (Beryl Reid/ Barbara Woodhouse); youngish showbiz bloke (Gary Davies/Mark Curry). Bottom row: bit of fluff for host to eye up (Carol Drinkwater/Linda Lusardi); zany comedian out to cause trouble (Kenny Everett/Spike Milligan); and ditzy singer/actress (Cheryl Baker/Lorraine Chase).

Thus seated, the celebs proceed to 'muck about'. Top Left engages host in 'we're both men of the world' banter. Top Middle refers to 'little man' under desk snatching the used cards. Bottom Middle acts up something rotten, filling host's every trip across the studio floor with nervous apprehension. And of course, Bottom Right overplays the 'ditzy' card for comic effect: 'Well first of all I put "pig" but then I thought nah so I put "dog" but that weren't right neither so I crossed that out then I thought "gorilla" but I couldn't spell gorilla so I tried to see what Kenny'd put but he wouldn't let me so then I wanted to put "crocodile" but I run out o' space so I changed it back to "pig".'

The host's role was to play weary supply teacher to this remedial primary-school class, which they did with gusto. Terry Wogan switched from floridly arcane banter to eye-rolling despair at the snap of a microphone wand, while Les Dawson began each show in full-on misanthropic mode and went swiftly downhill from there.

How on earth could such a knowingly knackered quiz become so popular? The clue's in the question. Lights on when you're ready.

RETROMETER: 9/10

Bluebird Sweets

The real reason kids learned about measurement

Peak year: 1982, before the pre-packaged generation took over

Not to be confused with their namesakes who made toys, Bluebird were responsible for the vast majority of sweets that sat in the jars on a high shelf in your local newsagent. The tradition had passed down for many years, and for the thrifty kid it was a good way to get more toffee without taking your chances on a bag of Revels.

However the most memorable aspect of Bluebird sweets came in their television advertising campaign. These proceeded much as every other sweet advert, until the last five seconds when the company's logo – unsurprisingly, a bird in blue – would appear on screen with a frankly terrifying flash of lighting and echo-drenched voice-over.

Adding an element of fear to the advert breaks in *Number 73*, this spookiness was probably loved by parents as it put kids off the brand completely.

We never enjoyed Squirrel's Nuts quite as much again.

RETROMETER: 6/10

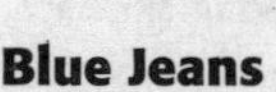

Blue Jeans

Next stop, Cosmo

Peak year: 1986: The year *BJ* revitalised a dowdy reader's look with a Lady Di quiff, a string of pearls and an oversized brooch

To be filed alongside *Patches*, *My Guy* and ***Just Seventeen***, *Blue Jeans* was indivisible from these publications, acting as the teenage girl's last stopping-off point before womanhood beckoned in the form of – well – *Woman*.

Packed with Paul Young, pop lyrics, problems (overly hairy nipples, usually) and pin-ups, it also dealt out photo stories about frizzy-haired girls despairing of ever getting a snog from the earring-sporting Steve, and fact-based features adapted from 'a reader's true experience'.

There were also regular vox pops on burning issues (which person would you take to a desert island with you? 'Simon Le Bon – he's gorgeous'), accompanied by photos of our nation's youth in its natural habitat: the shopping centre.

By definition *BJ* (as it unfortunately took to calling itself) and the like held onto its readers for two years at best, before they grew out of sixth-form meanderings and headed off into the real world, now equipped with the knowledge of how to apply blusher to a square-shaped face.

RETROMETER: 7/10

Blue Peter Books

Don't call them annuals

Peak year: 1977, Book Fourteen: ***Swap Shop***, Concorde, 'The King's Appendix', Jubilee painting winners – the full works

Debuting in 1964, these yearly dispatches from the pen of *BP* supremos Biddy 'replies to every letter' Baxter and

Edward 'cravat' Barnes adhered to a strict format from the off.

First came an opening 'Hello There!' collage of caption-less photos inviting readers to recall (a) a celebrity guest in a comedy pose (b) a pet climbing into a box and (c) a giant-sized prop 'borrowed' from another BBC production. Next up, some business at a stately home, with or without fancy-dress role play; half a dozen pages on the Summer Expedition ('Unlike a British wedding, everyone eats before the ceremony!'); recipes for an edible make; behind-the-scenes action from a BBC family favourite; gossip about the Appeal; short stories pitched at alarmingly young age ranges (*Paddington, Bleep and Booster*); an 'astonishing' truth about an obscure Victorian royal family member; and finally that perennial back-page competition to win a trip to a *Blue Peter* Party.

This roster never changed, because it didn't need to. Fantastic, ubiquitous slices of telly yesteryear, *BP* books were as reassuringly dependable as the seasons, and even the covers, whether sublime (Fourteen: John, Pete and Lesley in the *BP* control room with a million TVs) or half-arsed (Eight: John and Pete holding some oily rags) were great. They continue on top form, like their parent, to this day.

If you claim you bought number One when it came out, you're lying.

RETROMETER: 10/10

Bob Block Sitcoms 

Suburban pantomime capers

Peak year: 1976: *Rentaghost's* debut

Nowadays forty is considered pushing it for a 'youth' programme maker, so it's worth remembering radio comedy veteran Bob Block was fifty when he created his first children's sitcom.

1972's *Pardon My Genie!* was the tale of downtrodden hardware shop assistant Hal Adden and his genie (initially Hugh Paddick). The wish-granting calamities that ensued set the pattern for future Block stories, and its success allowed a lavish, all-star final episode set in the Thames studios.

Robert's Robots followed in 1973, detailing the misadventures of inventor Robert Sommerby and his misfit android creations, with an element of intrigue in the form of an espionage sub-plot.

Both programmes traded in slapstick, knowingly awful puns and disastrous misunderstandings, as did Block's first BBC series *Rentaghost*, although this programme's premise hardly seemed child-friendly. Bumbling young man Fred Mumford dies in a shipping accident. Wanting to keep his death from his parents, ghostly Fred sets up an Ealing-based spook-hiring agency, enlisting the help of haughty Victorian ghost Hubert Davenport and crazed medieval jester Timothy Claypole. This acknowledgement of death added an unusual tone to the series, perhaps best described as a ghostly *Goodies*, with the mismatched spooks attempting a different activity each week. Like *The Goodies*, it also had a cracking theme tune written and sung by a cast member (Michael 'Claypole' Staniforth).

Later, Mumford and Davenport were replaced by zanier characters like Hazel McWitch and Nadia Popov, and the show went for all-out silliness. Rentaghost owner Harold Meaker's permanently disgusted scowl, the addition of Christopher Biggins, a pantomime horse and dragon, and assorted 'visitors from the spirit world' kept things going until 1984.

In 1979 Block wrote a sitcom for Clive Dunn's *Grandad* character from his hit single, putting the kindly old duffer (named Charlie Quick) in chaotic charge of a rehearsal hall, with inevitable run-ins with both the young singers and dancers and the men from the council.

Block bowed out with 1985's *Galloping Galaxies*, a space-themed comedy with more complicated plots than before, but still lashings of puns, and Paddick's old radio sparring partner Kenneth Williams as the ship's computer.

Block's stuff is unfairly maligned these days – people tend to remember the time they hit puberty and felt themselves above the pies and punning rather more clearly than their younger selves lapping up Claypole and co – but for twelve years he was king of comedy for the under-tens.

RETROMETER: 8/10

Bob's Full House

In bingo lingo, clicketty clicks, it's time to take your pick of the six!

Peak year: 1984, when Bob's doors first opened for you

Lord Bob Monkhouse's bingo quiz remains, for our money, the finest game show ever screened on British television.

Four contestants faced Bob's questions and crossed off numbers on their bingo card for each right answer, although they had to beware of offering an incorrect response otherwise they'd miss a turn ('you're wallied!').

The winner of each round selected from a typically 1980s selection of BBC prizes (i.e. a foldaway bike), demonstrated by a dollybird ('sorry, you don't win her!').

The Monkhouse Mastercard round featured that essential element of all good quiz shows, the rotating structure, as the contestants selected questions from half a dozen categories, before the subjects were jumbled up ('mix those six, computer!').

Then it was into the final round, with Bob speeding up the questions and ratcheting up the tension ('Geoff, you NEED six, Muriel, you NEED seven!') and it could become edge-of-the-sofa stuff if the backmarker answered question after question to steal the game.

The first contestant to cross off all their numbers joined Bob for the nailbiting finale, the Golden Bingo Card. Now the aim was to uncover the numbers to reveal the letters behind that spelt out the destination of the prize holiday ('B! You're going to Bognor!') in the space of sixty seconds, although Bob would shamelessly help them.

Thanks to its brilliant format and a superslick compere, *Bob's Full House* became essential Saturday teatime viewing. Oh, and the credits appeared on the Mastercard's computer display, which was just brilliant.

RETROMETER: 10/10

Bod

A bald bloke in a dress – a sort of 1970s Matt Lucas

Peak year: 1981, with the fifteen-minute version well established

The intriguing thing about *Bod* is that the minimalist adventures of the titular protagonist were generally not the reason viewers watched. An extra feature was the big winner, despite not actually featuring the bald chap himself.

The reason is simple. The original incarnation of *Bod* was a five-minute show that featured our man making his debut to the brilliant dooby-dooing of Derek Griffiths, meeting friends Auntie Flo, PC Copper and Farmer Barleymow. This was popular enough, and the BBC repeated it a number of times over the next few years.

However, after a while, the Beeb wanted to add a bit more so it could fill up the entirety of the fifteen-minute ***See-Saw*** slot. So producer Michael Cole invented Alberto Frog and his Amazing Animal Band, who each week would help out someone in return for a milkshake. Cue much excitement in guessing the flavour. Add to that a game of *Bod* snap, and there was the extra time sorted.

For a while Alberto's antics weren't available on commercial video thanks to differing rights holders, but the two halves have now been pieced together for the full nostalgic experience. Of course, Griffiths' fantastic theme was worth the money alone, and indeed so fondly is it remembered that you can't rule out the possibility of it becoming the next national anthem one day.

RETROMETER: 9/10

The Book Tower

Hidden passages, spiral staircases, magic mirrors and teapots

Peak year: 1979: Doctor Who himself was our TV librarian

Boasting Andrew Lloyd Webber's *Variation 19* as its theme tune, the children's book-review programme was the scariest thing ever to lie in wait behind the Yorkshire TV chevron, thanks to the titular tower itself being a hugely foreboding gothic manor.

First hitting our screens in 1979, over the next ten years the show would eke out some of the darkest corners of the Spotlight directory in search of presenters, which included Bernard '*Carry On*' Bresslaw, illustrator Quentin Blake, Wincey 'ten seconds remaining!' Willis and Timmy 'Mallet's' Mallet.

However, the programme's best-remembered anchor was its first: Tom Baker, whose chocolate-brown tones and mesmerising stare heightened the programme's foreboding air.

At the end of each episode, the titles discussed therein would be displayed over the end credits, to encourage kids to order them up next time the **school book club** brochure came around. But it was a wasted effort. After 25 minutes in *The Tower*, most of the target audience were fearfully burrowing into their mother's breast instead of taking notes.

RETROMETER: 8/10

The Breakfast Show on Radio One

Benign dictatorship over bacon and eggs

Peak year: 1983: the mid-period pomp of Mike Read

Tenancy of the most fought-over watch on radio shuttled between six individuals during the 1970s and 1980s, starting with Tony Blackburn interrupting records to air his latest obsessions or entries from the studio joke book: 'I was talking to a tightrope walker the other day – he was saying his future's in the balance.'

Noel Edmonds wrestled control in 1973 and memorably exploited the slot's potential with prank phone calls ('your library book is 27 years overdue!') and lavish hoaxes (presenting an entire show 'flying' from Gatwick to Aberdeen).

A nothing-to-see-here interregnum followed under Dave Lee Travis from 1978 before the grand occupation of Mike Read began in 1981. Impersonating other DJs, the hormone-addled 'First Love' feature, celebrity namedropping – this was breakfast radio at its most regal. 'It just so happens I have the guitar with me . . .' Get away!

Read handed the baton to Mike Smith in 1986 for two years of dispensable business including the Breakfast Access Telephone ('the BAT phone' – do you see?) and piss-easy game Factasia, before Simon Mayo's decent stab at zoo radio introduced the titular 'crew' of newsreader Rod McKenzie and revolving weather/travel line-up Carol Dooley/Sybil Ruscoe/Dianne Oxberry, the well-hard 'Identik-Hit' quiz, and timely revivals for 'Donald Where's Your Troosers?', 'Kinky Boots' and 'Always Look on the Bright Side of Life'.

A loaded inheritance, the Radio One breakfast show – it could anoint or annihilate reputations at random. Those who survived intact (Edmonds, Mayo) most definitely deserved to.

RETROMETER: 7/10

'Bright Eyes' by Art Garfunkel

Hare-brained genius

Peak year: 1979

All through the 1970s the UK handed the chirpy, choirboy one out of Simon and Garfunkel far greater chart success than the grumpy, poker-faced one who'd written all the hits. Nursery rhymes about terminating your marriage? Give us songbook classics any time.

Mike 'Wombling White Tie and Tails' Batt enlisted Artie for the ditty he'd penned to appear in the film *Watership Down*, but ensured 'Bright Eyes' had bugger all to do with rabbits and instead contented itself with stabs at poetry ('There's a high wind in the trees') and loads of sweeping strings. The end product was pure class. From out of fretless bass swoops and ladles of reverb soared Artie's crystalline tenor, stepping up for a chorus that pulled off that trick of matching maudlin words ('How can the light that burns so brightly/suddenly burn so pale?') to uplifting tunesmithery.

Typically, it only appeared for about thirty seconds in the film. Still, Matthew Butler, the kid who dressed up as a bunny to sing it badly at the end of every *TISWAS*, was quids in.

RETROMETER: 8/10

British Rail

Ex-clunk-clicker plus warbling chorister attempt to popularise the Cheap Awayday Return

Peak year: 1976, when it was curtains up for the age of the train

Brainchild of boss Peter 'Mitsubishi' Parker, British Rail's first proper TV ad campaign was a whistles-and-bells extravaganza of cut-price offers and posh cinematic entreaties.

Dozens of Inter-City fleets, bodywork glistening in a perpetual rainstorm, plied forever-rolling countryside. Their cargo: the honourable Sir Jim'll Savile. His armoury: a dark suit, a Maxpax coffee, shockingly sensible hair and an endless amount of paperwork that had to be done before that pressing engagement with the man who makes the machines for the hospitals. Wine-bar funk played while the kid who sang 'Walking in the Air' (not Aled Jones, the other one) belted out, 'this is the age of the train'.

From a time when audiences were impressed by extended sequences of carriage exteriors, the ads did their job in leaving the slogan – somewhat meaningless out of context – in everyone's heads. They were then ditched for sighing chess pieces and a snoozing penguin.

RETROMETER: 7/10

British Telecom

Feathered Cribbins promotes long-distance relations

Peak year: 1979, when those Buzby soft toys were everywhere

When Bernard Cribbins, the voice of Buzby – a straggly, phone pole-dwelling cartoon canary in personalised vest – phoned his mum to tell her she was on telly, a nationalised industry dipped its toe into the heady world of merchandise.

Plush toys, stickers, combs, necklaces and badges sprang up. Buses and Commer vans carried his image everywhere. Buzby's adventures appeared in ***TV Comic*** and picture books detailing his laddish antics ('Buzby's Rock Group', 'Buzby's Girlfriend'). There was even an abortive attempt to privatise the company with the issue of 'Buzby Bonds'.

It all got a bit much, and he was eventually replaced with the less omnipresent (though more annoying) 'It's for you-hoo!' campaign.

RETROMETER: 7/10

British Wine

Rarely British, or indeed wine

Peak year: 1980, as the plucky Brits fought off the marauding Don Cortez

Nowadays even the *Daily Star* has a resident wineologist (probably), but until relatively recently the majority of British folk existed in a wine-free world, weddings and Christmases excepted. The holy trinity of Blue Nun, Black Tower and table-lamp-in-waiting favourite Mateus were as posh as it got, but slightly further downmarket were the British wines, or 'wine-style drinks' as they were often known, brewed in the UK from – shock horror – imported grape concentrate.

Perhaps feeling slightly guilty over this deception, marketing departments poured on the terribly English heritage. Rougemont Castle advertised itself with that old standby, a suit of armour. Country Manor cooked up possibly the worst slogan ever written: 'So light. So subtle. So buy some'. Playing to a slightly more continentally aware crowd, Concorde promised a bottleful of fun for under a pound.

At rock bottom, however, was the grape-free plastic-corked sparkling concoction known as Pomagne, the nine per cent proof prize in many a 'spin the arrow' local fete tombola which inspired countless teenagers to re-examine their breakfast. Long Life lager ('specially brewed for the can!') was the sophisticated choice by comparison.

RETROMETER: 7/10

BSB Squarial

The toff's satellite dish of choice

Peak year: 1989: Sky's big launch with BSB soon to follow

Satellite telly in Britain has been around since 1978; however, Sky Channel broadcasting Australian Rules football and looped episodes of *The Untouchables* to a few enthusiasts with giant dishes in their back garden doesn't really count.

The satellite age didn't really kick-off here until 1989 when a Rupert Murdoch-injected **Sky Television** went head-to-head against BSB. The stark difference between the two services was perhaps best symbolised by their radically different satellite dish designs: Sky's was an ugly, wire-meshy, nobbly affair made by the bloke who ran Amstrad, whereas the BSB squarial was of a majestic white, adhering to that aesthetic so beloved of home makeover programmes – clean, sleek lines. Undoubtedly the squarial was the more elegant of the two but whose carried the most popular service?

Well BSB offered state-of-the art D-MAC satellite technology and an eclectic mix of arts, sport and entertainment programming, but for those who chose Sky there was unlimited *ALF*, *21 Jump Street* and *The Price is Right*. Was it really a surprise when Murdoch's gang won out in the end?

RETROMETER: 6/10

Bullseye

Bit of Bully 'unbeatable', say lab

Peak year: 1989, when Jim got on the cover of the ***NME***

Yes, 'super smashing great' (which Jim claims he never said), and yes, the speedboats, but really it was all in the details with this show, which began on Mondays before being shifted to the legendary 'tinned peaches' slot on Sunday afternoons.

That includes Jim carefully denoting the ITV region all the contestants had come from, his question cards sticking up in a revolving table, and the magical incidental music – the board revolving to, seemingly, the intro to 'Lucky Star' by Madonna and the happy and sad variants of the theme depending on the outcome of the gamble.

It also includes the *Bullseye* tankards being given to each contestant, apart from the women who got a goblet instead. And, come to that, the deranged set of question categories, which at one point included the Bible, and for most of the run Spelling, cueing a brilliantly phrased poser ('Lots of us like to drink it, but can you spell it . . . champagne?'). Don't forget too the doggerel that Jim employed to describe the prizes ('There'll be laughter and whoops as you go through hoops with this fantastic croquet set!').

His sidekick Tony Green added to the fun, always imploring contestants to 'take yer time', to such an extent they probably got even more flustered. Everyone's favourite bit, though, was surely going into the break, when Jim pulled a wad of cash from his pocket and informed us 'it'll take me two minutes to count this out', topped only by his endless spiel over the credits ('We did the rooting, you did the shooting!').

Basically there wasn't anything about *Bullseye* that wasn't fantastic. After fourteen years it was dropped by ITV in 1995. The Battenberg's not tasted the same since.

RETROMETER: 10/10

Bunty

Absolutely 'for girls'

Peak year: 1981: Bunty and Buster (the dog) go on the piste for that year's front cover

While every Christmas Britain's boys took receipt of slim volumes of ultra-violence sporting adrenalin-soaked titles like ***Hotspur*** or *Warlord*, the nation's girls were reacquainting themselves with *Judy*, *Debbie* or *Jackie* and their obsessions with gymkhanas and ballet. Of these simply named titans it was *Bunty* which cast the longest shadow, dealing up the definitive in innocent girl-centric entertainment.

The 1971 *Bunty* annual was packed with wholesome titillation centred around the holy trinity of girls with aspirational occupations ('Rose Budd – Model Girl'); boarding-school antics (the legendary 'The Four Marys'); and equestrian pursuits ('Sue in the Saddle'). There were also the inevitable 'makes', billed as 'fun for nimble fingers' and – if things weren't white bread enough for you yet – four full-colour pages devoted to pin-ups of dogs.

Come the end of the 1980s, and seemingly little had altered. 'The Four Marys' were still stuck at St Elmo's School for Girls while the horsey stuff came courtesy of Jodie Fenton and her show-jumping phobia. There was even another canine pin-up. Despite that, times were a-changing and if you flicked to page 33 of the 1989 annual you'd find a crossword bedecked with the likenesses of Morten Harket, Terence Trent D'Arby and – in an out-and-out appeal to their demographic – Morrissey.

Things could never be the same after that.

RETROMETER: 7/10

Buster

Junior Andy Capp without the roll-ups

Peak year: 1984, as *Buster* rescues failing comics like a juvenile Red Adair

For four decades, *Buster* was the flagship comic of the Fleetway (and later IPC) stable. The eponymous flat-capped youth was the cover star from day one in May 1960, and was originally billed as 'son of Andy Capp' – recognising its status as a publication of the Mirror Group. The tagline was soon dropped, however, and in later years Buster had parents introduced in the strips who were better role models than the boozing, smoking Andy.

Initially the comic was split equally between funnies and adventure stories, but by the 1970s it was virtually wall-to-wall gags. In the end, perhaps the only *Mirror* hangover was the Old Codgers-style letters page, the fantastically titled 'Do Us a Favour, Buster', which aimed to settle playground arguments.

Buster's senior status was illustrated by the record number of comics that merged with it, as it eventually absorbed the entire Fleetway stable, starting with *Radio Fun* in 1961 and ending with ***Whizzer and Chips*** in 1990. However, this meant when its own readership started to decline, there was no alternative but to close it down.

The last issue in December 1999 fulfilled every editor's ambition by informing readers, 'don't place a regular order with your newsagent'.

RETROMETER: 7/10

Butterflies

The Laura Ashley sitcom

Peak year: 1982, the height of Ria's will-they-won't-they flirtation with businessman Leonard

Doubtless your mum's favourite sitcom of the day, *Butterflies* accurately depicted the bitter-sweet frustrations and regrets of suburban matrimonial life, although you only watched it for all the antics with the Union Jack Mini.

It might have had too many sequences of Wendy Craig shopping for breakfast cereal in soft focus and the symbolism of Geoffrey Palmer's mounted collection of butterflies was perhaps a bit excessive, but it remains the only decent comedy Carla Lane ever wrote.

The hint of sex and the prospect of adultery conferred genuine classroom cachet on being permitted to stay up late to see it, and more than made up for another gag about Craig's character being unable to cook, as did Palmer's patented sardonic minimalist persona and the presence of a trainee Nicholas Lyndhurst. Never let them tell you that middle-class sitcoms aren't funny.

RETROMETER: 8/10

Buzzfax

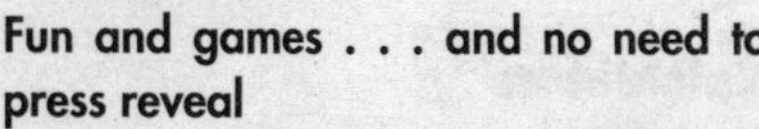

Fun and games . . . and no need to press reveal
Peak year: 1981, for one week only

Easily the most obscure Saturday morning kids' show of all time, ***Buzzfax*** was a one-off BBC summer experiment, linked by Buzz, a talking Ceefax sprite in a bowtie who introduced puzzles, quizzes and information on 'what to do today' in the gaps between the usual summer schedule of cartoons and ancient series, like *Battle of the Planets*, *The Monkees* and *Edgar Kennedy*.

Back then, seeing Ceefax on our normal old tellies represented a thrilling glimpse into the technological future, but even so, a blocky animated picture of Dinky Dog was never going to offer much in the way of competition to Noel Edmonds or Sally James.

RETROMETER: 7/10

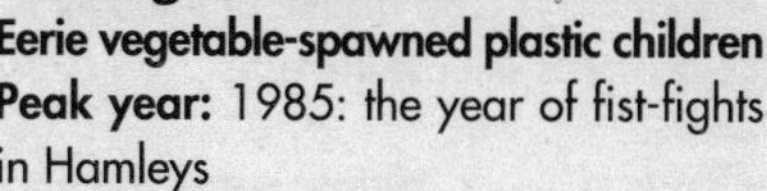

Cabbage Patch Kids

Eerie vegetable-spawned plastic children
Peak year: 1985: the year of fist-fights in Hamleys

The subject of a weary 'and finally' on the teatime news around Christmas in the mid-1980s, the Cabbage Patch Kids were the definitive toy sensation of the decade, provoking stand-up brawls in shops across the land as parents battled to nab the last one.

Ugly, podgy trolls (not to be confused with Trolls), they were the creation of sculptor Xavier Roberts, who had the smart idea of ensuring no two were ever exactly alike, thanks to a computer-controlled manufacturing process which made slight alterations to each creation.

When bought, they came with an 'adoption' certificate. Owners who filled this in would then receive a birthday greeting from the manufacturer a year after their original purchase.

In 1982, things really went nuts as Roberts sold the mass production rights to toy company Coleco, who proceeded to unleash the Kids onto the world. By 1985, the company was filing profits of $60 million as the seemingly acromegaly-afflicted vinyl and cloth playthings became the must-have accessory for all acquisitive Violet Elizabeth Botts who were prepared to soil their pants if it came to it.

However, as swiftly as the craze came

it went and, in 1988, Coleco filed for bankruptcy. The chilling coda: apparently there are 80 million of the ugly little bastards still out there.

RETROMETER: 10/10

Cadbury's Chocolate Machine

Not so much a toy, more some imprisoned confectionery

Peak year: 1971: decimalisation provokes countless headaches among junior sweetshop owners

For a brother or (usually) sister with an irritatingly fastidious nature, a toy cash register could provide endless hours of fun. But a Cadbury's Chocolate Machine added a whole new element to this faux shopkeeping business, and one that would pique the curiosity of even the most disinterested child – namely, chocolate. These red plastic contraptions could hold quite a number of those miniature Cadbury's Dairy Milk bars that hitherto only existed in big tubs of Roses. Said chocolate could only be legitimately released by inserting a two penny piece into a slot at the top, with the bar then collected from the dispensing tray at the bottom.

Inevitably boys grew jealous when sisters who owned one of the machines found it regularly stocked up courtesy of mum and dad, so they could innocently play 'shop' with their friends. This in turn prompted those disgruntled siblings to discover the joys of ram-raiding via forcibly cracking open the Cadbury's shop front whenever sis was busily engaged watching a musical on the telly.

RETROMETER: 7/10

Calculators

H-E-L-L-O

Peak year: 1973, when the Cambridge Sinclair felled log tables nationwide

On the surface it seemed preposterous: getting to bring your top birthday present to school and flaunt it in front of your mates all day long! Yet the infusion of these petite counting machines into classrooms was a slow one, lagging somewhat behind the pace ebulliently etched in *Tomorrow's World*.

British models tended to hang around long after being superseded by glossy Far Eastern imports, with Sir Clive's dimly glowing LED types all too quickly outflanked by Liquid Crystal Display efforts from Japan.

Regardless of make, however, the one thing all calculators possessed was the ability to – gasp – spell words, via a hasty 180-degree rotation of the screen. Hence 07734 was your all-purpose greeting, 58008 supplied adolescent sniggers, while simultaneously pressing 3 and 7 created a weird hybrid that resembled 't' and could be followed by 145 for guaranteed toast-of-the-playground hysterics.

RETROMETER: 8/10

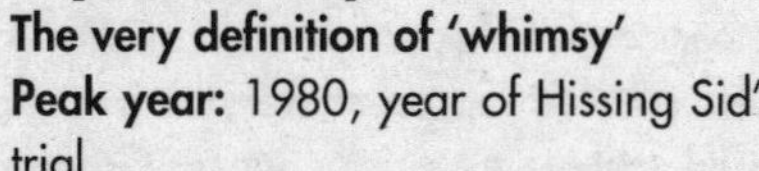

Captain Beaky

The very definition of 'whimsy'

Peak year: 1980, year of Hissing Sid's trial

They really were the greatest animals in the land. Captain Beaky and his band (from left to right: Timid Toad, Reckless Rat, Artful Owl, Batty Bat) were immortalised in verse by Jeremy "*Allo, 'Allo*' Lloyd, set to music by Jim Parker (whose recent *Ground Force* theme bears more than a passing resemblance) and recited by Keith 'Henry VIII' Michell.

Lloyd's doggerel tales of anthropomorphic derring-do, Parker's military pomp and Michell's deliberate, actorly relishing of the juiciest rhymes ('Owl's idea, the clever feller/to have a flying um-ba-rella . . . ') secured a number five chart position.

A second single, two albums and a BBC2 series followed in short order, detailing the further adventures of Beaky and nemesis Hissing Sid, plus a whole menagerie of zoological chums. Michell was helped out in the reciting department by the likes of Twiggy, Harry Secombe, Penelope Keith, Peter Sellers, Petula Clark, Noel Edmonds and, naturally, Peter '***Me and My Girl***' Skellern.

RETROMETER: 5/10

Captain Zep Space Detective

Help me help me if you can, space investigator man

Peak year: 1983, as Zep investigated 'The Lodestone of Synope'

The solar system's finest detective, Captain Zep worked for SOLVE (The Space Office of Law, Verification and Enquiry, since you ask), unravelling intergalactic crimes via the medium of **Colour Separation Overlay**.

In the BBC's shameless bid to cash in on *Tron*, the smart-arse kids of the SOLVE academy in the studio and the viewers at home were challenged to crack the case before the captain and his sidekicks.

Zep would introduce the action, which unfolded in front of moonscapes uncannily resembling airbrushed comic-book drawings, but just before the denouement, the action would dissolve back to the studio and it was down to the kids to unravel the clues. The SOLVE cadets, in their orange jumpsuits and hair gel, scribbled their solutions on 'futuristic' wipeclean clipboards. This was 2095, after all. Then Zep would reveal the solution, which you never got right because they cheated like mad.

The scripts were actually devised by Colin 'Mr' Bennett, and the mysteries had gripping names like 'Death on Delos' and 'The Tinmen of Coza'.

Paul '*Rosie*' Greenwood was the first Captain, before regenerating into Richard Morant, while his assistants were Jason Brown and Professor Spiro, who was later replaced by Professor Vana, aka Tracey 'Lynne Howard off of *Howard's Way*' Childs. If nothing else, the series boasted a nifty new-wave theme.

Stay alert!

RETROMETER: 9/10

The 'Casual' Font

A comic favourite in the days before Comic Sans

Peak year: 1988: *Grange Hill* adopts it for its end credits

In the days before desktop publishing, magazines and newspapers were limited to the typefaces they could use. Most relied on Letraset to physically stick down each letter they needed, so much so that the first issue of the *Sun* had to be creative with headlines as they could only afford three big 'E's.

In those days, the Casual font was much used as it was perhaps the only typeface that looked a bit like normal handwriting. Of course, it was just as uniform as your bog-standard Times New Roman, but somewhere along the line it became the official font of comics. ***Whizzer and Chips*** certainly embraced it with gusto, using it in every speech bubble and caption, and most other comics liked its juvenile quality. It also came to represent everything to do with school, especially when *Grange Hill* decided to use it for their end credits. The move was swiftly mimicked by more or less every other children's programme.

When Microsoft Word became commonplace, the Casual font started to fall out of favour, and for the most part was replaced by the ubiquitous Comic Sans. Nowadays this can most often be seen when an office manager is trying to make that demand not to steal their biscuits just a little bit more friendly.

RETROMETER: 8/10

Catweazle

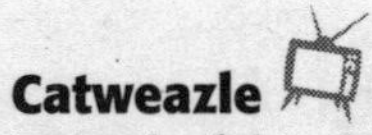

'Enough of this electrickery!'

Peak year: 1971, *Catweazle* wins a Writer's Guild award

Catweazle is perhaps the most good-natured television programme ever made. Its success was largely attributable to the performance of Geoffrey Bayldon, whose portrayal of the titular magician teleported from eleventh-century England to the modern day (well, 1970) was inventive and endearing. When he wasn't mispronouncing words in a curiously post-Stanley Unwin manner (referring to a telephone as a 'telling bone'), he was emitting a hugely entertaining stream of grunts and moans signifying his continual bewilderment at the world around him.

His appearance was also striking, with his straggly beard ensuring 'Catweazle' became the pop-cultural epithet with which to describe a dishevelled-looking person.

Even his modern-day companions, Carrot, and later Cedric, were on the money: enthusiastic and slightly spoddish but never quite nerdy as – say – Simon Randall from *Timeslip*. And given most of the action took place in the countryside, there were a goodly number of yokels on hand, the best of the bunch being big, thick Sam (played by Neil McCarthy), a labourer who looked like Jaws from *The Spy Who Loved Me* and generally ended up as the head-scratching butt of Catweazle's pranks.

RETROMETER: 9/10

Champ

Fisticuffs, football and frights for apprentice Terry McCanns

Peak year: 1984, when issue one boasted a free Super Soccer Slide Guide

Champ was DC Thomson's attempt at a 'gritty' action comic for bomber-jacketed lads more interested in *Murphy's Mob* and ***Minder*** than the traditional *'gott in himmel!'* brand of Dundee-originated derring-do.

Ten pages of each issue were devoted to 'We are United', the tale of a bankrupt football club rebuilding its fortunes under manager Joe Pearson. In contrast to ***Roy of The Rovers***, 'United' aimed for a more realistic approach, featuring financial problems, gambling addictions and hooliganism and, moreover, the team didn't win every match.

The team's stars included arrogant Welsh winger Terry Evans and maverick 'punk' midfielder Alex 'Hedgehog' Jones, and when the comic merged with stablemate *Spike*, legendary scrap-dealer-turned-goalkeeper Charlie 'Iron' Barr arrived at the club.

'Kids Rule OK' (no relation to the ***Action*** strip of the same name) followed the juveniles of Kingsway Comp, battling to save their school after it was threatened with demolition, while 'Storm' featured a bionic crimefighting dog.

Tales of mystery surfaced from 'The

Sinister World of Mr Pendragon', a bald bloke in a cape lurking around in the hedgerow, although they just couldn't resist sneaking in some of that wartime action now and then ('Hitler is reborn . . . and only Pendragon can stop his reign of terror!').

RETROMETER: 7/10

The Channel Four Logo

Seminal multi-coloured building blocks-type action

Peak Year: 1982: 'Good afternoon. It's a pleasure to be able to say to you – welcome to Channel Four'

The original Channel Four logo ushered in a new age of computer-generated miscellany arse-ing about on our screens betwixt the ads and programmes.

Designed by the soon-to-be ubiquitous Martin Lambie-Nairn (who'd go on to makeover BBC2 in the 1990s), the five-coloured '4' represented the meshing of disparate elements which were to form the then nascent Channel Four, but was nearly ditched at the planning stage when a C4 managing director asserted that all 'proper' TV logos should be in chrome. Thankfully, no one listened.

As well as representing a new way of branding, it broke ground by being created entirely on computer. Knocked up in the basement of an architects' office by boffin Tony Pritchett on a Teletronix 4054 (whatever that was) and finessed by the company who'd done all the snazzy bits in *Tron,* when coupled with a bombastic fanfare and Paul '*Catchword*' Coia's reverential tones, it provided Britain's fourth channel with an impressive start with which to segue into some anagrammatical fun with Richard Whiteley.

A genuine design classic, it was sadly responsible for prompting a swathe of spuriously revolving, obviously computer-generated idents across the whole of ITV-land throughout the rest of the 1980s.

RETROMETER: 6/10

Children's BBC

Phillip Schofield and friends fill the gaps on a budget of 50p

Peak year: 1986, and Phil was Mr Children's Television

Invented by Beeb head of presentation Pam Masters in 1985 as an attempt to bind the afternoon's programmes into one cohesive whole, *CBBC*'s simple format involved a camera being fixed to the wall in the BBC1 continuity suite and someone talking into it between *Eureka* and *Newsround.*

However, they had trouble finding a presenter and were reduced to auditioning members of the *Grange Hill* cast, until Phillip Schofield arrived, fresh from hosting pop shows in New Zealand.

Having to improvise all his links, Phil demonstrated his unflappability on day one when *Blue Peter* underran and he filled two minutes with nothing but a picture of Simon Groom and a giant sea-slug to hand. In terms of cost per hour, *CBBC* was perhaps the cheapest programme in television history – when Schofield invited viewers to write in for the lyrics to the theme of *Mysterious Cities of Gold*, it was he who put the songsheet together with a tape recorder and a photocopier.

After two years Phil went off to proper grown-up programmes involving such things as scripts and cameramen, to be replaced by Andy Crane, whose finest moment was reading out the top ten letter-by-letter during an endless technical breakdown. When he legged it to ITV, Andi Peters and then Toby Anstis stepped up for the job, but they were both less 'big brother' characters, more little sisters.

Then in 1994 the Broom Cupboard was abandoned and *CBBC* moved into a full-sized studio with a host of co-presenters. An era ended. They even had stylists.

RETROMETER: 10/10

Choose Your Own Adventure

If you decide to skip this entry then turn to the next page

Peak year: 1982; the series that 'teachers like too' hits its sixth edition

Over nineteen years from 1979, 184 *Choose Your Own Adventure* titles were published. Their unique selling point lay in allowing you – the reader – to make crucial plot decisions in the story by directing you to a particular page in the book dependent upon what choice you made – like whether you opted to 'walk toward the Indians and return the peace sign' (surely the right answer) or 'prepare to shoot it out'.

Indeed, one of the by-products of the series was an unwanted lesson in morality that taught us that to do the thing you think will be most exciting and violent will invariably result in your own abrupt death.

While perhaps the most ubiquitous, *Choose Your Own Adventure* was far from the only purveyor of such fare. TSR Hobbies (makers of ***Dungeons and Dragons***) knocked out a few under the banner of an *Endless Quest* and Puffin produced what seemed like hundreds of *Fighting Fantasy* titles, most of which were written by Ian Livingstone, Steve Jackson – or both. The big downfall with these books was that they relied on the reader rolling dice to determine whether or not they were successful in combat, and given that we couldn't be trusted to play a single adventure from beginning to end without cheating, the belief that we might actually abide by what a die said seems laughably naïve.

RETROMETER: 7/10

Chorlton and the Wheelies

Jump in, we'll take you for a spin around the Wheelie World

Peak year: 1977, and 'The Day of the See-Through Chorlton'

Trademark stop-motion surrealism from Cosgrove-Hall, depicting the battle of wits betwixt Fenella, the evil green 'kettle witch' and Chorlton, a jovial orange dragon in a yellow T-shirt who had been installed as a sort of guardian to a split-level community of humanoid trikes.

From her lair in an oversized kettle called Spout Hall, Fenella mounted repeated doomed attempts to depose King Otto and Queen Doris and seize control of Wheelie World, assisted by a talking German spellbook called Claptrap Von Spieldabeins, an Irish telescope named Riley, and a legion of spiky sentinels and sinister mushrooms.

Despite an impressive array of powers that included being able to transport herself around by propelling up and down through the Earth's crust at will, Fenella was inevitably thwarted each week by the chuckling Northern dragon ('Ta-ra, little old lady!'), who was christened after the Mancunian home of the Cosgrove-Hall studios.

Not the most obvious scenario, then, like most Cosgrove-Hall productions, but the thing managed to cram more imagination, humour and charm into ten lunchtime minutes than any kids' programme before or since. One episode featured Pablo Patito, a Latin American dancing duck, and another included The Welsh Travelling Stone Choir, led by a rock called Barry.

Erstwhile *Screen Test* inquisitor Brian Trueman supplied all the accents, from Fenella's Welsh screech to Chorlton's Lancastrian chortle. Remember, it's fun at any time of year, so put your wheels in second gear and hold tight, all right.

RETROMETER: 10/10

Christmas Card Post Boxes

The spirit of giving turned into classroom bastardry

Peak year: 1978: *Blue Peter* makes the 'tinselly Christmas card' and a million inspiration-starved teachers take note

As the school term wound up at the end of the year, teachers across the country looked for some form of activity to keep the kids 'making and doing' which wouldn't result in any take-home work for themselves.

Thus was created the tradition of the Christmas card post box, a two-pronged initiative that would not only keep the little bleeders quiet for a couple of afternoons, but also served as handy reinforcement of the most valuable lesson any of us ever learned in school: popularity is all.

First came the construction of the device. Generally inspired by similar-themed 'makes' on *Blue Peter*, these were manufactured from a well-known frosted cereal box and decorated with crepe paper (a material never glimpsed outside the classroom), tinsel and a shit-load of glitter-encrusted Marvin glue.

Once built, it would then be placed in the corridor by the fish tank for the whole school to use, awaiting the deposit of greetings cards constructed during class time (another afternoon taken care of, there), or those begrudgingly bought from the charity catalogue. Every morning a grandiosely titled 'card monitor' (read: spoddy kid) would then collect all the envelopes addressed to their form and distribute them to much excitement.

Cue kids comparing how many salutations they'd each received, and a harsh but valuable lesson for the odd-smelling 'seasons greetings'-less child at the back of the room.

RETROMETER: 6/10

Clive Doig's Programmes

So who actually did invent the potato crisp, the light bulb and the zip fastener?

Peak year: 1979: the start of *Jigsaw* and the birth of Noseybonk

Happen you were watching children's television anytime in the 1980s it is likely you would have chanced upon a programme with a theme tune that could only be described as 'boingy'. This would have undoubtedly been a Clive Doig production.

From *April Fool*, *Jigsaw*, *Eureka* via *The Deceivers* to *The Album* (not to mention the seminal *Vision On*), there was an undeniable house style to anything Doig worked on. Typically the series' format would revolve round a bookish concept such as inventions, word puzzles or blokes with big noses. Similarly, they would each feature one, some, or all of Doig's own informal repertory company. That roll call in full(ish): Mike Savage (the big scary one who played brash Americans), Madeline Smith (who portrayed ladies complaining about the tightness of their corsets), Bernard Holley (that bloke who used to read *Johnny Briggs* on ***Jackanory)*** and Sylvester McCoy (the standby comic gurner).

Inventive use of not-good-enough-yet technology was also something of a Doig trademark, with rather poor **Colour Separation Overlay** a constant source of terror for sensitive young viewers. In fact whatever it took to create an entertaining account of how cornflakes were invented or to reveal who played the first ever April Fool's joke, Doig would invariably utilise everything that his inventive mind and meagre programme budget could come up with.

RETROMETER: 8/10

Closed For Winter

Stay tuned to your local radio station for further details

Peak year: December 1981/January 1982

Put it down to a preponderance of dodgy Victorian-era heating systems or super-hesitant local authorities fearful of a kid's tongue freezing to a fork in the canteen, but even the mere dusting of snow used to prompt school shutdowns right across the country. Regardless of whether the weather was really that much worse in previous decades, a surfeit of exploding boilers, burst pipes, outside toilets and flooded assembly halls regularly combined to confine you to home (or rather outside, chucking snowballs, bits of ice, lumps of muddy slush and generally anything of an inclement icy hue at passing strangers).

The prospect of being actually asked to stay away from school during termtime was one of the greatest feelings ever, like being given an official licence to indulge in everything you'd normally have to put on hold at Sunday bathtime. It also forced a reacquaintance with BBC local radio DJs, who seemed to be the only people ever in possession of that crucial list of which public buildings were closed for the day.

If snowfall brought down power lines, as it did during the endless winter of 1981, then things weren't so much fun, not least because you couldn't watch any ***Programmes for Schools and Colleges*** and if you didn't have a gas boiler or a few dozen candles you were screwed. Still, if there weren't any battery-powered radios handy you could always deploy the excuse of not knowing when school reopened, and hence turn a couple of days holiday into a week-long seasonal skive. Hooray!

RETROMETER: 8/10

Closedowns

Don't forget to switch off your set

Peak year: 1974, when the Government imposed an energy-saving lights-out of 10.30 p.m.

No point staying on air once the nation's asleep, reasoned cash-conscious TV bosses. Besides, the transmitters needed to cool down or else they might blow up (fact – they claimed). So if you weren't in bed by the time all the networks pissed off, up came a clock, or the local ITV ident, accompanied by a cosy voice politely ordering you not to be so stupid as to watch this channel any longer.

Of course, staying up to actually see a closedown wasn't a chore, it was a privilege. This was exciting stuff, as you persevered past the point other weaker souls had given up, even though you felt you were somehow doing something wrong. Plus there was the chance to hear a continuity announcer cut loose, or catch an unbilled programme like a **Trade Test Transmission Film** or a demented **Public Information Film**.

It's weird to think that TV used to be rationed like petrol and eggs, but closedowns were compulsory by law for a time in the 1970s. It took ages to kick the habit – in 1983 the Beeb pulled live cricket from Australia at 2 a.m. as they thought nobody was watching. Nowadays more than a few seconds of black screen most likely means the death of a royal, or a power failure in the basement of Television Centre, and – in both cases – that Emergency Episode of *Dad's Army* is on the way.

RETROMETER: 6/10

A Clown Too Many by Les Dawson

His mother-in-law's outside in the car – he would've brought her in, but he's lost the keys to the boot

Peak year: 1985

Once the reader makes it past an unremittingly grim upbringing in Manchester, *A Clown Too Many* delivers precisely what's required: crappy venues and bemused audiences ('Well, I've gazed at the brutality etched on a lot of faces here and all I say is welcome to the show – and Heil Hitler'), run-ins with buxom boarding-house matriarchs, tryouts of iffy material ('A letter came through the door and it brought tears to my eyes – it was written on an onion'), and, of course, the delicate take on family relations.

Les doesn't say his mother-in-law's ugly, but when she sucks a lemon the lemon pulls a face; he keeps her photo over the mantelpiece to keep the kids away from the fire; and British Rail have banned her from putting her head out of a carriage window in case passengers think it's a cattle truck.

Stir in recollections of pantos in provincial fleapits plus ace tales of *Sez Les*, *The Dawson Watch* and the '**Blank**', and you've part gag-inventory, part deadly-sincere tribute to 'the loneliest job in show business' – as fine a tribute as the man deserves.

RETROMETER: 9/10

Colour Separation Overlay

'That's clever, how's that done?'

Peak year: 1978, as blue fabric festooned Television Centre

From the invention of colour television to the advent of digital effects, CSO (or Chromakey if you worked for ITV) was the most prevalent special effect in the business. Subjects were photographed in front of a plain blue (or green) background, which was electronically replaced with a starfield, library footage of the Grand Canyon or a picture of Joe Gormley, according to taste.

Limitations to this technique gave programmes of the era a distinctive look. The lighting had to be extremely bright, so the people in the foreground looked unnaturally washed-out compared to their background. Hair and shadows were the technician's nightmare, adding a furry blue fringe around the subject if they weren't careful – a sort of anti-Ready Brek glow. The result – every programme, from *Blake's 7* to ***Nationwide***, took on an eerie, fuzzy quality which just made telly all the more mysterious and imposing.

RETROMETER: 8/10

Comic Mergers

Great news inside for all readers!

Peak year: 1973, *Knockout* joins ***Whizzer and Chips***, so – what – is that three separate comics between the one front cover now?

While ***Whizzer and Chips*** made a virtue of being two titles amalgamated into one (indeed they had been joined at birth) the union of two separate comics was a cheap ploy to bin off a poor-selling title without having to actually break the terrible news to the reader.

What 'they' wanted you to think was the influx of characters from *Champ* into your weekly edition of ***Victor*** was great news for all parties, but bitter experience wrought at the hands of *Warlord*, *Starlord* or *Emma* suggested these 'thrilling' new features would last for only a few weeks, before they – and the title of the lower billed of the two comics – would discreetly disappear without so much as a by-your-leave.

There are a few exceptions to this rule, the most obvious being Bananaman, who can still be found today cavorting in the pages of the *Dandy*. But in the main, the only long-term repercussions of a merger were one less comic on the lower shelf in the newsagent and fearsome fights in households where siblings who had been regular readers of both titles were locked in battle for ownership of the new merged publication.

RETROMETER: 7/10

Commando 

'Silence, *schweinhund*!'

Peak year: 1976: 'Gun the Man Down!'

Commando pocket library books began in 1961, detailing the wartime exploits of brave 'Tommies' sticking it to either 'Jerry' (who'd eat leaden death with a scream of 'AARRGH!') or the 'Japs' ('AIEEEEE!').

These black and white stories came wrapped in lurid, full-colour covers usually depicting a soldier, with teeth grit, letting off a few rounds of ammo. On top of this was emblazoned the title of that issue's tale in the biggest, most jaggedy font imaginable ('INTO THE WOLF'S LAIR!').

If that wasn't proof enough that this comic was one hard bastard, then the final flourish of a bloody great dagger plunging through the 'C' in the logo sealed the deal.

In an age when ***2000AD*** pretty much admits it hasn't picked up a new reader since 1987 and the *Dandy* has turned itself into a jive-talking glossy just to stay afloat, it's astounding to note the hard-as-nails comic is still churning out 'war stories in pictures' to this day.

RETROMETER: 6/10

Copy Cats

Remembered now only for the bit at the end with the 'Copy Cats' each perched on stools

Peak year: 1985: Davro, Wilmot and O'Connor together – at last!

Some series just stink of their era, and this is undoubtedly one of them. Following on from the highly successful *Russ Abbot's Madhouse*, *Copy Cats* was ITV's attempt to make sketch-show comedy seem a bit more aspirational. From the wine-bar chic of the set to the freshfacedness of the 'Cats' themselves, everything about the series reeked of the 'new light entertainment mainstream' of the mid-1980s.

Indeed *Copy Cats* was just one of a slew of programmes that featured crap impressionists ('we're impressionists not impersonators' they used to say – as if that meant they were Monet or something) that for some reason the BBC and ITV used to sling out on Saturday nights (see also *Les and Dustin's Laughter Show* and *Five Alive*).

Copy Cats was jam-packed with mostly banal sketches featuring bog-standard impressions of yer Cillas, Jaggers and Carsons. Indeed no single sketch or gag can now be recalled from any one episode. Nevertheless, *Copy Cats* has found its way into our subconscious simply because it is the apotheosis of a certain type of comedy that you just don't get any more. Besides, any series that launched the careers of Gary Wilmot and Jessica Martin should never be completely forgotten . . . in case we make those same mistakes again.

RETROMETER: 7/10

Covering Your School Books

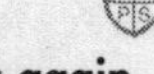

Old-time austerity bites again

Peak year: 1982, when photo spreads of the Dandy Highwayman were most often seen wrapped around a copy of *Chemistry About Us*

School kids during the 1970s and 1980s were no strangers to classroom economy measures. In a culture built on the premise of 'one between two', it came as no surprise that the few learning materials there were had to be cherished.

It therefore became the annual ritual that, when you moved on a year and inherited a new selection of textbooks, they had to be taken home and covered in thick paper (or 'backed', to use the vernacular), lest something terminal happen to the frontage, knocking a *Tricolore* out of circulation for future French classes.

A practical measure it may have been, but it was also an unrivalled opportunity for self-expression. Traditionalists took round-tipped scissors to a spare cutting of floral wallpaper, while the more image-conscious pressed posters of the Kids from *Fame* or Dexy's Midnight Runners into service. Then there were the creative types, who'd produce a collage of cuttings by way of textbook reinforcement, normally including a picture of *Danger Mouse* clipped from ***Look-In*** and something faintly subversive that would safely fly under the teacher's radar (classically, Neil from *The Young Ones*).

While carrying out this task, there was also ample opportunity to pore over messages and notes left in the margins of your *Macmillan Shakespeare* by previous custodians, which would range from the helpful 'turning point' scrawled across the start of *Romeo and Juliet*, Act Three, to the slightly less informative 'your [sic] a spaz'.

RETROMETER: 8/10

Crash

The daddy of all computer games mags

Peak year: 1985, when Oliver Frey artwork adorned kids' bedroom walls everywhere

For many budding journalists in the 1980s, the ambition was not to move to London, but Ludlow, Shropshire. This nondescript town became the centre of the gaming world when a small company selling Spectrum games via mail order launched a catalogue to promote their wares. So popular was this venture it was decided to turn it into a monthly publication.

Despite the massive success of video games, in 1983 most magazines considered them a waste of time, as opposed to more serious applications, and gave them as little coverage as they could get away with. *Crash* changed all that, concentrating on nothing but entertainment. Editor Roger Kean invited a bunch of teenagers from Ludlow's schools to come in and play the latest games for hours and tell him what they honestly thought, which he'd then turn into coherent text. At the Spectrum's height, dozens of titles were released a month, and *Crash* soon became the bible for games players, with its no-holds-barred reviews.

In time Newsfield, the publishing company, applied the formula to the C64, with *Zzapp!* (which was a hit) and the Amstrad CPC with *Amtix* (which wasn't). Meanwhile other publishers swiftly relaunched their magazines to compete, dropping the dense program listings and discussions on hex dumps in favour of relentless games. *Crash* was still number one, though, and regularly slagged off the competition (although one attack on rival publication *Sinclair User* was so savage they were sued and had to withdraw the issue).

However, rival publishers had tons of money to throw about, and were able to lure many of Newsfield's youthful staff across, eating into *Crash*'s share of the market. Poor financial management saw the company go bust in 1991 and, despite a buy-out that kept the titles alive, the following year it had to humiliatingly merge with *Sinclair User.* A sad end for a publication that had revolutionised the industry.

RETROMETER: 8/10

Cresta

Rumoured to be 'frothy', apparently

Peak year: The long hot summer of 1976

Most likely to be found stacked in a pyramid of cans on a chip-shop shelf, Cresta is best remembered for their relentless endorsement by a 'cool' dancing cartoon polar bear in sunglasses who sounded a bit like Marlon Brando ('D'you know what the bears drink up at the North Pole when they're toist-ee? The sea, man, the Arctic Ocean! Not me!'), for whom one slurp of this industrial-strength fizzy elixir sent him into some kind of ecstatic reverie ('Awoo-woo-woo! Cluck! Cluck! Cluck! Woooooo!') before signing off with his immortal catchphrase: 'It's frothy, man!'

Cresta came in 'five fruity flavours',

although the only one anyone actually remembers is strawberry ('The day they start making the Arctic Ocean in strawberry, is the only time this one here's going to drink it!').

RETROMETER: 8/10

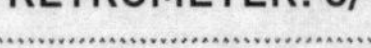

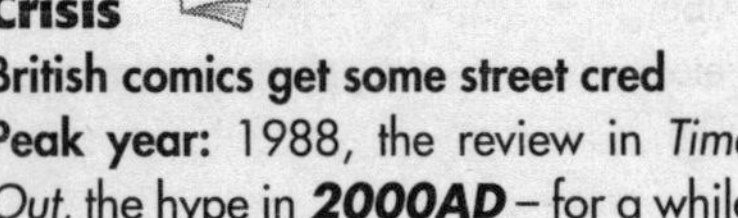

Crisis

British comics get some street cred

Peak year: 1988, the review in *Time Out*, the hype in ***2000AD*** – for a while it was all looking so good

It's 1988, and with 'adult comics' (or 'graphic novels' to use the accepted term) gaining more and more exposure in publications such as ***The Face*** and the *Guardian*, the time seemed right for the first ever widely available comic aimed at mature readers.

Crisis was a bold title that dealt with politics, sex and other 'adult' stuff. It initially consisted of two stories: 'Third World War', a convoluted and somewhat preachy account about the inherent evil of multinational companies; and 'The New Statesman', a highly convoluted tale about superheroes that was almost impossible to follow.

While the stories weren't much cop (and the lists of American and British atrocities that preceded each edition of 'Third World War' didn't exactly help in diffusing the comic's overly serious demeanour) *Crisis* did at least look stylish, thanks to designer Rian Hughes's military camouflage ethic.

However, right from the off it was clear the hip audience it was reaching out for didn't like the comic's preachy tone. A series of overhauls and new stories followed (including somewhat controversially a strip about Adolf Hitler), but still the young adults stayed away. Admirably Fleetway stuck with it for a while, but after 49 issues it changed from a fortnightly to monthly title. An influx of reprint stories soon followed and then after only a further fourteen months, *Crisis* – and the British adult comic boom of the 1980s – was all over.

RETROMETER: 6/10

Crosse and Blackwell Alphabet Soup in a Cube

Up there with Lucozade and How We Used to Live on a day off school

Peak year: 1982: well, it was very cold that year

If the bomb dropped, we'd still have Crosse and Blackwell soup to keep us company in the twilight. Indeed, the cubes were so small you could have fitted a couple of hundred in your Anderson shelter.

Along with Cup-a-Soup, soup in a cube was one of the by-products of the explosion of convenience foods in the 1970s. We often pondered how the Alphabet variety managed to fit all the letters in such a small space, but however they did it, it certainly made for a special treat when off school feeling sick – helping to settle your stomach by tasting of, basically, nothing.

Nowadays the cube seems to have disappeared again as a popular form of nutritional storage, even in the form of that football-ground favourite, Bovril.

RETROMETER: 8/10

Crown Court

Thrice-weekly legalese from Fulchester
Peak year: 1973, when Mr *Heads and Tails* himself took the stand

Derek Griffiths – yes, Derek Griffiths – sits in the dock, accused of swindling a family out of thousands. Surely it couldn't happen here? But it did, thanks to Granada's long-running daytime legal drama.

Crown Court, which, lest we forget, came to us from Fulchester long before *Viz* comic populated the place, brought the elderly and the idle one courtroom drama stripped across three half-hour episodes every week.

Following the hearings was a jury comprised of actual viewers, but even better than that was the array of talent on hand. While the likes of John Barron and Richard Wilson donned the wigs, an even more interesting line-up of faces shuffled in every week accused of drug-pushing, rape, arson and sometimes – whisper it! – embezzlement. Alongside your man Griffiths (as the unlikely-named 'Raoul Lapointe') you could spot Betty 'Mrs Mumford off of *Rentaghost*' Alberge, Lennard 'Granddad' Pearce, Peter 'Jason King' Wyngarde, Nigel '*The Charmer*' Havers and Pauline '*Pauline's Quirkes*' Quirke.

Running from 1972 to 1984, the show's format has been much imitated, but never bettered. That is until Fred Harris shows up in the dock somewhere on a public disorder charge.

RETROMETER: 8/10

Cue Frank! by Frank Bough

A tantalising glimpse into Uncle Frank's diary
Peak year: 1980

Cue Frank! is a classic of its kind, showcasing a man at the peak of his powers; Frank Bough, or 'Mr BBC', was at that point fronting both ***Nationwide*** and *Grandstand* and the nation felt that they knew him as well as his curiously named wife Nesta.

The most notable aspect of the book is Frank's bizarre writing style, which reads as if he dictated it to a ghostwriter who couldn't be bothered expanding it to full sentences, leading to a somewhat staccato structure: '1966. *Grandstand.* Studio E. Lime Grove. Five hours a week.' Nevertheless the glimpses behind the scenes at his two shows are fascinating.

At the end, though, Frank seemed to get somewhat overwhelmed, imploring, 'Tell me; is it too late? What should we all do next?'

This despair was lifted in 1983 when he got the *Breakfast Time* gig, which led to another marvellous publication. *Frank Bough's Breakfast Book* tells the story of the show, before falling into classic 'will this do?' tie-in territory with Debbie Rix's breakfast recipes and musings on the perfect boiled egg. Still, anyone after the real story behind Frank's relationship with Russell Grant ('we get along famously') were never to be disappointed.

We bet Eamonn Holmes couldn't do this.

RETROMETER: 9/10

The Custard Stops at Hatfield by Kenny Everett

Probably the most bonkers autobiography ever written

Peak year: 1982, at the height of his *Video Show* fame

You'd hardly expect Cuddly Ken to write a standard showbiz biog, and *The Custard Stops at Hatfield* is certainly not that. The title sums the whole thing up, and indeed musings on the north-south pudding divide are but one of the many highlights.

It's also got a completely different format to its contemporaries – published as an A4 hardback, with a different illustrator for each chapter, and Ken's writing style ensuring it comes across as one great big gossipy chat in the pub.

Given what we now know about Ken's private life, there are some fairly notable omissions from the text, but at the time this was a fascinating look into some notable episodes from his life – from tripping on a golf course with Freddie Mercury to knocking up an episode of *Captain Kremmen* in thirty seconds because he'd been snorting coke all night and forgotten about it. It's never depressing, though, and there's always a daft observation or great joke lurking around the corner.

The climax of the book is a transcript of a lunch meeting between Ken and his writing partners Barry Cryer and Ray Cameron, and is fascinating reading for anyone interested in comedy – not least for recording the exact moment Ken finally twigged why Barry decided to name a character 'Mary Hinge'.

RETROMETER: 9/10

D–L: The David Soul Gift Book to Lunchboxes

The David Soul Gift Book

'Hi! This is David Soul'

Peak year: 1978

With its scant 48 pages and price tag diligently snipped off by gran, *The David Soul Gift Book* is just one of many annuals based on similarly thin material.

The articles – such as they were – inevitably concentrated on Soul's role in *Starsky and Hutch* and included such exciting strap lines as 'they receive their scripts three weeks in advance' and 'we want people to enjoy the programme'.

Yet far from being the rip-off gran suspected it was, ***The David Soul Gift Book*** was actually a genuine source of excitement for young Hutch fans. Who really cared what star sign David was (Virgo), or whether he likes hot dogs ('so long as they are tasty and not merely pre-packaged convenience food') when herein you could gaze on countless photographs of the man decked out in denim, or preferably sporting one of his many admirable cardies?

RETROMETER: 8/10

Daytime in the 1980s

'A new way to spend your mornings'

Peak year: 1988: daytime came of age with *This Morning*

As recently as the mid-1980s, if you switched on the telly in the morning you'd either be stuck with ***Pages from Ceefax*** or the likes of Lesley Judd 'going' maths for ***Programmes for Schools and Colleges***.

This all changed on 27 October 1986 when BBC launched its daytime service targeted at 'shift workers, the elderly and retired, the unemployed and the housebound'. On screen, this translated into various short factual programmes (*Gardeners' World Special*, for one), the *Thought for the Day*-cum-poetry shop *Five to Eleven* and *Open Air* – 55 gleeful minutes of moaning about last night's telly.

Over on ITV, a proper daytime service didn't arrive until 14 September 1987 when Jeremy Beadle kicked off proceedings with game show *Chain Letters*.

Beadlebum was then followed by trash US soap *Santa Barbara* and the 'fags and slags' (© Danny Baker) of *The Time . . . The Place . . .* Over the years, ITV would shuffle the deck, essaying the likes of *Runway* and *Crosswits* in the *Chain Letters* slot, and quickly ditch the pappy US soap . . . for pappy US sitcoms. Yes, it was here *Out of this World* debuted, detailing the exploits of superpowered juvenile Evie 'swinging on a star' Garland.

But, of course, it was the launch of *This Morning*, hosted by Richard Madeley and his wife Judy Finnigan, the following year that gave ITV supremacy, prompting the BBC to sling out a million ***Pebble Mill at One*** clones – sometimes featuring [gulp!] Judi Spiers – in numerous doomed efforts to claw back the viewers.

All that, and the UK launch of *Neighbours*, gave a generation of lead-swinging kids even more reason to look forward to those glorious weeks of 'study leave' around exam time.

RETROMETER: 8/10

'Day Trip to Bangor' by Fiddler's Dram

All aboard the novelty folk-rock chara-banc!

Peak year: 1980

Blame Terry Wogan. One winter's morn, an obscure accordion-squeezing yarn about a works outing to a Welsh seaside resort inexplicably ended up amid his stack of Radio Two breakfast platters.

A couple of spins over the Quaker Oats later, the hairy, fiddle-brandishing ensemble had become almost a national obsession, thanks to their rollicking tale of a 'luvverly time' spent savouring the delights of 'chocolate ice', 'the big Ferris wheel' and 'a brass band that played a tiddly-tum-ta-ra-ra'.

If all this merriment now seems a little tame, at least the ride home darkly hinted at debauchery on the back seats, involving a 'bottle of cider' and a 'cuddle with Jack'.

The 'Dram found themselves ascending the festive charts, threatening a Christmas number one, before an unlikely alliance between Pink Floyd and Abba kept them from the top. But their status as the thinking man's Wurzels is forever assured. And all for under a pound, you know.

RETROMETER: 6/10

Deadline

'Comix' go alternative – with added *Generation Game* references

Peak year: 1989, Tankmania in full effect

Riding in on the tail of the late 1980s adult comics revolution, *Deadline*, the creation of ex-***2000AD*** artists Brett Ewins and Steve Dillon, bucked the trend for po-faced 'graphic novels' with an anything-goes editorial policy, and lashings of very British humour.

The flagship strip was Jamie Hewlett and Alan Martin's 'Tank Girl', a combination of ultraviolence, adolescent nudge-nudge japery and random references to *The Gumball Rally* and the Choices pension adverts. Also present were the more thoughtful meanderings of Philip Bond's oddly cute 'Wired World', existential violence from Pete Milligan and Ewins' ageing hitman 'Johnny Nemo', Nick Abadzis' spherically headed angstmeister 'Hugo Tate', and perhaps weirdest of all, 'Timulo', D'Israeli's Sheffield-based metaphysical fantasy mish-mash. None of these strips were written to editorial order, but for all the variety, they all seemed to have a slightly tapped 'something' in common.

Music interviews with the likes of The House of Love, Cud and Gaye Bykers on Acid, columns by *Channel Four Daily* presenter Garry Rice and counter-culture oddball Ron Merlin, and the occasional page-filling experimental splurge added to the ramshackle fun. If it sounds like a mess, it was, but in the early years at least there was enough of a house atmosphere to keep everything loosely together.

There really was nothing quite like it, before or since, though it was undoubtedly a product of the times – the editors even released a 'deep house' record that comprehensively failed to sell.

The comic started to wane as the 1990s progressed, however, and an ill-advised plan to sink assets into the long-gestating 'Tank Girl' film (which, being American, dropped all the gags about whinnets and *The Italian Job*, rather missing the point) led to its collapse in the mid-1990s.

RETROMETER: 7/10

Desmond Wilcox Documentaries

Devoutly ordinary folk parade in front of Mr Esther Rantzen's lens

Peak year: 1986, and two worlds collided: Wilcox and Pollard

Forever known round the BBC as 'Desmond's weepies', the stream of dowdy doccos that flowed from Wilcox during his long reign in the Beeb's features department could always be relied upon to interrupt a pleasant evening's viewing with another of life's Ugly Truths.

First came *Man Alive*, which Wilcox helped create in the early 1960s and quickly became his plaything, a weekly snoop into another suburban tragedy or gynaecological breakthrough. The big hit, however, was *The Boy David*, about a titular disabled Peruvian scamp Wilcox brought back to the UK for much-hyped face-building treatment.

Some efforts were not so sensitive. *Americans* found Desmond investigating people's business Stateside, and *The Marriage* followed the pre-nuptials of a boring couple in (as ever) painstaking detail, heaping on the pathos with title song 'Starting Together', badly trilled by Su Pollard, which promptly went to number two in the charts.

His eclipse was suitably epic, from the start of the 1980s when Wilcox and his missus virtually ran the BBC, to being axed as anchorman from crap ***Nationwide*** replacement *Sixty Minutes* after just seven weeks, to nothing. Apart from endless reunions with David, of course.

RETROMETER: 7/10

Desperate TV Tie-ins 

The stocking-filler telly treasuries you won't cherish forever

Peak year: 1984, when Ted and Dusty starred in book form

No Christmas morning stack of presents could ever be complete without a flat, rectangular parcel courtesy of a maiden aunt or kindly neighbour. Every single kid in Britain had to unwrap an annual on 25 December, by law.

As a result come Boxing Day afternoon, thousands of us curled up on the settee with a selection box, to leaf through some less obvious attempts to cash in on the Yuletide annual industry.

Like ***The Two Ronnies***, for instance. Messrs Corbett and Barker's bawdy wordplay might have been much-loved in the playground, but in comic-book form, something definitely got lost in translation.

The bizarre mix of illustrated sketches and monologues ('Good evening. Due to an EEC agreement, Christmas is to become Euro-Christmas!') ended up being heavily padded out with a feature on how television works, and unnecessarily large photos of the duo dressed as Sacha Distel and Nana Mouskouri.

Meanwhile, millions of kids tuned into Ted Rogers every Saturday, thanks to Dusty Bin and the exploding YTV logo, but that doesn't explain why Fleetway reckoned on publishing a ***3-2-1*** annual.

Puzzles, quizzes and a profile of the show's dextrous compere ('Ted, your stand-up comedian and master of the topical gag, has tasted life at all levels') were interspersed with leftover strips like 'Cap'n Codsmouth' and 'The Spooks of St Lukes', none of which had anything to do with McGuffins or The Brian Rogers Connection.

But although a bound volume of Dennis Waterman dust-ups might have seemed a more obvious proposition, a contractual oversight meant that one ***Minder*** annual could not legally feature George Cole. This minor problem might have deterred some publishers, but add a moustache, change the name to, er, 'Guv'nor' and bingo, a crafty manoeuvre even Arfur himself might have been proud of.

RETROMETER: 5/10

The Dick Emery Show

One-man rep from Ethel Meaker's brother

Peak year: 1972: *Ooh, You Are Awful!* played cinemas nationwide

He's rarely mentioned these days, but from 1963 until his death two decades later, Dick Emery was at the top of the comedy A-list.

For years the format went largely unchanged: a textbook giggling theme tune introduced sketches featuring Emery's cast of characters: Union Jack-clad idiot Bovver Boy, bucktoothed reverend, knackered ex-serviceman Kitchener Lampwick, sex-starved Hettie, boa-toting Camp Clarence, and Randy Mandy, begetter of that famous catchphrase as she playfully walloped the street interviewer for his perceived sauciness.

Sketches were written by an A–Z of Britcom talent: Dick Clement, David Nobbs, Esmonde and Larbey, plus Mel Brooks and even Harold Pinter. Towards the end of the series, some mutated into more ambitious mini-films.

Emery bowed out in 1982 with *Emery Presents*, a comedy detective serial that bravely ditched most of his regular characters.

RETROMETER: 8/10

Dingley Dell

Noel's other country residence

Peak year: 1981: with Perkins in tow

What is it with Noel Edmonds and whimsically named fictional stately homes? Whatever, this audio-only mansion was a lot more, er, stately than its manic telly descendant.

Noel livened up a Sunday morning Radio One slot with patented Funny Phone Calls (a money-spinning album came out in 1981), staid BBC newsreaders John Snagge and Brian Perkins reading out amiable nonsense (yep, Noel was the first to pastiche Perkins), John Gielgud reading *The Railway Children*, and the odd star guest, all playing along with the 'country house' conceit. (Though sometimes not – Noel: 'It's Dingley Dell, on a Sunday morning!' Billy Connolly: 'No, it isn't! Ye liar! There's just a man wavin' at us through the windee!' Noel: 'We don't have a windee!')

All cosy homespun stuff, to be sure, but that was your wonderful Radio One on Sundays – expect the expected. If you didn't hear ELO, Ray Stevens and *The Adventures of* ***Captain Beaky*** during Noel's show, a state of emergency would no doubt have been declared.

RETROMETER: 7/10

The Doctor Who Annual

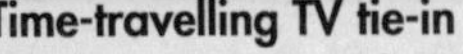

Time-travelling TV tie-in

Peak year: 1977: The Doctor visits the 'Eye-Spiders of Pergross'

From 1966 to 1986, Doctor Who enjoyed a string of adventures completely unrelated to his TV ramblings, courtesy of World Distributors and their series of annuals.

The 1971 edition was the first to feature the satin robes of 'Dr Who' Jon Pertwee, pitting the then fresh incarnation against 'The Ghouls of Grestonspey' and 'A Universe of Fred'.

Pertwee's run in paper hardly represented the golden era, with comic strips – the best bit by far – thin on the ground. Come the arrival of Tom Baker things got interesting, as the artwork went completely nuts.

Representation of the Doctor and his TV friends grew inconsistent and wholly dependent on what reference photos were available at the time. As a result, one story saw the Doc step out in Tom Baker's own jacket and sweater, as unveiled at a press call the previous year. Even more bizarrely, in a 1979 strip companion Leela turned into Adrienne Corri from *A Clockwork Orange*.

Things became less erratic as Peter Davison took over the TARDIS, although the pen-smiths struggled to capture his pleasant open-faced features on paper (cf: **Target Books'** series of Davison novelisations – see below).

The last *Doctor Who* annual was dated 1986. By this time, it was wall-to-wall text again, the Doc (now Colin Baker) dropping in on a repressed minority and leaving them to fight their own battle because 'the Time Lords have forbidden any direct interference in the development of any planet'. Unconvincing.

Aside from the lacklustre portrayal of the titular hero, the series was also infamous for its legion of features which bore a tenuous connection to *DW* itself, but filled out those pages a treat. Thus, in any annual you could generally find something on the comparative size of planets, an item on monsters from Greek mythology and a page just banging on about stars.

RETROMETER: 7/10

Doctor Who Target Books

'A tall man with wide inquisitive eyes and a tangle of curly hair'

Peak year: 1983: Target releases the novelisation of 'The Five Doctors' with a special shiny cover

When forced to visit the local library, one of the few saving graces (aside from having a quick finger through the occult section before you were caught) was being able to spend ages sitting on one of those sweaty plastic chairs looking idly at the covers of the countless Target *Doctor Who* novelisations on display.

The first few Target books were published in 1973 and featured among them a very evocative retelling of Doctor Who's earliest adventure with the Daleks. Unlike later books, author David Whitaker recounted the tale in the first person, and managed to confuse *Who* fans for years to come by taking major liberties with continuity (including making up his own account of how the Doctor came to meet his first on-screen companions).

By the late 1970s, several *Doctor Who* novelisations were being published each year, most written by one-time series script editor Terrance Dicks. Indeed in 1980 he wrote an incredible ten titles and still found time to contribute a story to the actual *Doctor Who* TV series. Unsurprisingly his prose style was very functional and some of his novelisations exceedingly brief.

Artists Chris Achilleos (tasteful stipple), Andrew Skilleter (1980s airbrush affairs) and Alister Pearson (overly complicated montages, with the initials of some girl he possibly fancied worked into the design) held similar dominance over the books' front covers and were loads better than the awful BBC publicity photos used for a spell in the 1980s when it was realised no one in the world could draw an accurate picture of Peter Davison.

By the late 1980s, the range focused less on the general reader and instead attempted to appeal to hardcore *Doctor Who* fans. This meant the final few titles (the Target novelisations concluded in 1991) were more complex in style – they explored the psychological depths of the baddies' motivations and featured excerpts from fictional characters' personal journals. Unsurprisingly none of these were written by Terrance Dicks.

RETROMETER: 9/10

Doctor Who Weekly

Happy times and places, every week

Peak year: 1979: Tom Baker peruses that 'fantastic first issue'

Doctor Who Weekly hit the newsstands in October 1979, its first issue trailing: 'Comic strips! Features! Pin-ups!'

Inside there were no less than three strips and a welcoming letter from the Doctor himself (he'd signed it and everything), which asked readers to write to his 'Terra-bound colleagues' with their thoughts about the new venture.

This being an era before every aspect of the series had been joylessly catalogued, the *Weekly* also ran perfunctory behind-the-scenes features which generally listed all the actors who'd played the Time Lord and left it at that.

And so it continued over the weeks, enlivened by the odd 'Crazy Caption' competition (an evil robot bears down on Sgt Benton – 'sorry sir, you can't come in here without a tie!' quips the soon to be pulverised squaddie); the occasional challenging reader's enquiry ('How is it that you can be a Time Lord from Gallifrey . . . yet in the story "An Unearthly Child" in your magazine's second issue it said you were a Doctor living in London?'); competitions to design new monsters for the show (we'd dearly loved to have seen the Doc go toe-to-toe with the 'Cyclopian Crabworm'); and most fondly remembered of all, the chance to enlist with the government's killing-aliens division via the special 'UNIT Hotline' page.

However, ten months after the launch, sales bottomed out. It seemed the Doctor was facing a cancellation crisis. Thankfully, the moment had been prepared for and in August 1980, the titular time traveller sat down with quill in hand to pen us his last letter from the confines of *Doctor Who Weekly*. In order to spread its cash further, the comic was regenerating into 'a Marvel Monthly'.

With the comic strips being gradually faded down in the mix, it went on to secure its place alongside the *Beano* on the lower shelves of newsagents right up to the present day.

RETROMETER: 9/10

The Domesday Project

All of Britain, at the spin of a trackball!

Peak year: 1986

A grandiose scheme involving BBC Micro computers, laser videodisc players and Paul Coia. Surely nothing gets more 1980s than this?

In 1983, BBC TV producer Peter Armstrong decided it would be a good idea to create a modern-day version of the guide to Britain first compiled under the reign of William the Conqueror. With the publication's nine-hundredth anniversary coming up in 1986, he swung into action. The new Domesday would contain text, diagrams and photographs, and – most importantly of all – it would all run on a microcomputer.

The country was divided up into twelve-square-kilometre chunks, and schools were asked to send their pupils out and about taking photos of their designated area, writing about whatever aspects they fancied. With few guidelines laid down, the results were at times whimsical. Photos of York covered a street scene, a row of houses and someone's mum doing the ironing – but didn't even give a glimpse of the world-famous cathedral.

When assembled, the data – 40,000 pictures and more than 27 million words – was converted into two video discs which allowed users to browse over maps, calling up photographic images from around the country at the twirl of a trackball. The future was here.

Of course, some twenty years later, the irony is that while the original Domesday can still be read, nowadays no one has the appropriate BBC computer hardware knocking around with which to access its 1980s update.

Still, it gave Paul Coia a nice little spin-off lunchtime quiz in the form of *Domesday Detectives* in 1986, so it had been time well spent.

RETROMETER: 10/10

'Don't Stop Me Now' by Queen

Toe-tapping scamper through Fred's thesaurus

Peak year: 1979: a textbook post-Christmas-blues money-spinner

Let's not be coy about this: the best Queen songs were always (a) written by F Mercury (b) opened with a bit of keyboard business from the man himself and (c) boasted capricious sound effects or vocal noodlings a-plenty. Forget Neanderthal drum and axe duellings – Freddie's piano was where the real gems lay, and 'Don't Stop Me Now' delivered the full works PLUS a few meaningless gossipy asides ('I like it!') for good measure.

Fred made his intention clear at the outset. 'Tonight I'm gonna have myself a real good time,' he promised, 'the world/I'll turn it inside out'. How he intended to accomplish this feat was then meticulously detailed courtesy of a brisk time change, the arrival of the rest of the band, and a staggering shopping list of similes in which our host meekly compared himself to a shooting star, a tiger, a racing car, a rocket ship, a satellite, a sex machine and an atom bomb. This exhausting roster unfolded over an evermore frenetic accompaniment until a none-more-1970s *nom de plume* – 'Mr Fahrenheit' – ushered in a complete breakdown, more conversational nattering ('Have a good time!'), Brian May's obligatory wankery and finally some suspiciously post-coital 'la la la' nonsense.

Expertly harmless, stupidly hummable, it was Queen the whole family could sing along to on long car journeys, and therefore indispensable.

RETROMETER: 9/10

Doomwatch

Scary finger-pointing early-1970s ecology drama

Peak year: 1970, as Toby Wren 'bought the farm' in explosive fashion

Ladies with impossibly bouffant hair, an obsession with anthrax, gents with impossibly bouffant hair and smoothies wearing cravats – that was *Doomwatch*, the BBC's hugely serious and impossibly exciting 'science fact' drama series of the early 1970s.

Very much an issue-of-the-day show, *Doomwatch*'s hallmarks were a few frighteningly accurate predictions of scary science, razor-sharp dialogue challenging the notion that governments were always open and honest (back then this was cutting-edge stuff) and heterosexual men referring to other heterosexual men as 'darling' in a manner that seemed quite chic and provocative at the time.

Over three series, *Doomwatch* touched upon subjects that would later become of great national concern: genetic engineering, euthanasia and chemical dumping. However, it also brought us giant mutant rats, people going mad because they lived in high-rise flats and fish that made men go sterile and attend cockfights.

The highpoint was undoubtedly the death of regular character Toby Wren (Robert Powell) after he failed to defuse a bomb. This provoked much angst from his boss Spencer Quist, ergo the predictable plotline in which the main character resigns, but returns not long after when they realise that they have the power to 'make a difference'.

By all accounts the series grew increasingly desperate for new issues and had run out of steam by 1972.

RETROMETER: 7/10

Dramarama

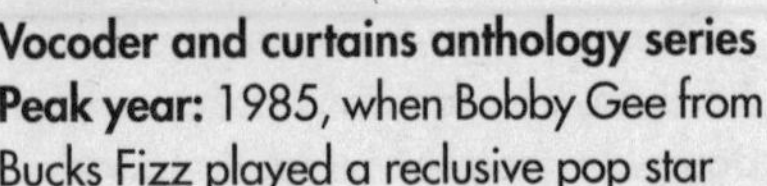

Vocoder and curtains anthology series

Peak year: 1985, when Bobby Gee from Bucks Fizz played a reclusive pop star

Originally billed as a scary kids' anthology series, the first batch of *Dramarama* (subtitled: 'Spooky' and shown in 1983) contained some of the most terrifying programmes ever broadcast in the name of children's television. In particular a story in which a girl's evil imaginary friend starts to manifest into something more real was truly bed-wetting stuff involving exorcisms, possessions – basically everything short of Max Von Sydow.

Other tales in that initial run dealt with time travel (including a sequence in which the second hand on a clock starts to go backwards, natch) and drowned sea captains coming back from the dead.

Later series would expand *Dramarama*'s remit to include knock-about comedies that were uniformly dreadful and worse still – experimental theatre. However, *Dramarama* was starting to get recognition for its issue-based stories. Of particular note were 'Look at Me', featuring a deaf boy befriending an older lad, and 'Play Acting', which dealt with an Indian girl's anxieties over betraying her cultural background.

Latterly the series grew increasingly fascinated with metatextualism and post-modernism. What either concept was doing on a kids' programme is a probably a good question. Sadly too many stories would end with the characters breaking the fourth wall, or delivering an ironic commentary on 'the meeja' when all we wanted to see was another shit-scary bit where a clock started going backwards.

RETROMETER: 7/10

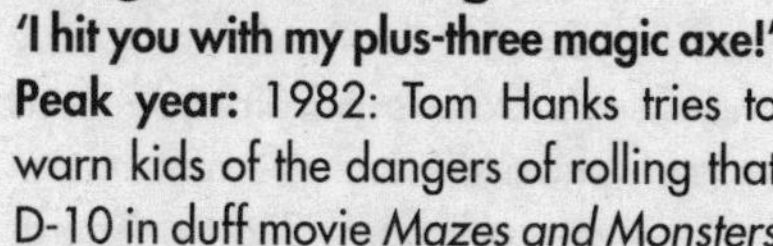

Dungeons and Dragons

'I hit you with my plus-three magic axe!'

Peak year: 1982: Tom Hanks tries to warn kids of the dangers of rolling that D-10 in duff movie *Mazes and Monsters*

Where to start? Not the dark and murderous pursuit as portrayed in that goofy 1989 episode of *Taggart*, nor the joyous roller-coaster ride-cum-trite morality play of the cartoon series bearing the same name, *Dungeons and Dragons* was instead a furious foray of hacking and slashing realised by the rolling of die and a lot of studious note-taking.

Mostly preying on naturally inclined chess champions in the early thralls of puberty, the game was traditionally played in the English lab during break time, or in aromatic bedrooms bedecked with airbrush artwork of large-breasted Valkyries in chain-mail fetish gear and bearded midgets waving big hammers about.

Marketed by US games company TSR, and based on an original premise by Gary Gygax and Dave Arneson, the D'n'D world existed in a sub-Tolkien milieu, where orcs, goblins and elves were your common Joes, and clerics were somehow exciting.

The action took place wholly in the imagination of its participants, events being described by an appointed 'Dungeon Master' (normally whoever had the most impressive collection of stationery) with conflicts resolved by the roll of an opaque many-sided dice (some of these things had ten faces!) and a lot of statistical paperwork.

Thanks to occasional moral panics in the 1980s linking it to the occult, the pastime was a regular cause of concern for parents unsure what their child was actually doing in that room with all his friends, and baffled by the mechanics of the thing – where was the playing board?

Nevertheless, it's still going strong today, providing a PE-fearing contingent with a harmless outlet through which they can express their aggression and paving the way for a future adult life of real beer, Marillion T-shirts, Terry Pratchett novels and black raincoats.

RETROMETER: 9/10

Duplicators

The pre-IT vanity publishing kit

Peak year: 1983: a godsend on the school trip to the local museum

Sure, with modern technology even the most technophobic teacher can knock up a perfectly attractive hand-out in moments, and print out hundreds of copies at the click of a mouse – but they don't have the special charm of the hand-cranked copiers that allowed for a smelly, feely, felt-tipped copy to be distributed around the class.

The most obvious use of the duplicator was creating worksheets to ensure the latest school trip wasn't just going to be an opportunity to mess about, but instead a spirit-crushing dreary traipse in search of boring facts about each exhibit.

Back when graduating from a pencil to a pen was a major watershed, the excitement of the duplicator from a pupil's point of view was possibly the first experience for many of the 'forbidden' adult stationery product Tipp-Ex covering up a slip of the pen. Truly the duplicator inspired a generation of temps.

RETROMETER: 5/10

Eagle

'This week's star names – Eddie Kidd, Mike Read and Steve Perryman'

Peak year: 1982, primitive photo tampering and a free space spinner signify the return of a publishing legend

Just how many boys were strong-armed by nostalgic dads into giving up their weekly fix of ***2000AD*** in favour of the relaunched *Eagle* is a question that remains unanswered to this day.

The original 1950s *Eagle* had been a highly influential and innovative boys' title; however, in the early 1980s innovation meant pointless celebrity columns (such as 'Read Mike Read' and Daley Thompson's 'Daley's Diary') and – even worse – photo strips.

As such, although 'Saddle Tramp' claimed to be set 'near the border with Mexico in the 1870s', it couldn't help but look like a bunch of pasty *Eagle* employees stomping around the badlands of modern-day Stamford Street and anywhere else within a bus ride of the office.

Yet the new *Eagle* did manage to produce a few memorable stories. 'Doomlord' was a creepy, skeletal alien supposedly come to Earth to judge us; and 'Thunderbolt and Smokey' told of two lads who competed together in curiously static football matches.

Unsurprisingly, the photo strips were dropped after just over a year, and *Eagle* turned towards more conventional storytelling techniques. However, it was clear the title was never going to match the popularity of its illustrious predecessor. Even the return of the 1950s' Dan Dare (drawn by one of the original artists too) failed to turn the tide, and finally in 1993 it was all over, allowing innocent kids to at last return to the ongoing escapades of Strontium Dog and the rest at ***2000AD***.

RETROMETER: 7/10

'Eat more of this!' campaigns

Nationalist food propaganda

Peak year: 1981, when QUANGOs ruled the Earth

It all started with the Humphreys – those unseen, drinking, straw-wielding beasts insidiously snaffling the milk from under the noses of Frank Muir and co. That advert was paid for by Unigate Dairies, but the general message was people weren't drinking enough milk, period.

For the next few years, a slew of these ads – not advocating a particular brand per se, and seeming more like a public service announcement as a result – were all over the telly.

The Humphreys mutated into the 'gotta lotta bottle!' campaign. British Cheese created a cartoon country club populated by well-spoken wedges of Double Gloucester and Sage Derby. A squadron of jacket-potato paratroopers asked, 'Sarge, when we get there, it will be butter, won't it? It won't be – gulp! – anything else?' The margarine threat was implicit: 'No buts, it's got to be butter!'

Meanwhile, the Meat Marketing Board were clearly worried about the encroaching fashion for vegetarianism. 'Wot, no meat?' cried a trio of Robin Askwith-like cheeky cockney lads, as they gate-crashed a couple's pork-free dinner and regaled them with an impromptu oompah ditty detailing a plethora of exciting serving suggestions for a nice bit of British meat, while posters in butchers' windows shouted: 'What's meat got? It's got the lot!' Later, a more sanguine Geoffrey Palmer urged us to 'slam in the lamb'.

It wasn't all animal-derived: 'Make room for the mushrooms!' sang a male voice choir of cartoon button-caps, marching onto the dinner table in a good-natured bid for fungal *lebensraum*, while minimalist cinéma *vérité* ads demonstrated faked documentary evidence of the soothing powers of 'tea – best drink of the day'.

But the least convincing of these broadcasts was not food-related at all: in the early 1980s, just as pit closures were starting to bite, a cosy family were shown relaxing by a fireplace warmed by 'Coal: the fuel of the future'.

Marketing can only achieve so much, you know.

RETROMETER: 8/10

Educating Marmalade

Bad girl warning!

Peak year: 1981, when Marmalade reached the Blessed Limit

Future telly drama overlord Andrew Davies was responsible for unleashing The Worst Girl in the World on an unsuspecting public. Played with perfect bubblegum-popping malevolence by Charlotte Coleman, she made her screen debut in *Marmalade Atkins in Space*, an edition of Thames Television's children's-play miscellany *Theatre Box* involving a dormobile space shuttle, moustachioed male nuns, a nodding dog and the secret of the universe.

Educating Marmalade followed in short order, a sitcom that detailed the desperate efforts of her parents (played by John Bird and Lynda La Plante) and education officer (who developed an increasingly elaborate nervous tick as the series progressed) to find an educational establishment that could control her. Marmalade being Marmalade, all such plans were doomed to failure – in her own words, she put herself about, driving everybody potty.

There was a sort of mini-punk sensibility to Marmalade's disinterested brand of mayhem, reinforced by a Bad Manners theme tune. In the second series, *Danger: Marmalade at Work* (in which various avenues of employment failed to contain the mop-haired wastrel) Coleman herself belted out a Sid Vicious-style opener ('Jobs! I've had a few/and most of them/were pretty grotty-ah!') But she's still firmly in the catapult-twanging tradition of Minnie the Minx et al. 'Marmalade Atkins, you are EXPELLED!'

RETROMETER: 9/10

'Eighth Day' by Hazel O'Connor

Doom-laden punk opera prophecy

Peak year: 1980

Hazel O'Connor acquired mass attention in the 1980 film *Breaking Glass*, in which the titular band (complete with junkie saxophonist Jonathan Pryce) got taken under the wing of shifty promoter Phil Daniels and rose up through the music biz, hindered by fascist police and public-sector strikes, natch.

The film ended with the climactic performance of this song, belted out by Hazel in a *Tron*-predating luminous printed-circuit body stocking in front of the classic early-1980s swirly blue dry-ice laser light tunnel. Then, still in the body stocking, she got on a tube train and had a nervous breakdown. Such is rock'n'roll.

The song was as much of its time as the film. Entering on a mighty burst of Wagnerian synth noise, Hazel favoured the cod-operatic declamatory vocal style for her tale of mankind's disastrous obsession with technology. He started off inventing neon lights, and things got progressively more horrific from there – on the third day 'we get green and blue pill pie' – until that harbinger of apocalypse: the silicon chip. The world ended with those merciless Texas Instruments taking over ('On the eighth day machine just got upset/a problem man had not foreseen as yet').

We may scoff, but such earnest brow-furrowing was once par for the course, sneering irony being a sign of shallow decadence as later single 'D-Days' (D for decadent) made clear ('Put on your face, put on your clothes/going out dancing, pose, pose'). O'Connor's only concession to convention was the wistful love theme 'Will You?' ('I spill my tea/oh, silly me!'), but by then Toyah had muscled in on the post-punk shouty scene, and the rest is (a big question mark in) history.

RETROMETER: 9/10

Emu's Broadcasting Company (EBC-1)

The best of 'that bloody bird'

Peak year: 1979: in the hallowed Sunday teatime slot

Rod Hull graduated from Australian television's *Super Fun Flying Show* to British infamy via a puppet emu he'd originally made for a ventriloquist act but binned when he found he couldn't cut it, vent-wise. The silent, vicious incarnation, however, was a Parkinson-baiting success, and the BBC offered Hull his own children's sketch show, which he wrote himself.

Set in a ramshackle TV station (to which the announcer 'handed over' before the programme), it featured acres of neatly observed, silly TV parodies – 'Yesterday's World', 'Open Emuversity' ('I'll just run over that again!'), 'Grandstand of Sport' – mixed with 'behind the scenes' control-room chaos (aided by technician Billy Dainty and tea lady Barbara New) and adverts for multi-purpose miracle household product Scunge, linked by poppy close-harmony jingles sung by a trio of loudspeakers with faces.

The 1980s brought a move to ITV, and the pastiches were swapped for pantomime whimsy and stage-school singalongs – a disappointing replacement.

RETROMETER: 8/10

Etch-a-Sketch

Magna Doodle's un-cooperative older brother

Peak year: 1980, when the toy came complete with an activity centre, and you could 'finish drawing the cowboy' or 'help Buzzy Bee find his way to the hive'

In our opinion the most disappointing toy ever when you actually got your mitts on it, from afar the Etch-a-Sketch looked like a piece of the future, a slab of plasma upon which drawings would appear via the twiddle of two satisfyingly chunky knobs.

Created by Arthur Granjean and brought to global attention in 1959 at the International Toy Fair in Nuremberg – surely the world capital of recreational fun and games – it was an ingeniously engineered device. A box full of aluminium powder and plastic beads, an internal stylus controlled by said knobs scraped a line on the underside of its dust-covered screen, thereby creating a thin black trail.

During the 1970s its manufacturer, The Ohio Art Company, released new versions in pink and blue frames, but the public remained committed to the traditional pillar-box-red livery. Around this time it was also promoted via a TV advertising campaign which lodged a shrill 'Etch! A! Sketch!' jingle in the minds of many.

However, despite the lure of magically creating magnificently detailed pieces of art, in reality it seemed to take the wrists of the world's supplest safe cracker and the endurance of a psychopath to draw anything more complicated than the ***Play School*** house, leaving most kids who didn't have the necessary idiot savant skills to disconsolately write kack-handed swear words across the screen instead.

RETROMETER: 9/10

Evel Knievel 

Accident-prone Yank's plastic incarnation
Peak year: 1975, when Evel did himself a mischief at Wembley

A Midwestern bike-shop owner with a taste for self-publicity, Evel somehow managed to hold great swathes of the international media in his hand as he set up ever more elaborate stunts with his trusty bike. Watching the yellow US footage on ***World of Sport***, British kids went mad at what they were missing.

Fortunately, it was the Ideal Corporation to the rescue in 1973, with the famed Evel Knievel Stunt Cycle, consisting of a semi-posable Evel figure and bike which hooked up to a red plastic 'energiser' with a chunky red handle with which you wound the vehicle's gyro. Then off he'd race, to jump over ramps, flaming hoops, cats etc. That he often ended up spiralling into a prone position several feet before actually reaching the ***Buster*** annual-supported ramp was a situation cleverly prepared for by the real Evel, who made sure he frequently did the same thing in real life.

Other merchandise included the Stunt and Crash Car (an odd-looking cross between a shark-nosed Citröen and – appropriately – a Thundersley invalid car), the Super Jet Cycle and Escape from Skull Canyon (some green plastic rocks for Evel to jump over). Eddie Kidd was scarcely a replacement.

RETROMETER: 7/10

Ever Decreasing Circles

'We're respectable people, not the London School of Economics'

Peak year: 1984: the dawn of Martin's mithering

Berthed in a similar Sunday-night slot to *Last of the Summer Wine* and posing as the same sort of casually spun unremarkable fare, *Ever Decreasing Circles* turned out – astonishingly, it's fair to say – to be meticulously hewn unforgettable farce.

With Richard Briers, Penelope Wilton and Peter Egan on board the show was always going to deliver something. What that was, however, took the viewer by surprise: a picture of suburbia that was the antithesis of the kind normally found in telly comedies, i.e. a place you actually recognised.

The Good Life creators John Esmonde and Bob Larbey pitched their central quintet of Martin and wife Ann, neighbour Paul and nearby residents Howard and Hilda into situations by turns ordinary, absurd and poignant, but always blessed with a twist of the unexpected. So when Martin's evil colleague, who could only be called Rex Tynan, managed to persuade him he'd slept with a prostitute in Amsterdam, the ghastly consequences played out in full three-piece freefall at, of all places, a dinner dance. When Paul bought another house on the Close and sublet it to people Martin thought would turn out to be insufferable pompous buffoons like his neighbour, they turned out to be real insufferable pompous buffoons like himself, and he hated them all the more.

Meanwhile, when Martin rounded on Anne for protesting in the shopping centre about Open University cuts, Howard rounded on Hilda for, well, just going to the shopping centre.

Ever Decreasing Circles: the only sitcom to look like your mum and dad's living room, and so much more than Penelope Keith falling on her arse in some mud.

RETROMETER: 10/10

Everest Windows

Double-glazing is amazing, don't you all agree?

Peak year: Ted and his feather reigned supreme throughout the 1970s

Burly agricultural lummox Ted Moult became a minor celebrity after being crowned *Brain of Britain*, but it's for his double-glazing commercials that he's best remembered.

Ted would go to fantastical lengths to demonstrate the effectiveness of Everest, fluttering a feather in front of his windows to exhibit the lack of draughtiness, before beckoning a noisy helicopter into his back garden to display their soundproofing qualities, and even swinging a demolition ball at them to illustrate their toughness. If all that didn't get you on the trimphone to ask the operator for 'Freefone Everest' and installing some 'Insulation for the Nation', then nothing else could.

RETROMETER: 7/10

The Face

Designing the decade

Peak year: 1988: its 100th issue

Heading the queue for a place within any 1980s-themed time capsule, *The Face* arrived at the same time as the decade it helped to define. The first edition came out in May 1980, boasting a crappy cover picture of Jerry Dammers and the dodgy strapline 'Rock's Final Frontier'.

Its editor Nick Logan, fresh from the ***NME*** and ***Smash Hits***, bragged of how the entire editorial team could fit in the back of a taxi, but once he switched the magazine's emphasis from music to style the staff – and circulation – ballooned.

Of course it was impossible to read a copy of *The Face* all the way through. The design was demented (headlines at right angles, pages ending mid-sentence) and the articles a mystery to anyone outside Greater London. However, you bought it because everyone else apparently did, and at least it didn't go on about 'the street' like *i-D*, or have endless photos of celebrities in silly spiky clothes like *Blitz*, its two rivals.

Still, *The Face* only worked when it was the 1980s and nothing but; once the decade ended, it had no place to go.

RETROMETER: 5/10

The Family

Proving that the decade between the 1960s and the 1980s was indeed brown with orange curtains and large patterned wallpaper

Peak year: 1974: watched by 5.5 million viewers, Tom and Marion wed in a blaze of publicity

This groundbreaking documentary serial recorded the day-to-day lives of the Wilkins family from Reading. There was Margaret, the tough-as-old-boots mum; Terry, the bus driver dad; Marion, the grumpy daughter; and Tom, Marion's boyfriend who did very little except wear his jacket with the collar up while smoking a skinny fag in the drizzle in that way that all good reprobates used to back in the 1970s.

Producer Paul Watson came in for a lot of criticism for having somehow hoodwinked the Wilkins into making some awful exposé of working-class Britain, but in truth all he did was film what actually went on.

Sadly Tom and Marion split up just a few years after the serial was transmitted – as did Margaret and Terry. There was a follow-up in 1983, and then in the late 1980s the whole thing was repeated once more.

Margaret turned up for a brief chat on *Wogan* and after that we never heard from the Wilkins again. However, Watson went on to make loads of other stuff including the equally infamous *The Fishing Party* and *Sylvania Waters*, before killing off the BBC's *40 Minutes* strand after it had been running successfully for thirteen years.

RETROMETER: 7/10

Fast Forward

***Hello!* for the Broom Cupboard set**

Peak year: 1989: Ma Boswell and company – now in comic-strip form!

Beeb might not have exactly flown off the shelves, but its failure didn't deter the BBC from launching another kids' magazine in 1989. *Fast Forward* was a more determined effort from the start, backed by what the BBC might not appreciate us calling an advertising campaign. The 'Fast! Fast! Forward! Forward! Forward!' jingle transmitted between the end of ***Children's BBC*** and the start of *Neighbours* remains lodged in the cerebral cortex of a million thirtysomethings.

The strips at the start included '*Grange Hill*' and '*Bread*' – the Scouse shitecom was massive with the kids – and the cartoon was as amusing as you'd expect. The best strip of the lot, mind, was 'TV Centre', featuring assorted BBC people having adventures – perhaps the most memorable involving Philippa Forrester trying to rig an edition of *That's Showbusiness*.

BBC branding included *Eggs'n'Baker* recipes and *Hartbeat* makes, while the pop page was later renamed *The O-Zone*, with a picture of Andy Crane at the top. The miscellany bit in the middle laboured under the name 'Flibbertigibbet!', the sports page was called 'G'Day Sport', and a lettuce edited the letters page. That's the kind of magazine it was.

RETROMETER: 4/10

'The Floral Dance' by Terry Wogan

Masterful novelty nonsense

Peak year: 1977: a powder-blue-suit-sporting Tel storms ***Top of the Pops***

The business of 1970s celebrities lending their pipes to the occasional 7" threw up the shameless (John Inman's monologue on retail strategies in 'Are You Being Served, Sir?' – 'Now I'd like my hand back/it's trapped between your thighs') and the brilliant yet back-of-an-envelope (Windsor Davies and Don Estelle as themselves, singing in character, but billed as themselves).

None, however, beat the union of the knowing, cod-olde-worlde declamation of Terry Wogan and the glorious strains of The Brighouse and Rastrick Band. Tel knew this ancient Cornish ode of old, and when the Band's instrumental version was released in late 1977 his impromptu on-air singalongs sent it climbing the charts. The inevitable followed: a rerelease with the great man mounting the ***TOTP*** stage armed with a Morrissey-esque bouquet of posies, assailing the throng with recollections of 'the curious tone/with cornet, clarinet and big trombone'.

Undeniable charm and a high oompah quota ensured a number 21 hit, and Tel was tarred with the song for life. Canny enough to know the odd burst of a chorus is what we all want, occasional memorable renditions on *Children in Need* show that Wogan can indeed still make the 'best of his chance'.

RETROMETER: 8/10

Flowers in the Attic

The overwrought pot-boiler that smells of incest

Peak year: 1979

Latterly described as a gothic novelist, and subject of her own *Critical Companion* academic text, Virginia (or sometimes VC) Andrews is today best remembered as the author of choice for twelve-year-old girls desperate to express their developing maturity. Her most famous work, *Flowers in the Attic* tells of four children who – after their father dies – are imprisoned by their mad mother and grandmother.

The book was a minor sensation back in the early 1980s, and was the title most likely to provoke the local librarian into phoning your mum before lending you a copy. Much talked about in girls' toilets, those excited exchanges usually concentrated on the volume's theme of incest and whether or not you would ever actually do that with your own brother in real life.

Andrews's other titles (and there were many) were further scandalising tales of imprisonment and sexual awakening, making them a literary training ground for those who wished to move on to the glamour and overt sexiness of Shirley Conran's *Lace* (a favourite with the fourteen-year-olds).

Honourable mention must also be made here for James Herbert's *The Rats*, which managed to find its way around both boys' and girls' changing rooms thanks to its carefully crafted blend of copulation and giant killer rodents.

RETROMETER: 7/10

Follyfoot

Heartfluttering horseplay

Peak year: 1972, when even Macca pined for the countryside

Yorkshire TV cleared its throat with this worthy series of yarns set amidst a rambling retirement home for ponies.

Follyfoot revelled in not just a top-notch cast (Arthur '*. . . Being Served?*' English, Desmond 'Q' Llewellyn) and heritage (the book *Cobbler's Dream* by Monica Dickens, great granddaughter of Charles) but also the titular mares' mansion was built from scratch on a posh estate near Harrogate at massive expense. Such investment helped turn trite tales of Q's niece Dora (Gillian Blake) petting over-the-hill nags into affecting fables of romantic Ruritania, which for a time sent the nation into a pastoral frenzy.

Star of the piece, the 'lightning tree' – a rotting stump superstition decreed everyone had to hurl a bucket of water over as they passed – supplied the subject of the show's gaudy theme, rendered in booming unison by The Settlers ('The lightning rent from the firmament!').

RETROMETER: 5/10

Free Gifts

If your squirt ring is missing, please see your newsagent

Peak year: 1976, the year of ***Krazy*** false teeth and the Super-Jet Joke Camera

Blatant circulation-boosting gimmicks they may have been, but nothing made a comic fly off the shelves like a free gift.

Easily the best remembered is the paper whiz-bang – that triangular origami construction that, when flung downwards, made a moderately loud bang. DC Thomson must have ordered a job lot of these some time before the war (World War One, probably), as practically all their comics gave them away every six months. Fun for anything up to five minutes.

In a similar vein was the balloon that, when released into the air, made something approaching a farting noise.

The same gifts seemed to come round again with frustrating regularity. ***2000AD*** launched in 1977 with a Space Spinner, a 'futuristic' mini-frisbee that turned up again on the front cover of the relaunched ***Eagle*** five years later.

Indeed, new comics always lured in the readers with a bountiful array of freebies. *Jackpot* launched by giving away a 'practical joke', a squirt ring and a Magic Numbers card game, while ***Krazy*** hit the shops with free comedy plastic fangs, fake camera and the 'top pop hummer' (i.e. a kazoo).

RETROMETER: 7/10

Free Milk

Playground fuel

Peak year: 1971: last orders

Besuited men behind desks considered it a nationwide dose of protein, but out in the field it was always a cheap and hasty alternative to breakfast or forking out for crisps at break-time. Free school milk had been on tap for all British state schools since the late 1930s, introduced to combat spiralling levels of childhood malnutrition and later becoming an enduring post-war tonic to supposedly ensure the next generation had good bones.

Notoriously prolific – crates of untouched curdling bottles were always hanging around the most over-heated corridor in the building – the hearty swig on a weedy straw through the blue or red-topped pints was, for ages, as much a part of the morning routine as running about whooping at a dog loose in the playground.

Then Margaret Thatcher famously curtailed universal guzzling of the white stuff when the country sank into yet another 1970s economic slump, though nursery and primary schools were allowed to continue siphoning it out for another decade.

The final deliveries were made in 1986 – until, that is, local authorities in Scotland recently decided to reintroduce it, thereby rather charitably allowing kids to partake in the right kind of nostalgia even before they could read or write.

RETROMETER: 8/10

Gambit 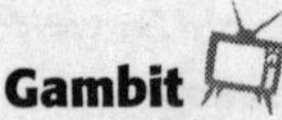

Fred Dinenage hosts a teatime quiz as only he knows (or dares) how

Peak year: 1982, when couples were desperate to be subjected to the wrath of Fred

People think Anne Robinson was the first person to give contestants a hard time on a TV show, but Fred Dinenage was doing it two decades earlier – though that wasn't always the intention.

Gambit, in anyone else's hands, would have been a straightforward teatime quiz to enjoy over the haslet; basically Pontoon on the telly, contestants were asked questions, getting a card for each one they got right, and whoever had the nearest to 21 would get the chance to play for Anglia-standard prizes of Mini Metros and canteens of cutlery on the mystical *Gambit* board.

So far, so ordinary, but the masterstroke was the casting of Fred as host, who brought something of an air of menace to the usual antiseptic atmosphere of these things. He wouldn't tolerate any talkback from his participants, once famously asking, 'you got a problem there?' to a contestant muttering during his link.

There was also the repartee with dippy hostess Michelle Lambourne, whose banter couldn't have received a frostier reaction had she been outside the studio. Rightly so, as in *TV Times* Fred claimed his show was 'an Olympics of the mind' and advised contestants to read an encyclopaedia every night in bed.

Sadly, in 1983 Tom O'Connor took over as host, and was far too polite to the punters. Unsurprisingly, the series ended soon after.

RETROMETER: 8/10

Game for a Laugh

'Watching us, watching you, watching us' – repeat ad infinitum

Peak year: 1981, which boasted a Christmas special with guests including Hercules the Bear and junior rockabillies, Showeenyweeny!

Originally presented by Jeremy Beadle, Henry Kelly, Matthew Kelly and Sarah Kennedy, an average edition of *Game for a Laugh* would consist of silly studio games (often involving patting the heads of bald men) and a few pre-recorded items (most likely featuring kids saying amusing things), followed by some of the people from said film standing up in the studio audience and waving superfluously.

However, the highlight of each show was undoubtedly the big hidden camera stunt. This might consist of a set-up in which someone's car appeared to get destroyed, or better still a person's entire livelihood sunk to the bottom of the Thames. Regardless, this sequence would play to rapturous laughter from the audience, and most probably the viewers at home too.

Yes indeed, *Game for a Laugh* is the 'daddy' of modern-day light entertainment. You want presenters running down a flight of stairs? How about Perspex trophies given out to contestants as a memento of their 'great day out'? What about the bit where the presenter goes up into the audience and says, 'of course we know all about embarrassing secrets, don't we . . . Sally-Anne Jones from Leicester'? *Game for a Laugh* did it all first, with the added lustre of a spurious once-a-season appearance from the Roly Polys.

RETROMETER: 10/10

The Generation Game

Brucie and Larry bring the nation together every Saturday night

Peak year: 1979, as 24 million people were entertained

The Gen Game was based on a Dutch format that mixed games, songs and sketches, though in the end the only part that remained was the conveyer-belt finale. Bruce Forsyth resurrected his flagging career with it in 1971 and stayed in charge for six years. It succeeded thanks to his ability to gently send up and bully the contestants while ensuring they remained the stars.

It could have gone belly-up when he quit for ITV, but the masterstroke was the hiring of Larry Grayson as his replacement. Larry played it hapless as a game-show host, seemingly unable to understand the mechanics of the show or even work out where he was supposed to be standing. But this ineptitude – much of which was put on – made him appear so lovable that the show was an even bigger hit. It was a staple of the Beeb's Saturday night until 1981, when it withered in the face of the brash new ***Game for a Laugh*** on ITV.

But the format was strong enough to inspire a revival in 1990, with Brucie back at the helm, and just as fresh and entertaining as the original. Sadly, one of the most perfect entertainment shows was sullied in 1995 when Jim Davidson replaced the Mighty Atom, and ensured the stars of the show were him, his mates and, worse still, Mr Blobby. Don't remember it this way.

RETROMETER: 8/10

The Gentle Touch

Britain's first female telly copper – just

Peak year: 1980, which brought our first glimpse of Jill Gascoine on the beat

Pipping *Juliet Bravo* onto TV sets by a matter of months was DI Maggie Forbes, denizen of London's Seven Dials police station, who spent her first sixty minutes' screen time dealing with the murder of her husband before opting for four years of pedestrian coppery and family angst.

Gascoine was the eponymous practitioner of tea-cosy conciliation, slipping merrily between accents as the weeks passed, having embarrassing grown-up chats with teenage son Steve (Nigel Rathbone), and holding forth on prostitution from behind a desk boasting a gigantic vase of flowers.

William Marlowe played pissed-off superior DCI Russell with recurring moustache, while Paul Moriarty was the irksome three-piece-suit-sporting DS Barratt.

Immensely popular appointment viewing throughout the early 1980s, *The Gentle Touch* was always one up on its Beeb rival thanks to the novelty of a DI having the bother of compiling her weekly shopping list before finding herself inconveniently caught in the middle of a grenade explosion. A half-arsed spin-off, *C.A.T.S. Eyes*, ruined everything.

RETROMETER: 5/10

Giles

Everyday family life, if the day was in 1932

Peak year: 1983, and breakfast telly keeps satire alive

For most kids, there was a limit to the number of comics you could enjoy each week, depending on the depths of your parents' pockets. Therefore anything that was a bit like a comic was enough, so dad's morning paper would normally be hijacked to find the cartoons. For readers of the *Daily Express* (the official grandparents' newspaper), the humour was provided by Giles, and his one-frame cartoons were obsessed over by budding artists.

Come Christmas, the year's highlights were compiled in a paperback publication, bought by wives for husbands and then, a couple of years along the line, passed onto kids during a clear-out.

Giles books were but one of the newspaper-strip compilations filling up newsagents' shelves come December. The likes of *The Perishers* and *Fred Bassett* also got the treatment. The latter's 1982 compilation was notable for the fact that all the year's strips were included, even the umpteen that were simply quasi-adverts for the forthcoming *Mail on Sunday* ('see me in colour from November 7th!') which made no sense at all after the event.

RETROMETER: 7/10

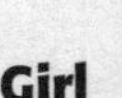

Girl

Mediocre reading for the plastic bangles and hairband set

Peak year: 1982: Paula Ann 'Claire Scott off of *Grange Hill*' Bland becomes a cover star

Nothing to do with the posh comic from the 1950s, the early-1980s incarnation of *Girl* was one of the great makeweights of juvenile publishing. The bridge between the cut-out-doll tweeness of ***Twinkle*** and acne-scarred problem pages of *Jackie*, it ploughed its trough in middle-of-the-road little lady-fare.

Initially focusing on generic horsey stories, it gradually became more cosmopolitan, sporting pop pin-ups and photo stories. Fashion tips were also available, as pictures of pubescents sporting fingerless gloves bigged-up the best cheapo merchandise from Chelsea Girl.

But, lest anyone think this was all too much, too young, the magazine still kept a foot in the old-fashioned comic-strip camp, detailing the low-action adventures of freckled-faced Patty and her 'World', orbiting antics with her better-looking friend Sharon and token boy Johnny Vowden.

Despite cautious swooning over the Spandau's and the like, the opposite sex were still yucky on the whole, as reader after reader sent in letters detailing incidents which showed up how stupid their brothers really were. 'What a nutter!' was the accepted pay-off here.

RETROMETER: 2/10

'Girls Girls Girls' by Sailor

Possibly not in Germaine Greer's record collection

Peak year: 1976

In the rich tapestry that is rock'n'roll, it's fair to say Sailor have never been afforded the respect they deserve for taking a sound pitched somewhere between Roxy Music and The Cliff Adams Singers, a sartorial image heavily indebted to flat caps, neckerchiefs and Richard O'Sullivan, and coalescing it all into something roughly approaching a workable proposition.

Sailor entered our consciousness in 1975 with a debut hit that invited us to 'get together' over a 'Glass of Champagne', but it's for their banjo-picking, wolf-whistling tribute to what the squash club set referred to as 'the fairer sex' that we shall remember them.

In three minutes flat, 'Girls Girls Girls' tipped its hat at any passing crumpet, from 'shy girls, sexy girls' to 'Miss World and beauty queens' to, well, anyone from Japan ('they know how to please a man!'), with an exuberant 1930s-style chorus that compelled the listener to launch into that Charleston-era, polishing-the-windows-with-both-hands routine, before essaying that crossing-over-hands-on-knees optical illusion-cum-dance.

In between the close harmonies, 'Girls Girls Girls' contained some invaluable practical advice for the budding accounts department smoothie ('don't rush, keep it nice and gentle, and sentimental').

If all this reeks a little of Brut 33, remember that this was a different time, an era when the respective merits of

Anthea Redfern and Miss Brahms off of *Are You Being Served?* were regularly debated in parliament. And there's always the nagging suspicion that the whole thing might have been tongue-in-cheek. Either way, hop on, the world is swinging, don't stop and twiddle your thumbs, get up and meet those pretty girls, girls, girls!

RETROMETER: 6/10

Gloy Gum

Half glue, half joy – that should have been the advertising slogan

Peak year: 1986: Halley's comet inspires a nation of frieze-makers

There are few things in life more satisfying than painstakingly peeling a dried bit of glue off the side of the bottle and rolling it between your fingers. Such was the excitement of using Gloy, the clear glue that managed to enjoy 99.9 per cent penetration of Britain's classrooms.

With memorable lower case 'gloy gum' logo, the product came in plastic squeezy bottles with a nubbly dispenser on the top which, inevitably, would get good and gummed up after a few squeezes onto crepe paper and therefore require stabbing with a pair of scissors before you continued.

Eventually the rise and rise of Pritt Stick saw Gloy fall out of favour, not helped by the fact that some kid would always make a right mess with it and stick everything to the table.

The same was true of its less transparent 'rival', Marvin, meaning those essential little green spatulas soon fell into disuse.

RETROMETER: 6/10

Gobots

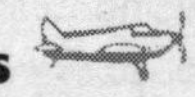

'Mighty robots, mighty vehicles'

Peak year: 1986, Hanna-Barbera release the cinematic masterpiece *Gobots: War of the Rock Lords*

The whole 1980s vehicle-that-changes-into-a-robot phenomenon was an extremely confusing and perilous scene for the uninitiated and if not too careful could result in tantrums as little kids were given Optimus Prime by a well-meaning relative when what they had asked for was Giant Zrk.

While less well known than the ubiquitous Transformers, the Gobots were actually first to hit the market. Released by Tonka toys in 1984, they were based on the already existent Machine Robo range that had been created by Bandai.

The original Gobots were a lot smaller than the Transformers and came in packaging depicting a cartoon version of the toy you were purchasing that looked far more impressive than the actual thing itself. Much like other products of this ilk, the robots were necessarily oddly designed, such that Cy-Kill (the first Gobot out of the factory) had rather obvious motorcycle wheels for shoulders. The extensive range covered all forms of transport including planes, dumper trucks and police cars.

Although aesthetically there wasn't much between them, the Transformers were marketed far more aggressively and successfully positioned themselves as the hipper of the two lines. Indeed by the mid-1980s, the poor kid who owned the entire Gobots line was something of a laughing stock – as was his dad who still insisted on recording all his favourite TV programmes on Betamax.

RETROMETER: 9/10

The Golden Shot

'Up a bit, down a bit, left a bit – fire!'

Peak year: 1974, Bob's second coming

By the 1970s, ATV's Birmingham-based archery game show had survived a dud of a launch – with dull original host Jackie Rae traded in for the more agreeable Bob Monkhouse – to carve out a niche for itself as the weirdest thing on telly.

Trotting out an array of lame contestants (including, on one occasion, a partially sighted woman with a nervous twitch) or a spurious guest star ('welcome, Alf Ippititmus!') to train a crossbow on an apple secreted in a glam-rock-inspired diorama, it also brought a mix of topicality ('the work to rule is over!' decreed Bob during a 1970 edition as the power workers' strike came to an end) and social action (the Kidney Machine Stamp Appeal) to Sunday teatimes.

Reliable for sporting at least one technical cock-up per episode, the whole package was must-see stuff. But then something bad happened.

In 1972, Bob was 'let go' and stand-up comic Norman 'swinging' Vaughan brought in. Visibly nervous on screen, he didn't prove to be a natural raconteur, hopefully asking a contestant, 'listen Dennis, what shall we talk about?' when attempting the traditional getting-to-know-you chat.

Vaughan was soon out, to be replaced by *The Comedians* star Charlie 'keep smiling all the time!' Williams – but things didn't improve. Permanently befuddled, the comic stumbled his way through edition after edition exclaiming: 'We don't know where we are!' and: 'They keep changing things. Don't tell Williams, he's only t'gaffer!'

As viewing figures dropped, there was just one thing for it. The 1974 series boasted a new theme (featuring Stephanie De Sykes), a slightly rejigged format and – yes! – Bob, who'd done a nifty deal to return, on provision that ATV also let him commandeer a new show they'd just acquired – *Celebrity Squares*.

RETROMETER: 9/10

Gold Spinner

Dairylea's trendy rival

Peak year: 1978, St Ivel sponsors the Gold Spinner Frisbee Championships

In the admittedly small world of foil-wrapped triangular processed cheesy spreads, Dairylea reigns supreme. It was not ever thus: the 1970s played host to St Ivel's Gold Spinner, a tenacious paste of solid milk which sought to steal a march on Kraft's creation.

Firstly, it upped the zany flavours ante with a multifarious assortment of tomato, pickle and onion-augmented wedges. Secondly, a cartoon ad campaign was cooked up, featuring Roderick, a gawky, accident-prone preteen in outsize baseball cap, who got into amusing scrapes as his frizzy-haired lisping sister and pet dog looked wryly on.

This seemingly watertight approach was no match for Dairylea's **stage school showcase** campaign, and the brand didn't make it far into the 1980s.

RETROMETER: 6/10

The Gossamer Albatross

The Lighter Side of NASA

Peak year: 1979, and THAT Channel crossing

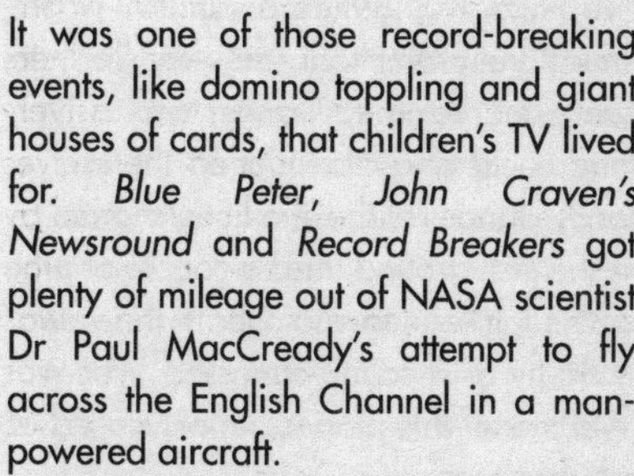

It was one of those record-breaking events, like domino toppling and giant houses of cards, that children's TV lived for. *Blue Peter*, *John Craven's Newsround* and *Record Breakers* got plenty of mileage out of NASA scientist Dr Paul MacCready's attempt to fly across the English Channel in a man-powered aircraft.

Luckily for pilot Bryan Allen, after all the media build-up, the backward-facing, all-plastic contraption with bicycle-powered propeller didn't fare as ridiculously as it looked – the crossing was made in a shade under three hours, and children briefly forgave NASA for their unconscionable dallying over the space shuttle.

RETROMETER: 5/10

'Got to be Certain' by Kylie Minogue

Back when we still knew her as Charlene

Peak year: 1988; we're not sure if anyone else released records that year

The KLF once noted that every Stock Aitken Waterman record began with the same tune as the chorus, thus ensuring they started buzzing around your head as soon as possible. 'Got to be Certain' is the perfect example, and dates from the period when Matt, Mike and Pete could do no wrong.

While it's obvious that the song is basically 'I Should be so Lucky' part two, such was Kylie's popularity at the time none of her fanbase were likely to complain. All they wanted was a lyric they could sing along to on the bus, a fancy dance routine they could practice in the playground, and a couple of nice outfits for them to coo over in the video.

Sadly a Childline-endorsed *Wet Wet Wet* meant this glorious effort stalled at number two.

Of course, following Kylie's success, virtually every resident of Ramsay Street was after the PWL shilling. Her squeeze Jason Donovan managed equally impressive (initial) success, but even *Neighbours'* massive status couldn't give Stefan 'Don't it Make You Feel Good?' Dennis a hit.

RETROMETER: 8/10

The Grange Hill Annual

Your yearly record of the General Collapse of Secondary Education

Peak year: 1980: *GH*'s first annual

Despite the long-running kids' TV drama being infamous for its near-the-knuckle content, its series of annuals were far better behaved.

Well, almost. The first *GH* book had a bit of attitude, as evident in its comic strips, one of which featured Tucker Jenkins arsing about with water bombs – 'What nut-job did that? I'm SOAKED!' Alongside that, there was an interview with producer Colin Cant who rightfully moaned: 'at first you don't think it's necessary to have kids swearing or whatever, but after a while you begin to wonder.'

Alas, the following year things blanded out. We were now into the realms of finding out what nicknames pop stars endured at school (Bob Geldof was 'Liver Lips'), loads of quizzes, 'true-life confessions' ('I punched my teacher') and spurious pin-ups of the cast. Curiously, from this point on there also seemed to be some sort of embargo on depicting *GH* uniforms, resulting in a mélange of Adidas sweaters, dungarees and anoraks.

Thankfully, series creator Phil Redmond remained a constant presence, penning his yearly letter to *GH* fans asking for their input and flagging up future developments: 'There are plans to create another series following Tucker's life after leaving school . . . with a bit of luck you may be seeing more of his ugly mug!'

The annuals wound up in ignominious style with the 1988 edition, which suffered from the publishers apparently only willing to shell out for a lousy eight photographs to illustrate the whole book. Flippin' 'eck!

RETROMETER: 5/10

'Green Door' by Shakin' Stevens

A riddle wrapped in an enigma shrouded in some unnecessarily tight jeans

Peak year: 1981

The man with the biggest apostrophe in pop, Shakin' Stevens conquered Boots' record department armed with little more than some faded denims, a tub of Brylcreem and a pair of surprisingly elastic knees.

Dads everywhere might have muttered something like, 'bah, I remember this from the first time round', from behind their *Daily Express* before sitting back in their Parker-Knoll, but Shaky's one-man rock'n'roll revival machine soon had kids and mums alike on board.

By the summer of 1981, the winklepickered Welshman was in his pomp, toppling 'Ghost Town' by The Specials from the top of the charts in the week of the royal nuptials with a remake of 'Green Door'.

In this enigmatic finger-clicking shindig, a restless Shaky, tired and unable to sleep, stood midnight sentry over a, er, green door, contemplating the secrets that lay tantalisingly behind its façade.

Fortunately, Shaky had established a few basic facts about the beguiling high-jinks beyond this emerald egress. Firstly, there was an old piano, and they were playing hot behind the green door. Moreover, although Shaky didn't know what they were doing, certainly they were laughing a lot behind the green door. Dammit, just what was going on in there?

But further attempts to penetrate the lime portcullis met with little success. Not unreasonably, Shaky tried knocking, only to have it slammed in his quiff. And when he tried the old 'Joe sent me' manoeuvre, someone laughed out loud behind the olive aperture.

From that point on it became clear that Shaky would never identify the owner of that 'eyeball peeping through a smoky cloud', and not even another burst of the mid-air splits on *Razzmatazz* could make up for that.

RETROMETER: 6/10

Green Shield Stamps

Perforated alternative currency unit of old Albion

Peak years: the 1970s, when only a fool paid cash for a toaster

In an era before Nectar Cards and Air Miles, shopping loyalty schemes were a little more basic, but a lot more fun. Back in the 1970s, supermarkets and petrol stations across the kingdom liberally dished out Green Shield Stamps with every purchase, to be saved in albums and bartered for household goods at the neighbourhood 'redemption centre'. Indeed, Bob and Thelma's house in *Whatever Happened to the Likely Lads?* looked like it had been entirely furnished out of a Green Shield Stamps catalogue.

The best thing about the mint-coloured tokens was that the privilege of 'licking and sticking' was usually afforded to the most junior of the brood, although the fact that every kitchen drawer and glove compartment brimmed over with thousands of the things meant this was a laborious process that frequently resulted in acute dehydration. However, the promise of a Spirograph from the catalogue usually prompted a swift recovery.

Indeed, hours could be whiled away gazing at the tempting bounty featured in the literature, and pondering just who had the time, resolve and financial resources to collect enough books to procure a free speedboat or Ford Cortina Mk3.

RETROMETER: 10/10

Halfpenny Sweets

Decimalisation-defying delights

Peak year: 1973, when even blackouts failed to deplete the nation's bell jars

When the *Financial Times* famously grumbled 'the half penny is a most miserable coin, we really do not want to be handling it', you knew they'd never bombed down to the nearest newsagents in order to compile a pocket-sized inventory of sugar mice and Fruit Salads.

Halfpenny sweets were, of course, invariably nothing of the sort, eventually costing upwards of 3p a pop, but the notion ('one Black Jack please!') prevailed for an admirably long time, as did the singular parade of liquorice whips, bubblegum balls, candy necklaces and, in that bell jar on the top shelf that was always suspiciously dusty, ABC letters.

RETROMETER: 7/10

'Healthy Living' Produce

Tuck in and slim

Peak year: 1985, when Daley Thompson liberated Lucozade from the sickbed

A simple switch of diet, so the breezy adverts claimed, could revolutionise your lifestyle without depriving your tastebuds. A penchant for fizzy drinks? Trade in your Coke for Britvic 55 ('55 per cent orange juice!') 'What can cope with all your calories?' trilled Victoria Wood, seated at a piano bizarrely sequestered on a giant pontoon. 'One-Cal can!'

Any number of 'very very tasty' alternatives to bacon and eggs conspired to turn breakfasts into entire agricultural ecosystems (Branflakes, Fruit and Fibre, Special K). Your tea, meanwhile, could be left to technology: microwaveable Lean Cuisine platters, or look-alike non-meat nibbles from the kitchen of Linda McCartney.

Of course, to shed pounds you had to shed pounds sterling – this was fast-track weight loss for the well off. At least Daley's sweat-drenched hurdling to the sounds of Iron Maiden defined Lucozade as the brew of the people.

RETROMETER: 6/10

Heinz Noodle Doodles

Picture-book pasta in tomato gloop

Peak year: 1978, perfectly complementing a round of grilled Sunblest

Don't play with your food, scolded mums at the dinner table, a directive inexorably doomed to failure after Heinz unleashed their latest brand of canned merriment on the nation's teatimes. Endorsed by an animated character known only as the Noodle Doodle Man ('Yes, the Noodle Doodle Man!'), who sounded alarmingly like Jon Pertwee, pasta crafted into novelty shapes was plainly what toast had been invented for.

The Noodle Doodle Man explained in song how he had come to town with lots of straight spaghetti, twisted it around and round and this is, he averred, what you get-ee: Noodle Doodle motor cars, Noodle Doodle houses, Noodle Doodle butterflies, eek, Noodle Doodle mouses! And you never got that with Spaghetti Hoops.

RETROMETER: 6/10

Hergé's Adventures of Tintin

Not so innocent Belgian boy reporter romps

Peak year: 1972, as Middle Eastern adventure *Land of Black Gold* appears in English

The tufty, plus-four-wearing boy journalist with the tiny dog and typhoon-thundering sea-dog sidekick may have been created in the late 1920s, but English translations of the meticulously drawn hardback comics didn't start appearing in numbers until the 1960s and 1970s, and were an instant hit, aided by TV cartoons introduced with a proudly bellowed 'Heeeergéee's Adveeeentuuuures of Tiiintiiin!'

And what wonderful things they were – exciting, amusing (the bumbling, unrelated Thompson Twins became iconic) and for the most part fascinatingly educational. As with ***Asterix***, there was no inkling to the young reader that they were – ugh! – learning stuff from this, but learning they were. Hergé, who died in 1983, never slackened his draughtsmanship, or his meticulous research of the locations he sent the lad to, though his final completed work *Tintin and the Picaros* made a fatal error – those plus-fours were updated to flares, which was, of course, all wrong.

RETROMETER: 8/10

Hi-de-Hi! Annual 1983

Based on the BBC Television Series – very loosely

Peak year: 1983

Stafford Pemberton Publishing might not be a printing powerhouse like Simon and Schuster or Faber and Faber, but their distinctive, if somewhat bizarre logo (a cartoon vulture) adorned many a stocking-filler back in the 1970s and 1980s.

The 1983 *Hi-de-Hi!* annual is archetypal of their work, featuring the usual mix of text-based stories, vaguely recognisable watercolours of members of the cast, barely relevant crosswords, comic strips that fail to capture the essence of the series and, most importantly, endless full-page publicity photos.

The *Hi-de-Hi!* annual's crowning glory, though, was its superfluous articles about the 1950s. Given the upper age range for these publications must have been about twelve we know not why the writers thought the readership would be in any way interested in a potted history of Buddy Holly. But then, given the target market at the time would have had a whole load of titles to choose from (ranging from *The Professionals* to *Rentaghost*) then we can't quite understand how this annual made it onto the shelves in the first place.

RETROMETER: 3/10

High Street Liveries

Before the concept of branding meant every logo looked the same

Peak year: 1977: brown and orange are the official colours of the decade

How many high street store logos can you recognise these days? It seems they all tend to merge into one – sans serif letters on a pastel background to create something almost offensive in its inoffensiveness. But back in the day, you knew where you were when you were shopping, thanks to those many distinct logos.

In those days, retailers knew that there was just one colour that would stand out from the crowd – crap brown. WH Smith were the masters of this, going for a chunky 'WHS' in bright orange, forming a cube on a brown background. Everyone was at it – J Sainsbury (as it was officially called then) and Tesco also used a similar colour scheme, the latter winning points for its marvellous 'typewriter' font. It was almost as if colour was as rationed as petrol at the time.

Today, finding a store still decked out in its 'classic' livery is as rare as spotting a skylark, but there are always a few in the quieter high streets where head office haven't got round to supplying any new signs just yet.

The other side effect is that we can never concentrate during the exterior scenes of old episodes of *Only Fools and Horses* without being distracted by the branch of Woolco or Gateway in the background.

RETROMETER: 9/10

The Hit

Get to the back of the *Q*

Peak year: 1985 – its only year

An attempt by ***NME***'s paymasters IPC to create a glossy version of the inkies, *The Hit* promised to 'Hit Harder than the Rest' through interviews with Hipsway and competitions to win Barry McGuigan's gloves.

The first issue resembled a proto-gay lifestyle mag, thanks to a cover picture of a fey Paul Weller in a pink T-shirt, and even boasted *John Craven's Newsround*'s Terry Badoo among its luminary contributors. But though its knowing take on rock and its obsession with LP charts anticipated the launch of *Q*, *The Hit* was pretty much doomed when the real thing arrived twelve months later.

Fellow glossy casualties of the decade included *Zig Zag*, erstwhile punk bible relaunched as a Goth-obsessed weekly then relaunched again as a dire Madchester/world music talking shop which disappeared after one edition; *Jamming*, home of think pieces on the GLC and pictures of Kid Jensen 'reading' an upside-down copy of the mag with fingers hilariously inserted in ears; and *Flexipop*, an open invitation for kids to nick the eponymous cover-mounted discs and leave the rest of the issue languishing on the shelves.

RETROMETER: 2/10

The Hotspur Book for Boys

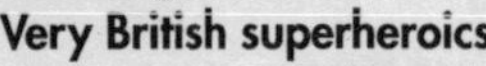

Very British superheroics

Peak year: 1982: 'King Cobra to the rescue at Niagara Falls!'

Although a weekly issue of *Hotspur* always seemed a rare find down Mr Newsagent's, its annuals were a staple part of any bloodthirsty boy's diet.

In contrast to ***Victor*** and *Warlord*, by the mid-1970s *Hotspur*'s USP had become its array of colourful fantasy figures, bordering on the (whisper it) superhero territory – an area British comics had traditionally left to its more vulgar American cousins.

Chief exponent was King Cobra, who made his first appearance somewhere around 1976. By day, reporter Bill King (and can you see how they're working that surname?), by night a reptilian crime-buster thwarting plans to blow up dams and stuff with his electrified mitts and unimpressive-sounding 'flying-squirrel wings'.

Other notable crime-fighters included Red Star Robinson (essentially, a bloke with a red star on his sweater), Nick Jolly 'The Flying Highwayman' (who'd been transplanted from the 18th century to the present day by 'an amazing time ray' – well, it was all we needed by way of explanation back then), X-Bow (a crossbow-wielding motorcycle nutter) and the Iron Teacher (a bin-like automaton who did little in the way of educating).

Aside from the fantastical stuff, *Hotspur* also held its end up in terms of sports and war stories, but, to be frank, these were largely interchangeable with what you'd find in any other boys' annual.

The final *Hotspur Book for Boys* was dated 1992, some ten years after the weekly folded.

RETROMETER: 9/10

House of Dübreq

Mini gizmo empire

Peak year: 1977, as those Trumps roll off the presses

Despite sounding like a minor European royal family from a *Dynasty* end-of-series special, the House of Dübreq was, initially at least, three blokes called Ted, Burt and Brian, who augmented their film sound dubbing and recording business (dub-req, see?) with the invention of the Stylophone in 1967, got Rolf Harris on board, and never looked back.

Paul Daniels was the next celeb to lend his face to the firm, endorsing a collectable series of rhomboidally packaged magic tricks with colour-coded difficulty ratings, which he plugged in a basic telly campaign shared with Rolf's squeezy paint-filled art brushes. 'All from the House of Dübreq!' chanted the unlikely pair in unison.

But these were mere diversions from their flagship product, the truly inspired **Top Trumps**. Sadly this wasn't enough to keep the business afloat, and the early 1980s saw the company close, flogging the Trumps to Waddingtons. A new incarnation, however, recently rose from the ashes, helmed by Brian's son Ben. What fresh aural mayhem they'll unleash remains to be seen.

RETROMETER: 7/10

How 

Like having three granddads on the telly

Peak year: 1978, alongside *Magpie* as an ITV staple

How was perhaps the simplest concept in the history of children's television. Simply get four people to find out how various things work, and then ask them to explain it around a table. Probably the lasting legacy of Southern Television, it's enjoyed two lengthy runs on ITV.

The first incarnation featured the avuncular country gentleman Jack Hargreaves and mad scientist Jon Miller as the stars, with everyman local news anchor Fred Dinenage playing the fool and getting to do all the daft stunts. Add to this the motherly charms of Bunty James and Marian Davies and you had absorbing (and cheap) telly.

Hargreaves was the star (and also an executive at Southern) and was often seen smoking his pipe on air. On at least one occasion he got so carried away he forgot it was still in his pocket and burnt a hole in his jacket.

The series came to an end in 1981 when Southern lost their franchise, but it was back in 1990 with Fred returning to the table, this time accompanied by Gaz Top and Carol Vorderman. Fred's combover is perhaps the most famous symbol of the South of England.

RETROMETER: 7/10

HR Pufnstuf

The Krofft original

Peak year: 1970, as the big screen beckons for Seymour Spider, Ludicrous Lion and co

After designing the *Banana Splits* and their bizarre house, puppeteer brothers Sid and Marty Krofft set up as television producers in their own right in 1969 with Day-Glo *Wizard of Oz* parable *HR Pufnstuf*.

Jack *'Oliver!'* Wild played the regulation clean-cut kid who, along with Freddie his talking flute, was lured away to the Living Island by the evil Witchiepoo. In among the lurid talking trees and mushrooms (the brothers pooh-poohed suggestions of drug references) he encountered the island's titular mayor, a rather big-headed, un-dragon-shaped dragon.

The scene was set for knockabout adventures, always resolved happily with a cheerful 'see you next week!' It was popular enough to merit a film spin-off, called simply *Pufnstuf*, with guest witch Mama Cass.

RETROMETER: 6/10

Ice Lollies

Can I have a frozen Zoom, please?

Peak year: 1981, when everyone walked around with Funny Feet

The stampede for stick-based refreshment in the phew-what-a-scorcher summers of the 1970s meant the Department of Transport had to alert motorists to their refrigerated menace in The Highway Code, noting that nippers queuing at the ice-cream van 'may be more interested in ice cream than traffic'.

And rightly so. Nobody's going to pay any attention to the imminent threat posed by an oncoming Austin Maxi when you could be unwrapping a Lolly Gobble Choc Bomb, the three-in-one Lyons Maid caper featuring strawberry ice around a solid chocolate 'flavour' centre, all encased in more choc and tiny sugar balls. Or a Fab!, the enduring strawberry, vanilla and chocolate jamboree smothered in hundreds-and-thousands and originally endorsed by Lady Penelope.

The Cider Barrel was rumoured to contain 'real' Bulmer's scrumpy, and if sucked in combination with a swig of contraband **Top Deck** on the school trip back seat, had the power to convince the class Pogo Patterson that he was feeling 'a bit drunk'.

In the late 1970s, the time-honoured link between ice cream and the cinema ('Lyons Maid – in the foyer now!') heralded a wave of blockbuster tie-ins. Lyons Maid cashed in with a *Superman* lolly in the never-popular 'cola' flavour, as Christopher Reeve soared to success at the box office. In a revolutionary move, plastic lollysticks emblazoned with 3D figures of characters from the film were introduced. Few kids could resist the prospect of owning Marlon 'Jor-El' Brando captured in lifelike polythene.

But despite the perennial competition from the Mini Milk, the Lemonade Sparkle, the Orange Maid or the Strawberry Mivvi – whatever a 'mivvi' is – nothing could top Wall's Funny Feet, the majestic frozen pink size seven.

And of course, the fun wasn't over once the ice cream had all been licked, thanks to the vaudevillian mirth of the traditional lolly-stick joke. What dance do empty tins do? The can can! Oh, watch out, there's a car coming . . .

RETROMETER: 10/10

Ice Magic

Shape-shifting garnish

Peak year: 1986: the perfect side-order to dinner in front of ***Masterteam***

This begrudgingly sickly yet alluring pudding feature enjoyed a window of mid-1980s ubiquity when any mum with a modicum of sense made sure a substantially filled bottle was always ready in the cupboard.

Ice Magic lived in a crappy plastic squirty pyramid at room temperature, but when applied over ice cream turned from runny liquid to a rock-hard solid, forming – depending on the application – a wafer-thin veneer (for wimps) or a massive crust (for die-hard dessert denizens). The only problem was you had to wait fifteen minutes for the thing to harden, by which time you'd invariably excavated all the ice cream and were left with a lump of chocolate you may as well have got from out the biscuit tin.

RETROMETER: 4/10

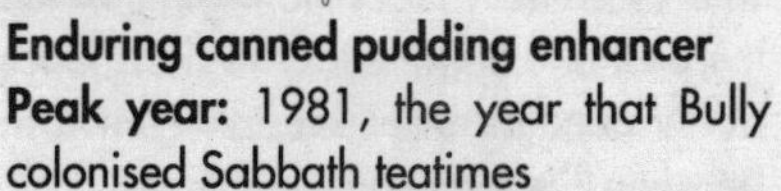

Ideal Milk

Enduring canned pudding enhancer

Peak year: 1981, the year that Bully colonised Sabbath teatimes

The finishing touch to a million Sunday afternoon desserts, Ideal evaporated milk from Nestlé's (pronounced 'Nessles', never 'Ness-lay') brought a dash of creamy richness to any bowl of jelly, fruit cocktail or peach segments.

Evaporated milk etiquette demanded that one made a hole in the top of the blue can with a tin opener, before decanting it into a jug. Rivalry came in the shape of Ideal's nemesis Carnation, prompting a Coke vs Pepsi-style battle of red and blue tins.

In the 1980s, evap, as the connoisseurs called it, faced new challenges, not least from Nestlé's own Tip Top, a Bernard Cribbins-impersonating concoction ('Whoops-ooh, aren't you looking slim, mum?') and, fatally, from Anchor Cream in a can. Sunday teatimes with Jim Bowen and the Man from Del Monte were never the same after that.

RETROMETER: 6/10

Instant Sunshine

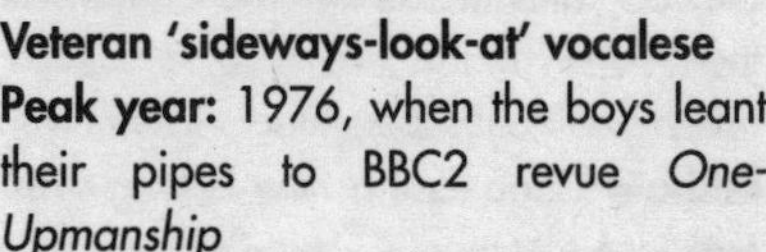

Veteran 'sideways-look-at' vocalese

Peak year: 1976, when the boys leant their pipes to BBC2 revue *One-Upmanship*

Unapologetic graduates of the straw boater/starched spats school of wordplay and whimsy, the light-hearted magazine programme of the 1970s and 1980s that didn't call upon capricious ensemble Instant Sunshine to supply a full stop to a line-up of topical chat, consumer watchdoggery and cut-price cuisine was scarce indeed.

Erstwhile medical students Alan Maryon-Davis, David Barlow and Peter Christie had swapped their lab coats for blazers in the late 1960s, moving swiftly from college hops to the Edinburgh Fringe to cabaret supremacy. With Christie penning the tunes and new recruit Miles 'Franglais' Kington wielding double bass, the tantalising prospect of not one but four Richard Stilgoes waxing wry about everything from government subsidy ('We're awfully keen on the Arts') to liturgical controversy ('Who mowed the lawns of Eden?') to package holidays ('Los Peckham Ryos') became a reality.

They were covered by the King's Singers. They were permanent fixtures in the grubby foyer of ***Pebble Mill at One***. Their appeal spanned the ages from kids on ***Jackanory*** – semi-musical tales including 'The Search for the Source of the M1' – to remuneratively challenged pensioners listening to Radio 4 ('Financial review is long overdue/don't let money stew – with profit in view/what you must do is tune to *Money Box*').

They were regulars on Robert Robinson's *Stop the Week* for decades, slipped effortlessly between the world's cocktail lounges and literary festivals, and outgunned and outpunned rival harmonisers Harvey and the Wallbangers ten to one. Side projects, including Alan's stint climbing in and out of giant polystyrene capillaries on BBC1's *Bodymatters*, failed to derail the 'Sunshine's state, though Miles eventually buggered off to do more newspaper columns about funny foreign accents.

Thankfully they're still going strong today, with David's son Peter now on bass and the repertoire bolstered by ice-cube chinking winners like 'Don't tell the Abbot', 'Cucumber Sandwiches' and 'Conservation Conversation'. Scat's the way to do it.

RETROMETER: 9/10

In-vision Announcers 

An army of chummy, bearded men killing time before *The Sweeney*

Peak year: 1979, due to the endless strikes they had to talk their way around

It's all fancy computer graphics and smartly edited trailers these days, but in the past it was up to your region's team of ITV announcers to keep you tuned in between the programmes. Some companies made do with off-screen voices, but most stuck the affable host in front of the camera, despite many seemingly having great faces for radio. And for some reason they all seemed to have beards – possibly a condition of employment.

It was the BBC who started the policy of in-vision announcers, but they dropped them in the early 1960s claiming they were too cosy. That's probably why ITV took it up, and many of those picked became celebrities in their regions. In those days announcing was considered a career all of its own, but many were multi-skilling before the word was even invented – they would often write their own scripts, read the local news, voiceover trailers and deal with technical breakdowns.

The announcer's faithful friend was ***TV Times***, which they would parrot information from whenever there was an awkward gap.

Some, like *Miss World* MC Peter Marshall (Thames) and *First Post*'s Sue Robbie (Granada) went on to present real programmes, but many were happy enough to simply pop up for a few seconds before *Corrie* to tell you of the delights to come.

Sadly the practice went out of fashion in the 1990s and now you're more likely to see Ant and Dec dancing around between the programmes instead.

RETROMETER: 9/10

I-Spy

Pocket-sized trainee MI5 snooper manuals

Peak years: The 1970s, when no motorway journey was complete without one

The staple of a million back-seat car excursions or idle summer afternoons, *I-Spy* books recruited a generation of adolescent Philby and Macleans into a sinister mass surveillance operation, presided over by a mysterious figure known only as Big Chief I-Spy, from his base at the 'Wigwam on the Green'.

From the jetset glamour of *I-Spy Civil Aircraft* to the rather more prosaic *I-Spy on the Pavement*, the aim of this series of pocket-money pamphlets remained the same – to go around looking at stuff and ticking it off. Perhaps the most demented of the lot was *I-Spy Car Numbers*, which challenged readers to note down every combination of letters used on British registration plates.

Once you'd collected the set, you posted off the book to Big Chief I-Spy to . . . well, nobody was ever quite sure what happened then, because they'd always included some kind of rarity housed at the Beaulieu motor museum, or the FA Cup, or Princess Michael of Kent, rendering the prospect of anybody ever completing the book practically impossible.

Exactly what anyone got out of all this frenzied activity remains unclear, beyond learning that Jimmy Tarbuck drives about in a limo bearing the number plate COM 1C, but *I-Spy* succeeded in tapping into the adolescent collect-the-set, tick-the-box mentality. *Odhu Ntinggo*!

RETROMETER: 10/10

ITV Idents

Those animated badges representing the ITV regions

Peak Year: 1976, when colour sets first outnumbered black and white in the UK, and we got to see those idents in their blue and yellow glory

Back in the day, ITV was a bustling fiefdom, populated with a dozen or so separate regional companies that served their local audience, as well as punting the odd programme at the network to be shown UK-wide.

For viewers used to their own local TV station's branding, the chance to catch a yawning Thames skyline, striped LWT ribbon or a lesser-spotted Border 'chop sticks in a bowl' was the cause for some excitement. Now we were going to see how they did telly in another part of the country.

And so the various idents which preceded each region's offering came to take on characteristics of their own. The revolving Anglia knight was wholesome, unthreatening, and only ever cued in *Tales of the Unexpected*, *Survival* or ***Sale of the Century***. Meanwhile, Granada's static 'G' with an arrow up top spoke of gritty, traditional works, and carried the weight of a regional big-hitter.

Then there were the rarely seen players: HTV's warm symphony of moving lines and synth, and Southern's delicate star accompanied by a sub-'Classical Gas' acoustic guitar workout.

But the daddy of them all was the ATV ident. A bombastic fanfare (that's four trumpets and four trombones you're hearing) and a portentous kettledrum accompanied the merge of three coloured circles into two yellow eye-like shapes sat on top of each other, at which stage the station's three letters would appear. Pure class, and better yet, a fair sign *TISWAS* was up next.

RETROMETER: 10/10

Jackanory

Low-key literary leviathan

Peak year: 1980: Kenneth Williams read *The Dribblesome Teapots*

The ultimate in non-television telly, *Jackanory* lumbered through the schedules for thirty years: an epic parade of personalities in uncomfortable chairs, pretend storybooks on their laps, reading an autocue for fifteen minutes every weekday.

Its worthiness was never in doubt, but the thing always stood or fell on the choice of host. Inevitable successes (and recalls) went to Kenneth Williams (a dozen appearances), Willie Rushton for limerick tomfoolery, and numerous Doctor Whos including Tom Baker (*The Iron Man*) and Peter Davison (*The Sheep-Pig*). The monotony was broken further by gimmicks including write-your-own-story-and-we'll-read-that-instead contests, and illustrations done 'live' in the studio, usually by Quentin Blake or John *Littlenose* Grant.

Increasingly out-scored by Yorkshire TV's ***The Book Tower***, the *'Nory*'s credentials nose-dived in 1984 when the Prince of Wales turned up to read self-penned fancy *The Old Man of Lochnagar*. It somehow soldiered on until 1996 and an appropriately boring rendition of *The House at Pooh Corner* from Alan Bennett.

Programmes for Schools and Colleges did this sort of thing way better.

RETROMETER: 4/10

Jingles 

Singalonga-branding

Peak year: 1978: the great odyssey across Medium Wave

The launch of 'One-derful' Radio One brought proper, polished, people-in-alarmingly-close-harmony jingles to Britain (albeit produced out of Dallas), and it was Tony Blackburn, unsurprisingly, who led the advance, peddling reminders of the station name, his own name, how great he was, and if possible all three ('Tony Blackburn is number one one, one, one, one, one, one, one').

The 1970s were awash with them, from 'It's the Happy Happy Sound' to '247 Radio: Rolling Out the Music for You'. For the consummate marriage of host and jingle, however, Mike Read's breakfast show was hard to beat. Strains of Mari Wilson's 'Mike Read, just what I've always . . . wan-ted' and the timeless 'Mike Read/Mike Read/275 and 285/Mike Read/Mike Read/national Radio One!' still rattle round a generation's heads, not least as the latter was turned into a spin-off single promoting the values of, erm, living in a tower block.

But it wasn't all whimsy. Jingles enjoyed the status of **Public Information Films** in 1978, when the entire national BBC radio network got shunted around as part of an international agreement divvying up the Medium Wave. Frank Muir wisecracked, **Terry Wogan and Jimmy Young** crooned, and Radio Three announcers did their utmost: 'The new kilohertz number is 1215 – the date of Magna Carta!' Best of all, though, was The King's Singers' a-capella hymn detailing how the new frequencies 'will be chang-ed' and, because Radio Three was occupying 247m, 'it will be renamed One-derful Radio Three'.

RETROMETER: 9/10

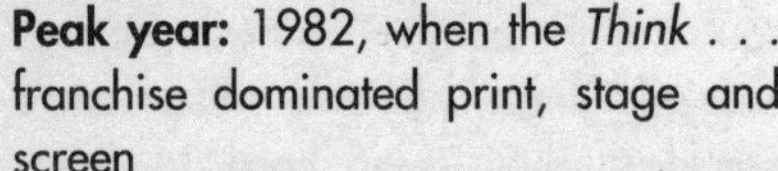

Johnny Ball and the Think . . . Programmes

A master at work

Peak year: 1982, when the *Think . . .* franchise dominated print, stage and screen

A CV boasting nightclub comedian, Redcoat and ***Play School*** host was always bound to lead somewhere great. So it proved for Johnny Ball in his decade-long berth as definitive preteatime crisps and pop telly.

Think of a Number came first, applying arcane arithmetic to card games, rope illusions and how to make a hexahexaflexagon out of a bit of newspaper. *Think Again* on inventions, *Think Backwards* counting down from ten to one and *Think it, Do it* on – eek! – career choices followed, but the format rarely changed: a studio audience of kids, magic tricks ('it's a trick!'), and a set comprising loads of massive cupboards, flung open by our host to reveal some pre-recorded clippage featuring Johnny in preposterous historical garb retelling some fable or other, ending in a suitably lame punchline ('one thing I can tell you about pasteurising milk – you certainly need . . . a lot of bottle!')

Think . . . spin-offs were just as ace, running to factsheets, paperbacks and a legendary stage show which for people of a certain age was like seeing the Beatles at Shea Stadium. One of the greatest kids' presenters ever, to this day Ball does the lecture circuit to packed audiences. 'What a handsome chap!'

RETROMETER: 10/10

Junior Choice with Tony Blackburn

Housewife's choice goes from playlist to playpen

Peak year: 1982, the year Tone gatecrashed Cheggers and Maggie Philbin's wedding

Having whiled away the late 1970s blubbing down the microphone about blood sports and how his wife had left him, Tony Blackburn was finally turfed off Radio One weekdays at the turn of the decade for the milk-teeth merry-goround *Junior Choice*.

The show was such an obvious dumping ground it's amazing Tone stuck with it for four years, especially as he moaned afterwards how it was 'souldestroying'. Perhaps it was because his only other fallback, Tony Blackburn's CB and Electrical Centre, had folded after three weeks.

Under his stewardship *Junior Choice* chiefly ran to a cut from the latest volume of ***Captain Beaky***, a child ringing in to complain how their mum and dad argued over breakfast and Tone's long-serving gimmick Arnold the Dog: a tape loop of someone scraping the inside of a dustbin in an attempt to create the sound of a barking mongrel. Why he never used a real dog was never explained.

Later he conscripted ***Swap Shop*** stalwarts Keith Chegwin and Maggie Philbin for support, shamelessly hyping up their nuptials to the extent of babysitting Cheggers in a Leicester hotel the night before the ceremony.

Lunatic OBs from Mount Snowdon, however, could not delay the inevitable. When Tone left for Radio London in 1984 the *Sun* offered their condolences. History fails to record whether it was for his old or new employers.

RETROMETER: 3/10

Just Seventeen

'Prince, Pat Cash and Nino Firetto in colour'

Peak year: 1985, when Hillier's Hunks adorned the Superfresco

Launched in 1983 by ***Smash Hits*** guru David Hepworth, teen mag *Just Seventeen* rapidly established itself as essential training-bra reading for the nation's Calley Doningtons and Ronnie Birtles.

Just Seventeen fearlessly tackled the burning issues of the 1980s, like modelling ('You don't need to be 6ft and beautiful to be one'), additives ('should they be given the big E?') and, of course, hair disasters ('how to avoid them').

And like all self-respecting teen magazines, *Just Seventeen* had its advice pages, as Melanie counselled a generation of adolescents ('I was shopping with my friends and they started stealing . . .').

But it wasn't all serious fare, as acres of space was devoted to the pin-ups of the day on the 'Hillier's Hunks' page (selected by editor Bev Hillier), including Tom Cruise, Phillip Schofield and, er, Pat From *Brookside*.

The Spy pages vox popped the magazine's readers for their thoughts on life ('Lisa Adams is 15. Likes: clothes, parties and boys with spiky hair. Dislikes: skinny boys and *Albion Market*'), and celebrity features included 'A Day Out With Sam Fox' ('It's into a cab for an interview with Gary Davies!').

And brilliantly, in between the ads for Wella Shockwaves, Dr White's and NatWest OnLine, *Just Seventeen* featured short stories, like 'Waiting For a Train' ('Jess's watch showed the time at ten minutes to eight, but no-one had arrived at the station, not the fat man or the boy in the crumpled jeans. Stranded in silence, she blinked herself awake time and again while she waited . . .')

RETROMETER: 7/10

Kenny Everett Radio Shows

The bijou jockette!

Peak year: 1977: the inception of Captain Kremmen

Cuddly Ken's Radio One career started the 1970s in fine style, when a joke about the Transport Minister's wife passing her advanced driving test got him the sack. By popular demand, the Beeb's 'mahogany men with mahogany minds' reinstated him via a stint in local radio purgatory, followed by a heavily vetted Radio One show pre-recorded at his Welsh farmhouse.

Everett compensated for the lack of spontaneity by creating ever more complex pre-recorded bits and pieces. Sound effects, speeded-up voices and multi-tracking enabled him to have conversations with assorted characters (Crisp the butler, Gran), croon cod-1920s jingles which ambled off into awkward confusion ('now on BBC it's time to have a competition/and you may or may not enter it . . . upon your own volition') and, when in doubt, blow up Broadcasting House.

Ev defected in 1973 for a live breakfast show on the nascent Capital Radio, where he carried on winding up management with stunts like an entirely silent interview with Harry Nillson, and a competition to win a Ferrari (Ev after the switchboard melted: 'all this fuss over a Dinky toy!'). There was also the All-Time Bottom Twenty: crap records by Jimmy Young, Jess Conrad etc. Spoof space adventure '*Captain Kremmen*' was his trump card, a brilliantly produced five-minute wonder of explosions, silly names and lashings of innuendo, which resurfaced with animation on his Thames TV series.

Ken returned to BBC radio for weekends on Radio Two in the early 1980s, with a (slightly) more sedate pace and Beatles singalongs ('we'll take away the vocal sac and leave you with the backin' whack!'), before nipping back again to Capital Gold, where he remained for the rest of the 1980s and beyond.

RETROMETER: 9/10

Ketchips

Potato products for those who can't even be bothered to open a bottle of ketchup

Peak year: 1988, when convenience outflanked taste

Ketchips were the type of fad product that would catch your eye while traipsing around after your mum during the weekly Presto or Gateway shopping expedition.

The high concept at work here was taking the humble chip and inserting tomato ketchup in the middle. As a feat of engineering brilliance it was up there with the Cadbury's Crème Egg; however, the appeal of the ketchip was not quite as enduring as that fondant delight.

Indeed, the ketchip was not so much a chip, more a big, soggy potato croquette seemingly made up from a wad of Smash mixture and laced with a vinegary tomato-type sauce that was the condiment equivalent of watery squash.

Yet during an era in which high street culinary tastes were rapidly expanding, the ketchip seemed just as plausible a product as a prawn cocktail sandwich or even butterscotch **Angel Delight**.

RETROMETER: 6/10

Know How

The layman's DIY bible

Peak year: 1977, the first issue – with a hammer on the cover

A pioneering partwork from Orbis covering every aspect of the burgeoning DIY culture, *Know How* was a Herculean undertaking, promising a 'week-by-week DIY course in 96 parts'. Such workman's arcana as 'Choosing Sinks' and 'Repairing Gutters' were expounded with step-by-step instructions.

In the age of the Workmate and the easy-fit bathroom tile ('I'm 'avin' a spot of bovver!') such sage practical advice was lapped up by intrepid would-be grouters.

A suspiciously similar publication, *The Knack*, was launched in 1982.

RETROMETER: 6/10

Krazy

Adventure? Excitement? Plots? No, just loads of jokes

Peak year: 1976, but the annuals kept running for years

Just look at that name! You're laughing already, aren't you? By the time *Krazy* arrived on the newsagents' shelves in the mid-1970s, Fleetway's comics had more or less cast off the old tradition of including numerous 'serious' strips and just went for non-stop laughs.

Krazy took its name to the extreme, by simply cramming in as many jokes as possible; indeed, the paper eschewed British comic conventions by treating the entire publication as one whole, with everything spilling into everything else and strips running throughout the pages. The main focus was on 'The Krazy Gang', the leader of whom was the repulsive Cheeky.

So popular was the main man, and so regularly were Fleetway launching new titles, that he was inevitably spun off into his own comic, the predictably titled *Cheeky Weekly*. These strips kept up the stream-of-consciousness style by generally involving our hero wandering around and meeting stock characters who would each tell him a joke. However, such silliness had a short shelf-life and both titles soon closed down. Our parents weren't made of money!

RETROMETER: 7/10

The Krypton Factor

Colour-coded middle management Olympiad

Peak year: 1987, when fourteen million tuned in for the final

Billed as the quest to discover 'the UK's Superperson', *The Krypton Factor* resembled nothing less than the initiation test for the paramilitary wing of MENSA. However, it has to be said that the original Superman, whose planet inspired the programme's title, built his reputation on a bit more than shuffling around hexagonal perspex bricks and sliding down a rope.

Invigilator Gordon Burns oversaw four contestants – typically systems analysts and recruitment consultants – through six demanding rounds. First came Mental Agility, Burns posing questions such as 'what day is ten days before March 3rd?' through headphones to aid concentration. Next up was Response, in which the contestants attempted to land a Jumbo Jet in a flight simulator, with chuckling commentary from Gordon ('Bit of a bumpy landing there!').

The Observation round followed, which initially featured film clips ('Which knight was second to the left of the knight holding the sword?') and an identity parade, but later included spot-the-difference comedy skits starring a fresh-faced Steve Coogan. Physical Agility came next, the participants donning colour-coded tracksuits and tackling a 400-metre Army assault course ('It's a course that demands respect') complete with water jumps and rope slide.

Next came the Intelligence round, the bit that everyone remembers, in which the contestants had to solve an intricate three-dimensional geometric puzzle (Gordon: 'The secret with this puzzle is to start at the bottom . . .'). Finally, it was General Knowledge, with the four contestants lit in profile in a quickfire cerebral death race.

For all its intellectual airs, *The Krypton Factor* revelled in its shameless gimmickry, with its spiky theme by The

Art of Noise and luminous computer graphics, and instead of boring old scores, the contestants were deemed to have 'a Krypton Factor of 26'. But let's face it, *Mastermind* was never this much fun.

RETROMETER: 10/10

Lada Jokes

Ah, the grand tradition of British satire

Peak year: 1982, when Jasper Carrott was king of comedy

If you had to sum up the cars made by Lada in the 1980s in one word, it would probably be 'boxy'. The rather unique aesthetics made it a sitting duck for sniping from comedians, regardless of how often their loyal customers emphasised their efficiency and ease of use.

Indeed, in an era that brought us the Austin 1100 and Fiat Panda, you could question why Lada was subjected to so much ridicule. It wasn't alone, with the Skoda (falls apart) and Reliant Robin (won't go) also familiar punchlines to tabloid spoofs. Eventually *Lada*, presumably thinking 'if you can't beat them . . .', hired comedians to appear in their ads. Unfortunately, said mirth-makers were Cannon and Ball.

In later years the company gained further publicity thanks to Maureen Rees's hapless attempts to learn how to use one in *Driving School*, and so thrilled were they with their return to the public eye, they gave her a free one. Sadly, this, coupled with Skoda becoming respectable, meant the jokes started to ring hollow. Now all we could chuckle over at the car dealers was what Fiat Punto translated to in Spanish.

RETROMETER: 7/10

Ladybird books

Corner-shop Encyclopaedia Britannica

Peak year: 1984, when you could scrawl in them as well as read them

Pride of the East Midlands town of Loughborough – attracting schools from across the county to its guided tours and factory giveaways – Ladybird Books furnished improvised bedroom bookshelves of at least four generations of kids.

These perennial last-present-in-the-Christmas-stocking slimline publications emerged in 1940 with the same rock-hard covers and weird parchment-like innards they still boasted in the 1990s. Never more than a few dozen pages in length, they nonetheless delivered facts, playground talking points and line drawings on everything from natural history (*What to Look for in Spring*) to traditions (*The Stories of Our Christmas Customs*) to literacy (the *Peter and Jane* dynasty).

Illogically sequenced reference numbers flagged up collectable franchises including 'Fiction' (*Aesop's Fables*, ancient legends, plus, excitingly, *Deeds of the Nameless Knight*) and, most enduring of all, 'Learnabout'. This ran through everything from making your own transistor radio and cooking *Easy Meals* to the minimalist *Knots* and the wonderful *Codes and Ciphers*, with dazzling explanations of 'The Ancient Spartan Skytale' and the 'Superencipherment and Encicode'.

Those Ladybird bods were anything but complacent, however, embracing the 1980s with a stream of one-offs for national events like the Pope's visit to the UK, the Royal Wedding and, in 1984, a guide to the Olympics that daringly included space for you to write in the results. They were onto an obvious winner with *Loughborough – Past and Present*, and even tried the tourist market with a guide to London ('You can stay as long as you like in the places that interest you and not spend so long in those that don't').

Even though they left Loughborough in 1999 to become part of Penguin, Ladybird now do just as sterling work online as well as in print, ensuring as many as possible are still able to find out that if a man could jump as well as a flea, he would be able to jump over St Paul's Cathedral.

RETROMETER: 9/10

Laser 558 

Never more than a minute away from the music

Peak year: 1984: 558 was the biggest thing on Medium Wave

The biggest pirate radio station of the 1980s, Laser 558 blasted a mix of back-to-back hits and fast-talking American DJs across England from a ship anchored in the North Sea, the *MV Communicator*.

In an era when Gary Davies's 'Bit in the Middle' was as edgy as pop radio got, Laser's star-spangled 'all hits, all the time' sound allegedly earned it nine million listeners, including Paul and Linda McCartney, while the station came fifth in the 1984 best radio show poll in ***Smash Hits***.

The DJ roster included Jessie Brandon, Holly Michaels and loudmouth Charlie Wolf, who hosted the late show. Inevitably the authorities cottoned on to Laser's success and attempted to force it off the air, dispatching a spy boat in a bid to halt supplies to the station.

Ironically, while 'Eurosiege 85' failed to take it off the airwaves, mounting technical problems forced the *Communicator* to head for port, where it was impounded, to the dismay of one T Blackburn, who had once quipped: 'Laser's more fun than another pop station I don't care to mention. I hope it will give the legal stations the kick up the bum they deserve.'

RETROMETER: 7/10

'Laughing All the Way to the Leeds'

There's liquid gold in them thar hills

Peak year: 1988, when the ads went into heavy rotation

Even though George Cole made the effort to swap his trilby for a flat cap, everyone knew that was really Arthur Daley up there dishing out the financial advice in a series of polished 60-second capers.

Told in rhyme, Cole would regale us with stories from his life which – inevitably – involved him popping into the Leeds at some point to add a little something to his Liquid Gold savings account.

Best remembered of the bunch was his exploit with a greyhound which was lured away from him by a crook and a string of sausages. Thankfully, our man got the better of the situation, and: 'Down at the track/he soon came back/when Fifi caught his eye', Fifi being, of course, a toy poodle, because they're your actual canine sexpot, right?

Equally noteworthy was George's tangle with mortgages, as he told the tale of his klutzy son-in-law and daughter who were moving out of his house for a place of their own. The pay-off? 'Now I got quite emotional/on the day that they moved in/tears of sadness for my girl/and tears of joy for him.'

RETROMETER: 8/10

'Left to my Own Devices' by Pet Shop Boys

Che Guevara and Debussy to a disco beat

Peak year: 1988

If nothing else, Neil Tennant and Chris Lowe's high-kicking existential stomper at least encapsulates two basic Pet Shop Boys obsessions – 'drinking some tea' and 'shopping' – inside the first ninety seconds.

Neil proceeds to deadpan his way through his itinerary for the day, from getting out of bed ('at half past ten'), phoning his friends, watching the telly, leafing through a holiday brochure, going out, coming home again and, well, this all carries on for four minutes and 47 seconds.

In between, Neil mulls over his solitary childhood ('in a world of my own at the back of the garden') and the pressure to conform ('I was always told to stick with the gang if you want to belong'). Not exactly typical *Chart Show* fodder, but the PSB's customary wit and style ensured another top ten standing ovation for the duo.

Produced by flamboyantly bespectacled pop boffin Trevor Horn, with a profusion of operatic flourishes, 'Left to my Own Devices' turned out to be a sort of 1980s 'A Day in the Life' in a long black coat and a Boy baseball cap, right down to the orchestral crescendo at its triumphant climax.

RETROMETER: 8/10

Lego

More than just knobbly plastic bricks

Peak year: 1982, Lego release the cool-sounding Technic I kit

Everyone has a Lego story to tell, be it fights with older brothers over the best Lego spaceship or the dog chewing half your collection. Indeed, the world's most ubiquitous toy (well we think it is anyway) has long since become part of the – ahem – very building blocks of growing up.

Invented in Denmark in 1949, the Lego brick was first marketed as the 'LEGO Automatic Binding Brick with four and eight studs'; however, this was truncated to the rather catchier 'brick' just four years later. After that initial hiccup it would quickly come to dominate the world of kids' building blocks.

Over the years there were many innovative additions to the range, including: 1957, Lego bricks with lights inside; 1974, the Lego family (leading inadvertently to the world's first Lego transvestites as kids stuck dad's head onto mum's body); and of course in 1982, the introduction of the formidably complex and Meccano-esque Lego Technic range.

Yet, despite this multitude of produce, it is those shared experiences of the toy that bind us together; like the fact we all used to keep our Lego bricks in a big blue plastic box; or that at one time or another we each tried stickle bricks at school and were mystified as to what you were meant to make out of them beyond some vague approximation of a cactus; or even that regardless of the complexity of the kit, while boys constructed a *Battle of the Planets*-style fleet, girls used the same bricks to build rectangular houses with neatly arranged multi-coloured walls.

All of these are happy memories, certainly more so than that other unifying Lego experience – namely the excruciating pain of stepping on a stray brick.

RETROMETER: 10/10

Leyland Cars

Great cars and a great deal more

Peak year: 1977, the year the Marina, the Dolomite and the TR7 rolled off the Longbridge line

British Leyland might have produced more material for Jasper Carrott and *Not the Nine O'Clock News* than they did successful cars, but the commercials for the nationalised behemoth and its umpteen quintessentially English marques ('Austin! MG! Triumph! Mini! Jaguar! Daimler! Princess! Morris! Rover!') invariably strove to evoke an image of world-beating British know-how. Hence the appearance of a French smoothie parked in front of the Eiffel Tower and improbably proclaiming, 'zees Allegro iz ze best foreign car ah've ever owned!', while a quartet of sheiks crammed into a Mini –

'well, even they've got to watch the petrol, haven't they?'

RETROMETER: 7/10

Lift Off with Ayshea

The antithesis of *Whistle Test*

Peak year: 1973: Mud! Slade! The Sweet! Er, Lieutenant Pigeon!

It's a serious business now, but in the past pop music was more or less entirely confined to children's television. This meant the likes of Roxy Music and Roy Wood would tend to find themselves nestling alongside ***The Tomorrow People*** and *Out of Town* in the teatime schedules.

Lift Off with Ayshea was the first in an endless stream of pop programmes produced by Muriel Young at Granada, with the titular Brough adding a little bit of glamour to the otherwise mumsy kids' presenters popular at the time. Virtually all the stars of the day appeared, along with a whole host of novelty acts that made the Cheeky Girls look dignified.

The show later mutated into *Get it Together*, with the less alluring Roy North in charge, and comic interludes provided by *Ollie Beak*, aka a puppet owl operated by Wally Whyton. Perhaps something like that would liven up modern-day ***Top of the Pops***.

Sometimes the stars themselves would get their own vehicle, such as the Bay City Rollers' seminal *Shang a Lang*. Perhaps the most notable of all the Granada pop series was *Marc*, where a dumper-bound Bolan sung his own songs and introduced guests, most famously David Bowie, who managed to get about three bars out of his duet with the host before falling off the stage.

RETROMETER: 6/10

'The Lion Sleeps Tonight' by Tight Fit

'Wimoweh a-wimoweh' indeed

Peak year: 1982, when the 'Fit went top of those pops

In the early 1980s ABBA-derived pop acts came in all sorts of shapes and sizes, but perhaps none were so mercurial or contrived as Steve Grant, Julie Harris and Denise Gyngell's Tight Fit.

The 'Fit first saw chart action in 1981 with a medley of old 1960s standards helpfully titled 'Back to the Sixties'. However, it was in April 1982 when the group really hit the pop big time with their majestic reading of the variously titled, seminal 1939 Soloman Linda and the Evening Birds' platter 'The Lion Sleeps Tonight'. The Fit's version went careering to the top of the charts, helped in no small part by Grant (or whoever)'s falsetto providing easy comedic copy for the likes of Little and Large or Paul Squire.

Tight Fit were to return to the top five later that year with the ABBA-baiting 'Fantasy Island'. As finely crafted a slice of Euro pop as ever there was, the song raised some eyebrows when it was noted Steve Grant's voice sounded completely different to the proto-Thom Yorke warbling of 'The Lion . . . ' Then ABBA's management allegedly weighed in, apparently threatening to sue the threesome for stealing the Swedish group's patented 'sound'.

Evidently the burden of top-flight popdom became too much for Tight Fit. They released another single – 'Secret Heart' – but it failed to breach the Top 40. Steve then fell out with Julie and Denise, and roped in another two girls. However, by then Tight Fit's lip-synching magic had deserted them for good. Steve subsequently shacked up with Eartha Kitt and Denise became Mrs Pete Waterman – thus ensuring the baton of plastic pop was passed on to the next generation.

RETROMETER RATING: 7/10

Load Runner 

The Galaxy's First Computer Comic

Peak year: 1983, the year the 'Runner duelled with Horace and the Spiders

From the Dragon 32 to the Oric-1, The Great Bedroom Computer Boom of 1983 had many casualties, but few as improbable as *Load Runner*.

Intended to cash in on the mania for anything with a Kempston joystick and a dodgy RAM pack, the comic never seemed quite sure if it was meant to be ***2000AD*** or the *Home Computer Course*, and consequently ended up stranded in the middle. It didn't exactly help that a few strips appeared in photo-story format, like *My Guy*.

The comic's star was the titular 'Runner, a maverick computer gamer who somehow got himself 'sucked' into programs (cf: *Tron*) every fortnight, while 'Andy Royd: Rogue Star' envisioned a dystopian future society where a maverick footballer took on soccer-playing robots. And 'Mindwarp' depicted invaders controlling an army of roller-skating teenagers brainwashed through personal stereos.

Load Runner also included a technical advice page called 'Brainy's Brainbox', and those endless type-it-in-yourself programs printed in the tiniest font imaginable, that always crashed because you'd missed out a semi-colon in line 2390.

One issue had a free flexidisc featuring a track by Mainframe, an electronic musical project 'masterminded' by Chris Sievey, aka the bloke inside Frank Sidebottom's papier-mâché head. Mainframe's bleeps and bloops were accompanied by a program that, in theory, played a sort of primitive video in time with the song, in the unlikely event of anyone ever getting it to work.

But after just thirteen issues, it was game over. The galaxy's first computer comic, as its cover had proclaimed in futuristic 'digital' font, had become its last, and it was left to ***Crash***, *Zzap 64*, the short-lived *Big K* and that impenetrable Pi-Man strip on the back page of *Popular Computing Weekly* to entertain the kids.

RETROMETER RATING: 5/10

Look and Learn

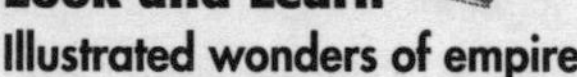

Illustrated wonders of empire

Peak year: 1975, the merger with *World of Wonder*

An oasis of calm bookishness in the reprehensible world of comics, Fleetway's stalwart educational paper sallied forth in 1966, bringing factual nuggets of nature, history and geography to the nation's short-trousered masses. Its 'improving' agenda made the annuals an acceptable present for aunts to dole out to wayward nephews in the hope that a bit of extracurricular scholarship would result.

All this was dashed, however, when it merged with *Ranger* comic, and proper adventure strips started seeping in between the diagrams of glaciers. Most popular was epic sci-fantasy 'The Trigan Empire', with battles aplenty, top-notch artwork and a factual content of roughly nought. A rather dry annual was thus made palatable, until it finally became extinct in 1982.

RETROMETER: 6/10

Look-In

'Look out for *Look-In!*'

Peak year: 1974, footie pundit Brian Moore makes for the most unlikely cover star of all time

Look-In could have simply been a load of free advertising for ITV programmes, but thanks to the comic's eclecticism, first-class artwork and brilliance at coming up with exciting strip adventures for the likes of the Osmonds, the Bay City Rollers and *ALF*, it was – for the majority of its tenure – the most star-packed and exciting comic you could find in the newsagent.

Admittedly it suffered a little from the down-market tag that still dogged ITV even into the 1980s, but assuming you could persuade mum to cough up the necessary dosh, then behind its beautifully painted cover (usually featuring loads of stars on a yellow background, invariably created by film poster artist Arnaldo Putzu), you could revel in a heady mix of comic strips cashing in on the latest craze, get quizzed by mum as to what cartoons about *Benny Hill* or *Man About the House* were doing in a 'kiddie's' comic, or wade through the fearsomely difficult-to-navigate TV guide that attempted to list all of the programmes of interest to children showing on all of the different ITV regions that week.

Having begun way back in 1971, *Look-In*, by the 1990s, had conspicuously failed to adapt to its target audience's interests (where were the *Home and Away* and *Blind Date* strips?) and so was cancelled, but somehow ever since glam rock died it had been all over anyway.

RETROMETER: 10/10

The Look-In Television Annual

'All your TV favourites!'

Peak year: 1978: Mike 'Flintlock' Holoway, Lee Majors and Abba adorn the cover

The yearly dispatch from the ***Look-In*** offices was a fine companion to the 'junior ***TV Times***' weekly fare.

The run, which would span twenty years, started in style with the 1972 annual, sporting a fetching still of a decidedly *louche* Roger Moore on the front. Inside were the standard-issue comic strips ('*Timeslip*', 'Crowther in Trouble' etc.), bolstered by an array of text features ('Magic Whiskers – another look at the strange old wizard, Catweazle'); loads of *Magpie*-obsessed nonsense ('Puff's Paddock Playmates!'); quizzes (including a ***Please, Sir!*** crossword); that old staple, a 'board game' (this one based on *Survival*, and set in an African nature reserve); and, best of all, photographic endpapers.

These impressive dioramas would usually feature a studio snap taken from some high-up gantry featuring cameras, lights, crew and all. 1973's *Junior Showtime* exposé is an expansive masterpiece, rivalled only by 1978's bird's-eye view of ***The Tomorrow People*** set, complete with a belt buckle-clasping Nicholas 'John' Young centre stage.

The template for success had been pretty much perfected right from the off, with the only significant changes the following year being the adoption of those iconic painted montage covers featuring a brace of TV and pop personalities huddling together and the inevitable alterations in the rolling stock of TV programmes suitable to cover (cheerio ***Please, Sir!***, hello *The Fenn Street Gang*).

And so it continued up until 1991. Somewhere along the way, the painted covers had been ditched in favour of photos, but otherwise business remained as usual. However, the market was no longer there for comic-strip adaptations, 'Fact Files' and word searches, and the series bowed out that year, denied the chance to develop its new-found obsession with New Kids on the Block.

RETROMETER: 10/10

Love, Curiosity, Freckles and Doubt by Pat Phoenix

'I hesitated at the doorway. Now, remember, Pat, I told myself. Sparkle, sparkle'

Peak year: 1983

As she'd published *All My Burning Bridges* some ten years earlier, most Pat 'Elsie Tanner' Phoenix fans must have hoped a second volume wouldn't be forthcoming, lest they be forced to navigate the actress's tortured prose for a second time. Sadly for them, Phoenix was far from done, and by the early 1980s there was a mountain of material to be squeezed into a new tome.

Named rather grandly after a line from the poem 'Inventory' by Dorothy Parker, the book jumped around a bit (as if dictated by Phoenix sitting at the end of a slightly down-at-heel wine bar), taking in Pat's failed marriage to actor Alan Browning, various tales from rep days and copious praise for the cast and crew of *Coronation Street*.

Yes indeed, Pat name-checked anyone and everyone at Granada Television, including 'the girls on the switchboard whom I adore, secretaries, people throughout the building for whom I have great affection', and it was rare a single person was mentioned without their name being prefixed with the words 'my great friend'.

Yet many people undoubtedly loved *Love, Curiosity, Freckles and Doubt*. Phoenix was the type of tragedy-tinged celebrity who attracted hardcore fans who would happily return to her autobiography whenever they found themselves in a lull between their next *Mills and Boon*, ***Reader's Digest*** or true crime fix.

RETROMETER: 6/10

Lunchboxes 

Air tight food carry-cases

Peak year: 1984, the year the fight with the Visitors from *V* spilled out into the lunch hall

Not just any old lunchboxes, though. Just to make it clear it's those incredibly tough, plastic affairs with a clasp fastener, a kids' TV or toy favourite across the front and an accompanying thermos flask.

Another product of the perennial requirement for school children to bandy about their favourite personalities wherever they went, the lunchbox married functionality (an airless compartment for that cheese sandwich and packet of Smith's Square Crisps) with form. Normally brightly coloured, the only drawback was that your picture of Kermit the Frog, Strawberry Shortcake or *the A-Team* would inevitably peel off after several vigorous scrubs from a hygiene-conscious grown-up. Bah! Them!

RETROMETER: 6/10

M–R: The Magpie Annual to Rupert: The Daily Express Annual

The Magpie Annual 

'Packed full of exciting items for boys and girls!'

Peak year: 1976: a nation demanded to know, 'what on earth does Puff do all day?'

The yang to ***Blue Peter Books***' ying, *The Magpie Annual* could always be relied upon to blend its glam rock leanings (disturbing psychedelic endpapers festooned with stripy numbers, smiling moons and laughing clowns – the only thing missing being a freaked-out Malcolm McDowell and a machine gun) with some good honest educational fare ('Fanny is the diminutive of Frances, which appeared in England in the Tudor period') and the inevitable 'makes' (an 'Arab belt', an 'orange surprise', a 'tote bag' or a 'live wire game').

Your typical *Magpie* annual would breakdown as follows: a bonkers contents page, presented in the form of a maze built around the titular bird; 'Hello and welcome!' – an end-of-year report detailing all the exciting things Mick and the gang had been up to over the last twelve months ('Colin Bloy talked about his collection of shells'); a couple of animal features ('Seals and Sands' in 1978's *The Magnificient Magpie Book*, 'The Life and Times of Puff and Other Horses' in the 1974 edition); random pieces on commonplace aspects of everyday life ('What's an Adventure Playground?' mused John Birtwhistle in 1976); the mandatory stills of Mick, Susan, Doug and Jenny in historical garb, commandeering go-karts or looking dreamily into camera; and best of all the perennial rundown of the Byzantine rulings which dictated how and when the eleven *Magpie* badges could be issued.

But curiously, little – if anything – on Tommy Boyd.

RETROMETER: 9/10

Making the Most of the Micro 

BASIC instinct

Peak year: 1983: the year of the BBC Micro owl

Bill Gates and Tim Berners-Lee might disagree, but for our money the real pioneer of computing was a middle-aged bloke in a jumper called Ian McNaught-Davis.

The avuncular 'Mac' fronted the television series promoting the BBC's computer literacy mission, which aimed to get everyone cataloguing their stamp collection and filing their accounts on their home computer, but largely resulted in a generation of kids getting hooked on *3D Ant Attack*, spending their Saturday afternoons messing about in Lasky's computer department ('10 PRINT "HELLO"/20 GOTO 10') and dreaming of emulating Matthew Broderick in *War Games*. It did, however, succeed in bringing the BBC Micro into practically every primary school and rich teenager's bedroom.

The first series, *The Computer Programme*, featured Mac and Chris Serle as his everyman stooge, frowning at the intricacies of GOSUB routines and I/O ports, with Kraftwerk's 'Computer Love' as the theme tune. Mac then went solo for *Making the Most of the Micro*, taking a more detailed look at programming ('and we'll be returning to machine code later in the series') and the computer industry on Sunday mornings, transmitted from a black studio with yellow metallic shelving.

Making . . . spun off into *Micro Live*, an epic four-hour special from Pebble Mill, with Mac, Lesley Judd and the mighty Fred Harris showcasing the BBC Buggy robot, which broke down on cue, while hackers inveigled their way into the programme's Prestel link live on air. It became a weekly BBC2 magazine, with some American bloke called Freff contributing reports from Silicon Valley, and even spawned a rival in Tony Bastable's *4 Computer Buffs* on Channel Four.

Infamously, Mac once managed to enrage the kids by slagging off computer games as a waste of processing power. But it didn't stop him turning up on ***The Adventure Game*** alongside Sheelagh Gilbey and the school caretaker of the year, masterfully cracking the 'how many Argonds round the pond?' challenge.

RETROMETER: 8/10

Malory Towers by Enid Blyton

'Gwendoline, you goose!'

Peak years: Er, the 1950s?

Redolent of an era when schoolgirls still had names like Daphne, Connie and Jean, brandished a lacrosse stick and organised midnight feasts, the *Malory Towers* books chronicled the progress of Darrell Rivers, from 'hot-tempered' first-former to head girl of her idyllic cliff-top Cornish boarding school.

The staff at the 'Towers comprised headmistress Miss Grayling, rotund French teacher and perennial victim of classroom pranksters *Mam'zelle* Dupont, firm-but-fair form mistress Miss

'Potty' Potts, 'manly' equine enthusiast Miss Peters, and a teacher called Miss Parker who had a big nose and, well, you get the idea.

Meanwhile, the roll-call of pupils included Darrell's best friend Sally, scatterbrained maths genius Irene, scatterbrained artist Belinda (there wasn't an awful lot of skilful characterisation going on here) and practical jokers Betty and Alicia, forever dreaming up hell-raising schemes that usually involved sneezing powder.

Trademark Blyton tomboy Wilhelmina 'Bill' Robinson owned a horse called Thunder, who almost had a fatal brush with colic, while her friend the Honourable Clarissa Carter had a weak heart and a horse named Merry-Legs.

Darrell's enemies included bossy Moira (described as, er, 'a hard, domineering creature'), spoilt Gwendoline Mary Lacey and doormat 'Saint' Catherine.

The storylines revolved around jealousy, mysterious thefts and poison pen letters, a formula that ensured *Malory Towers* engrossed generations of girls who liked ponies and ballet, not to mention their brothers sneaking a read to discover just what schoolgirls in nighties got up to in their 'dorm' at night.

RETROMETER: 7/10

Mandy

'Stories [of suffering] to brighten your days!'

Peak year: 1976, when would-be ballerinas were duffed up once an issue

Launched in the mid-1960s, *Mandy* mixed a potent array of ponies, magic, school japes and winsomeness with a liberal sprinkling of cruelty.

While the gym-slip brigade loved to see what gentle nonsense the title character and Patch the pup were getting up to this week ('Mum's in bed with flu so I'm doing all the cooking'), the real meat was the regular beatings dished out on the never-say-die cast of parentless girls, junior witches and plucky young cripples.

So, no sooner had 'Secret Ballerina' orphan Cindy Reeves saved up eighty pence to cover her bus fare to the Crystal Shoes Trophy dance-off, when she was brutally mugged by the evil Dolly Platt and cronies.

Tragedy also weighed heavily on 'The Girl Who Gave Babies Away'. Terminally ill – yup! – orphan Betsy Deakin may have been on a race against time to find good homes for her brothers and sisters, but she at least had the consolation of being voted 'top' by *Mandy* readers.

Over the years the title merged with many of its 'rivals', sporting their wares within its own pages (the 'famous *Debbie* photo story' for one), but it never strayed far from the stone-throwing and torture, and at least three stories every issue climaxed on a shot of a tear-streaked heroine sat alone in her bedroom wondering why the world hated her so.

RETROMETER: 8/10

Mary, Mungo and Midge

Picture-book urban primer

Peak year: Made in 1969 but repeated ad nauseum for the next decade

'Do you live in a town?' inquired the matching-tie-and-cufflinks tones of Richard Baker at the start of every instalment of this durable high-rise gazetteer for the ***Play School*** set. 'Mary, Mungo and Midge live in this town. They live with Mary's mother and father in this tall block of flats.'

So who were this trio? Well, they were: Mary, sensible latchkey child in a pinafore dress; Mungo, lumbering but faithful canine; and Midge, mischievous mouse who played 'Three Blind Mice' on a piccolo.

Filmed in the same stiff but colourful animation style that John Ryan had previously used on *Captain Pugwash*, each episode depicted the trio descending in the lift, Midge cadging a ride aboard Mungo's nose to press the button, and heading for another escapade on the streets of their town.

The programme explained hospitals, airports and so on to the audience, and gently highlighted the perils of metropolitan life. Nobody who saw it could fail to be haunted by the heartbreak of 'Mungo Lost'.

For all the lazy gags that would now be levelled at a series featuring characters living at the top of an urban block of flats ('Midge would be a drug dealer, right') and a style of narration that Brian Sewell might consider 'a bit posh', *Mary, Mungo and Midge* had a real charm that endured repeat after repeat throughout the 1970s.

And remember, you must always wait for the lift doors to close.

RETROMETER: 10/10

Masquerade

Greensward-knackering hippie picture quest

Peak year: 1979, when the first copies came out, and the country went mad

Reclusive painter Kit Williams published a book in September 1979 containing fifteen dense, surreal paintings surrounded by cryptic text, which promptly went on to sell over a million copies. The reason was that the pictures contained clues to the whereabouts of a hare-shaped jewel worth £5,000 buried somewhere in the country.

Masquerade mania exploded all over the media. Williams received hundreds of letters a day from zealous puzzlers, great swathes of countryside were dug up, and the book became a national obsession.

The puzzle was finally solved in 1982 by a 'Ken Thomas', who, it turned out several years later, wasn't who he claimed to be, and had apparently cheated – he knew an ex-girlfriend of Williams' who had a good idea about the hare's location (Ampthill Park in Bedfordshire).

A sequel, *Untitled*, followed in 1984. The puzzle this time was to work out the real title of the book, and present it in a wordless manner. The (genuine) winner was Steven Pearce, who was awarded the prize – a golden bee – on an edition of *Wogan*, during which his mechanical 'answer' unfortunately broke on camera.

RETROMETER: 7/10

Masterteam

'Let's play!'

Peak year: 1986: acme of the pre-teatime roustabout

Before Michael Grade's daughter talked her dad into utilising it for 'another appointment with those Antipodean. . .' *Neighbours*, 5.35 p.m. on BBC1 meant any number of reliably featherweight fancies served up to satiate rumbling stomachs and wandering minds.

One of the more memorable efforts was *Masterteam*, a charming parlour game featuring Angela Rippon behind a huge desk helming tournaments of whimsically monikered ensembles of workmates and/or publicans (The Uttoxeter Weavers, The Ely Eggheads). To Angie's cry of 'let's play!' teams grappled with general knowledge teasers, riddles and the intriguing 'pot pourri' round, forever pedantically clarified as 'a mixed bag, a random mixture of questions, we don't really know what we're going to get' – a description that always implied things were a bit more disorganised down behind that quizmaster's gantry than Angela would've liked.

Other perennial 5.35-ers were US hand-me-downs such as Scott Baio-bulwark *Charles in Charge* and *All in the Family* spin-off *Gloria* ('But you know what, Joey? We'll be OK').

Then there was the devoutly British *Fax*, the telly equivalent of the very bottom section of a broadsheet newspaper puzzle page. Here Bill Oddie, 'Mr Trivia' Billy Butler and either Wendy Leavesley or Debbie Rix would perch awkwardly on chrome stools to clear up Women's Institute coffee morning-esque talking points like 'was ration Britain a fitter Britain?' and 'where do birds go to die?', pausing for occasional abrupt mood-changes such as when *Blue Peter* dog Shep died and John Noakes turned up to blub through an outrageously tortuous eulogy.

And if that wasn't enough infotainment before the onset of Nicholas Witchell, then there was always *First Class*: Debbie Greenwood and computer 'Eugene' presiding over rival schools trying to master the 'rather complicated spring and vault' of Konami's *Hypersports*, or spot the Duran star behind the gold disc.

For some, Ramsay Street couldn't come soon enough.

RETROMETER: 7/10

Match of the Day

Almost always father's favourite programme, but seldom appealing to mum, claimed The Chin

Peak year: 1977, when you were just as likely to see Rochdale vs Scunthorpe as Liverpool vs Arsenal

MOTD, to give it its unmemorable acronym, started in 1964, but the show's golden age was undoubtedly the 1970s after Jimmy Hill joined from ITV. Jim linked the whole programme and analysed the action as well, and could be relied upon to say something to irritate the fans of all 92 league clubs each season.

However much you hated him, you had to watch as it was one of the only places to see any football at all. The sport's authorities only let the BBC screen an hour of action each week, involving just two matches, and they were obliged to show a set number of ties from the lower divisions. If both games ended goalless, tough luck. John Motson, Barry Davies and Tony Gubba were behind the mic for the normally mud-splattered encounters, staying until Davies quit in 2004.

Throughout the golden age, the programme's 'rival' was *The Big Match*, Hill's old stomping ground on Sunday afternoon LWT, which was somewhat more glamorous with Elton John and Raquel Welsh making appearances. In 1980, the two programmes were obliged to swap slots for alternative seasons, with Jim donning open-necked shirts for his Sunday outings. However, the rise of live action meant that the nation's boys no longer had to stay up in their pyjamas to see the bearded one analyse and patronise.

RETROMETER: 7/10

Match of the Day Annuals

Tony Gubba probably still has them on his CV

Peak year: 1980, if you were a Kevin Keegan fan

Despite being a post-watershed show for much of its life, the Beeb knew that a huge percentage of the ***MOTD*** audience was made up of pyjama-ed schoolboys staying up, so for four years published spin-off annuals for the Christmas market.

The first, dated 1979, was a fairly generic tie-in, with quizzes, pin-ups and fact files, including an interview with celebrity fan Don MacLean and a piece on their Scottish sister show *Sportscene*, which was notable for describing host Archie MacPherson as 'a man with hair resembling rusty steel wool'.

From the 1980 edition, the format consisted of articles 'written' by the commentators, who were all pictured on the back, making for the most impressive collection of comb-overs ever printed.

Jimmy Hill, of course, relished these opportunities, and during the annual's lifespan answered letters from female viewers about spitting and made suggestions on the future of the game, memorably asserting that top clubs would soon provide a 'car jockey service' for supporters.

The rest of the team lived up to their personas – John Motson's pieces were packed with statistics, Barry Davies wrote in a florid style, Des Lynam exhibited a dry wit and Tony Gubba was, well, Tony Gubba ('like the Mad Hatter with 1/6 on his hat, Trevor Francis will have his million pound price tag hanging over his head for years to come').

The 1980 annual was virtually a Kevin Keegan fanzine, as he appeared on the cover and was mentioned in every article, Jim suggesting 'any mother would be pleased to welcome him as a son-in-law'.

Who said there's too much sex in football these days?

RETROMETER: 8/10

Me and My Girl

Reliably harmless Friday night aperitif

Peak year: 1985, when it ran unfettered on our screens for almost half the year

Precious little summed up the end of a 1980s working week finer than the sweet strains of a multi-tracked Peter Skellern swooning through the theme to *Me and My Girl*.

'Sometimes it seems,' he sighed among a cocktail of pizzicato strings and lush synthesisers, 'I shatter her dreams/with some careless word/a foolish lie!' Skellern's pipes, when coupled with the title sequence's portfolio of soft-focus stills depicting the titular 'Me' (Richard O'Sullivan) and his growing-up-too-fast offspring 'Girl' (Joanne Ridley) indulging in textbook 'oh you!'

reactions, perfectly summed up both sit and com.

The nub was always Sullivan's redoubtable widower Simon Harrap playing the field while struggling to cope with his similarly emotionally wayward daughter Samantha. Cream in the coffee, though, was Harrap's simultaneously undignified efforts to make a success of his advertising agency, the brilliantly named Eyecatchers, in the face of hapless partner and brother-in-law Derek Yates (Tim Brooke-Taylor) and his dependable comedy staple, the off-screen tyrannical missus.

Simple yet sublime, as LWT's only decent primetime sitcom of the whole decade it's no wonder *Me and My Girl* clocked up over fifty episodes. Better still, every one felt reassuringly the same.

RETROMETER: 8/10

Meg and Mog

Pre-school occult fun

Peak year: 1972, in their first ever adventure Meg and Mog meet up with Jess, Bess, Tess and Cress for some Halloween hi-jinks

Once ubiquitous on the travelling library circuit, and every school bring-and-buy sale, *Meg and Mog* may be a distant memory to most of us now, but back when you were as high off the ground as your knee-caps are now, Meg – a skinny, big-nosed witch suffering from alopecia (well, she only seemed to have five strands of hair) – and Mog – the feline familiar, who looked like a cross between a cat and a wasp – were a central part of our bed-time story ritual.

By simple virtue of featuring a witch in the lead role, the books were imbued with an element of rock'n'roll credibility Peter and Jane and Pat the dog couldn't hope to match, and just to seal the deal, the first six adventures (all published in the early 1970s) featured an octopus, a dinosaur and even some astronauts – all of which were drawn by Jan Pienkowski, whose rather simple style occupied that grey area in art of being very simple and easy to copy, but also somehow really very good too.

RETROMETER: 8/10

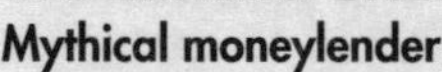

The Midland Griffin

Mythical moneylender

Peak year: 1984, the year griffin dictionaries took over classrooms

The Midland Bank's bizarre, intimidating choice of a mythological lion/eagle monster for its emblem was softened in the early 1980s with a series of animated ads in which said griffin, quaintly rendered like a big-beaked Country Life butter man and speaking with the voice of Richard Briers, helped various customers get the most out of the listening bank.

Quick to note the child-friendliness of all this, Midland launched the Griffin Savers account, in which juvenile capitalists were treated to griffin-branded pencil cases, folders, wallets and the *Oxford Griffin Savers Dictionary*, a copy of which could at one time be found in the school bags of one in three children. Stick that in your NatWest piggy bank!

RETROMETER: 7/10

The Mighty World of Marvel

Excelsior!

Peak year: 1972: the Thing and the Human Torch battle a huge lizard monster – but only on the front cover

US comics might have sported full-colour throughout and longer stories, but for some reason the UK's legion of **Cresta**-quaffing, nose-picking kids just weren't interested.

Hence, in 1972, American giant Marvel launched a new publication designed to win over the Brits. Taking its lead from the indigenous comics market, *Mighty World of Marvel* took several of the company's most successful titles, stripped out most of the colour, and hacked the stories into seven or eight-page chunks. These were then thrown together to create an anthology title packaged to ape the other weeklies on the shelves.

But, it just wasn't right. Too often the covers would sport action that didn't actually appear inside, the artificial breaks in the story were much too jarring and – well – it was all too American.

'Dear Editor,' wrote reader John Bishop from Norfolk in one issue. 'Can you explain why the Hulk is affected by gamma rays, Fantastic Four by cosmic rays, and Spider-Man by radioactivity? Is this based on any scientific fact?' You see? We wanted scientific fact!

RETROMETER: 1/10

Mike Yarwood: Impressions of My Life

Through the laughter and the tears . . . a celeb autobiography from the old school

Peak year: 1986

Much loved in the 1970s and then largely forgotten about after that, Mike Yarwood finally got round to releasing his autobiography in 1986 (perhaps missing the boat a little there).

Published by Willow Books, its front cover was a classic of the genre, featuring the comic performer in a couple of humorous guises (Patrick Moore and Robin Day) with the inevitable larger, proper portrait of Yarwood ('this is me!') positioned slap bang in the middle.

The book took a relatively brisk and self-deprecating route through the author's early life, first appearance on *Sunday Night at the London Palladium* and later struggles with drink and marriage. All of this was recounted in a breezy manner with Yarwood obviously none too keen to analyse his past in any level of detail.

Ably assisted by ghostwriter Linda Dearsley, one imagines Yarwood and scribe spending hour upon hour trying to come up with enough anecdotes to fill this rather slim tome. As a result, the reader could enjoy such tales as the time Harry Worth complained to a waiter that he couldn't find his spoon only to be shown that it had been resting beside his soup bowl all along; the occasion upon which Max Bygraves advised Yarwood that a two-piece suit should always be worn with the jacket buttoned up; and – perhaps most memorably – the moment when Cliff Richard reprimanded Mike for using the expression 'knickers in a twist'. Truly a memoir from another age.

RETROMETER: 9/10

Minder 

'So good for you' fisticuffs, farce and spurious nudity

Peak year: 1983: Dennis Waterman and George Cole assailed the UK pop charts with 'What are we Gonna Get 'er Indoors?'

The quintessential post-teatime bit of rough, *Minder* became the show most beloved by teenage boys thanks to its once-an-episode punch-up quota, squealing tyre action, cast-iron comedy and reliable bare boobs moment.

Originally intended as a vehicle for Dennis Waterman, freshly demobbed from the slags and shooters of *The Sweeney*, *Minder* coupled ex-con Terry McCann (Waterman) with entrepreneur Arthur Daley (George Cole) whose malapropisms and sharp practices quickly established him as the show's out-and-out star.

Although blessed with a stomping pub rock theme supplied by Waterman himself and the fantastically named Dennis Waterman Band, the series got off to a poor start due to scant publicity (thanks, ITV strike of 1979) and a general sense of bemusement as to what the programme was meant to be – although billed as a thriller, it was stacked with gags.

Despite lukewarm ratings, the programme returned and hit critical mass by its third series, whereupon it had become a national obsession, with

Waterman rightfully crowned as Britain's hardest man in playgrounds nationwide.

When he threw in the towel in 1989, it looked like the game was up, but new bloke Ray Daley (Arthur's Perrier-swilling nephew, played by Gary Webster) turned out to be not half bad, letting the show go out on a relative high in 1994 – despite the essential Waterman-warbled lyrics being dropped for an amped-up guitar workout.

RETROMETER: 7/10

Misty

'The paper with bite!'
Peak year: 1978, with the *Carrie*-esque 'Moonchild' in full swing

Girls' comics weren't all pillow fights, ponies and iron-on David Essex patches. On 4 February 1978, the brief but well-remembered reign of *Misty* began, a supernatural story paper tailored to a proto-goth female readership.

The comic's figurehead, Misty ('daughter of the mists, sister to the shadows, gatherer of tales') – bizarrely resembling the young Julie Burchill – provided a page one 'message' of 'dare you read . . ?' atmospheric portentousness similar to Herbert van Thal's in the ***Pan Book of Horror Stories***.

Serials such as 'Paint it Black', 'The Ghost of Golightly Towers' and 'Moonchild' (written by the ubiquitous Pat Mills) shared space with one-off stories like 'Finders Creepers', 'Uncle's Nasty Hobby', 'Happy Birthday, Spooky Sue!' and 'The Hag of Hattersley Hall'. Recurrent themes included cats ('Some people can't stand cats. Some people fear them. Others . . . WORSHIP THEM!') and getting picked on for being 'different' ('In every school there's a girl who all the others pick on. But what happens if the girl discovers she has . . . THE POWER!')

Sadly, Misty's Cavern of Dreams wasn't popular enough for her IPC overlords: on 12 January 1980 came the chilling words 'important news for all readers inside!' and the comic merged with *Tammy* the following week.

RETROMETER: 7/10

Monster Munch

'The biggest snack pennies can buy'
Peak Year: 1977, when 'saucy' was a legit flavour

The Monster Munch ads were populated by four Honey Monster-esque creations who would happily chomp on Smith's Crisps' corn snack representation of their own monikers, and get pretty competitive about it in the process.

That goggley-eyed fab four in full, then. The pink one with the long neck and huge nose; the short spherical fella with the New Romantic fringe; the one-eyed chap with the red nose and grey lips; and the blue bod in the Noddy Holder hat with the floppy ears.

In their allotted thirty seconds, the quartet would arse about in some kind of sketchily defined prehistoric jungle, conspiring of ways to eat more than their share of the crisp that came in three great flavours – pickled onion, roast beef and the worryingly generic 'saucy'. 'However, while he's enjoying his dream, guess who's enjoying his Monster Munch?' Indeed.

RETROMETER: 6/10

Mr Angry 

I'm very, very angry!

Peak year: 1986: Steve Wright and Mr Angry stormed the pop charts with 'I'm so Angry'

Back in the day (1982–94 actually) *Steve Wright in the Afternoon* seemed totally different from all other radio shows. It had a group of superfluous people (originally called the Afternoon Boys and later renamed the Posse) and – even better – loads of comedy characters ranging from the camp Gervaise to the self-explanatory Mr Mad, right through to Sid the Manager. The only commonality between this disparate, fictional bunch seemed to be a laboured line in obvious stereotypes; however, when sitting in the back of the car on your way home from school they were the most subversive creations since your mate constructed that penis out of Plasticene during double Art.

Of them all, though, Mr Angry (from Purley) was the undoubted pinnacle. Here was a biting satire on the 'Disgusted of Tunbridge Wells' brigade, a conduit by which Steve and the Posse could make achingly clever observations on the absurdity of modern-day life simply by mentioning a given subject and having Mr Angry 'phone up' and proclaim that he was very angry about it in, yes, a comedy angry voice.

Sadly Mr Angry has long since been rested by Wrighty. These days Steve is more focused on promoting his love song compilations than bringing dangerous comedy to the masses. Are we angry about the situation? Well perhaps a little terse.

RETROMETER: 8/10

'Mr Blue Sky' by ELO 

National Anthem-designate

Peak year: 1978

There's no doubting Jeff Lynne's finest hour. Whether as bedrock of ELO or pretending to be George Martin, his unquestionably majestic stab at the rock über-anthem, 'Mr Blue Sky', is unsurpassed.

Whereas so much other ELO output boiled down to addled pseudism on a slide guitar, here nothing was superfluous and everything had its place: the thumping oompah piano accompaniment, the nicely finger-clicking pace, the trademark strings bouncing cheerily along, and atop of everything the most preposterously mundane yet somehow instantly infectious wittering about, well, the weather being nice. 'See how the sun shines brightly,' chirped Jeff, 'in the city, on the streets/where once was pity/Mr Blue Sky is living here today!'

As with all champion lyrics they looked crap written down, but matched up with call-and-response-style vocalese (to aid those playground singalongs), tons of Beatle-styled orchestral flourishes, and, the crowning glory, a soupçon of *Sparky's Magic Piano*-esque vocoder dabblings, they became a hymn to the way life is, generally, for the most part, all right.

By the time you reached 3 mins 40 secs, with melodramatic sci-fi-sounding chords and a noble strings and piano epilogue, you felt like getting to your feet and saluting.

RETROMETER: 9/10

Murder Casebook

Serious investigations into the 'ultimate crime' – handily bundled into a newsagent part-work

Peak year: 1989, a special *Murder Casebook* dossier case accompanies the first ever issue.

In the late 1980s Marshall Cavendish was the king of the high street part-work. Their up-market publications about famous artists and the like could be found littering the waiting rooms of posh dentists the land over. However, in 1989, this once genteel publishing house launched *Murder Casebook* – perhaps the most gruesome high street title ever.

Issue one kicked off with an examination of the Yorkshire Ripper, and was followed by a look at Dennis Nielsen. As the weeks went by there was a steady stream of murderers of diminishing repute (evidently the editorial team had prioritised their slayers in order to kick off the range with the most marketable ones). However, the format of each issue remained unchanged. Sections entitled 'Early Days', 'In Focus', 'Murder in Mind' and 'Talking Point' attempted to add gravitas to what was basically a load of articles about horrible killers.

The fact that each edition proclaimed it had been compiled with the help of a number of consultants (including *Rough Justice* presenter David Jessel, billed somewhat grandly as 'the magazine's media and planning consultant') did little to shake the vague feeling of prurience that descended upon you whenever you tried to read it.

RETROMETER: 4/10

Music and Movement

Get yourself into a space

Peak year: 1970: the eleven-plus had been abolished, but half-naked prancing lived on

The theoretical practice that stated a child's cognitive skills could be enhanced by encouraging association with physical movements certainly enjoyed one of the more remarkable passages through history, starting off in the rarefied climes of the Geneva Conservatory in the early 1900s but ending up with a bunch of barely clothed barefoot six-year-olds jumping up and down on a splintery wooden floor.

Music and Movement first turned up in British schools after World War Two in the shape of BBC radio workshops helmed by the starched-voiced Ann Driver. Infants were instructed to act out an activity in time with a piece of music picked out in lacklustre fashion on a battered piano – a simple enough instruction, but one hedged about with much mind-expanding hyperbole.

Hence you would start off pretending to bounce a ball or skip a rope. Then came a bit of transmogrification: swim like a fish, or slither like a snake. Next, existentialism: flutter like a leaf, even sigh like the wind. Finally, all pretence of realism was ditched and it was time to 'do our wide dance' and other favourites from the catalogue. The principle (and the frugal dress code – was it still the Blitz?) persisted pretty much unchanged for decades. But you joined in because everyone did. You were only just out of your pushchair after all.

RETROMETER: 8/10

My Little Pony

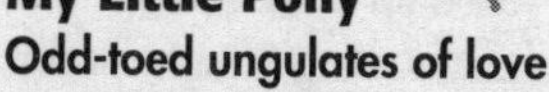

Odd-toed ungulates of love

Peak year: 1984, the inevitable cartoon appears

We're not afraid to name names, here: Charles Muenchinger, Steven D'Aguanno and Bonnie D Zacherle patented 'an ornamental design for a toy animal' in August 1981. The original concept actually had some character to it, exhibiting a sort of Eeyore-like resignation, but toy company Hasbro quickly supplanted that nonsense with wide-eyed Day-Glo cutesiness.

Plasticky and bright, with comb-able polyvinyl manes, they were essentially quadruped versions of 1970s favourite Trolls. Trolls, fatally, didn't get their own cartoon. If they had, it might have been more interesting than the Ponies' non-threatening escapades alongside

Moochick and the Bushwoolies. No wonder that original little nag looked so pissed off.

RETROMETER: 2/10

National Garages 

'Excellent, lovely Smurfs!'

Peak year: 1978: the summer of Smurfmania

The three-apples-high ambassadors of Smurfland had colonised mainland Europe and the columns of ***Look-In*** before they rolled up on your local forecourt. In a marketing masterstroke, National Garages lured in the kids and their harassed Talbot Horizon-driving dads by giving away collectable plastic Smurfs with every tankful of four-star, while Windsor Davies got in on the act by narrating the animated commercials in full-on *It Ain't Half Hot, Mum* mode ('now, car drill! Smurf yourselves, Smurf yourselves!') before the indefatigable blue sprites reprised their hit single to proclaim in song: 'National, the one place on earth, you get service with a Smurf!'

We're not entirely sure where Father Abraham was in all of this, mind.

RETROMETER: 8/10

Nationwide 

Majestic teatime institution

Peak year: 1974: a consummate mix of ironing boards and inflation

Always so much more than freaks jumping on eggs, *Nationwide* was THE definitive curtain-raiser to a night in front of the box.

It began in September 1969 with a lonely-looking Michael Barratt 'co-ordinating' rickety monochrome link-ups between fledgling Beeb regional outposts armed only with a standard issue Corporation telephone. Three-way discussions on overheated British Rail axle boxes soon gave way, however, to a bigger set, dispatches from the likes of James Hogg and Bernard Falk, and Cook of the Realm competitions.

The famed opening titles, adorned with spinning mandala and ace theme tune, arrived in 1972, the same time Frank Bough joined Mike and Bob Wellings on the main desk.

Imperial *'Wide* really began in October 1973 when the Consumer Unit opened for business with Valerie Singleton keeping a beady eye on that enduring 1970s concern, 'prices', while Richard Stilgoe fielded letters from people with six fingers on one hand and diligently documented the collapse of the economy through song.

Mike, Frank and their ever-expanding team became a family of friendly faces, segueing between

National Nursing Awards, *It's a Knockout* scoregirl competitions and visits from Prince Philip with ease. During the three-day week they even sought to revive the population's spirits with the cry '1973 – Was it Really that Bad?' The country was safe in their hands.

After Mike left in 1977 – via a regal 'tour' of the nation on his own customised train – the glory days continued for a while until, eventually, the team started to disintegrate and the Beeb meddled with the format, first trying ***Pebble Mill***-esque lifestyle fodder, then parachuting in David Dimbleby (billed above Frank in ***Radio Times***: wrong!) to lecture viewers about Iran. The curtain fell in August 1983 when it was axed for the indisputably crap *Sixty Minutes*.

Nationwide: the definitive beans-on-toast/doing-the-pots telly. Bring it back now!

RETROMETER: 10/10

'Naughty . . . but Nice' 

The height of Lorraine Chase-inspired chirpy comedy

Peak year: 1979, when they were the height of sophistication

While *Mr Kipling* ran its sedate, well-mannered commercials for decades, boringly recounting scenes not witnessed in normal households for centuries, Lyons decided that a more modern approach was required. The basic theme of the 'Naughty . . . but Nice' campaign was that, yeah, the cakes might have loads of sugar and cream in them that may be bad for your figure, but who cared when they tasted as good as this?

The slogan is said to be the creation of Salman Rushdie, trying to raise a few bob to pen novels by working as a copywriter. Perhaps if he'd stuck to writing about cream cakes then he wouldn't have had so much hassle in later years.

In fact Rushdie is not alone in taking the commercial shilling over the years – legendary sports commentator Murray Walker may have been well-known for his garbled English, but in a previous career he'd informed the nation that 'a Mars a day helps you work, rest and play'.

RETROMETER: 6/10

Nescafé 

Showbiz at its best

Peak year: 1984, when Gareth was in his cups

The campaign that begat a National Gesture, the mid-1980s Nescafé adverts were a prime example of how to succeed in advertising without really trying.

The premise was so-so: middle-of-the-road showbiz faces (Gareth Hunt and Una Stubbs at the core, augmented by the likes of Peter Davison and Diane Keen) relaxed in suburban splendour, discussing the product's 'special blend and roast' and 'richer, smoother flavour', while bizarrely producing handfuls of coffee beans from nowhere by shaking a clenched fist next to the ear. Such unpretentious advertising can only be cherished with hindsight, but who nowadays wouldn't swap a multi-million-pound boreathon with surfers and horses for compact classics such as 'Gareth's Garden' or the award-bypassing 'Gareth's Cups'?

As the 1980s really kicked in, Nescafé decided to up the ante, and the annoying Gold Blend couple was born. The sexual speculation foisted on Gareth and co by topical gag merchants up and down the land was spelt out in clunking innuendo, and a happy era of innocence and sweaters ground to a halt.

However, in 1989, Richard Briers and Penelope Wilton performed an 'ironic' postscript, showing the sainted Dickie rehearsing for a Hunt-style commercial, only for Penny to leap in with 'the gesture'. 'I wanted to do that bit!' moaned Briers, childishly. So did we all, Mr B.

RETROMETER: 7/10

'New Song' by Howard Jones

Did someone mention mental chains?

Peak year: 1983

In the list of Great Howards of the 1980s, the Buckinghamshire electro minstrel is right up there with Howard Stableford from *Beat the Teacher* and Richard Briers's neighbour off of ***Ever Decreasing Circles***.

The jump-suited synth troubador's debut, 'New Song', was a slightly nebulous anthem to free-thinking that encouraged us to get 'challenging preconceived ideas', punctuated by a twiddly middle bit that a generation of teenage boys tried and failed to master on their Casio SK1s.

Jones forever looked like a student teacher who'd unaccountably become a pop star overnight. The kind of guy who, hey, knew how to have fun (cf: spiky hair) but had a sensitive side too (cf: vegetarianism), practically all his songs contained Some Kind of Message – a combination that made him the perfect man to serenade rail passengers at Bristol Temple Meads station during a special edition of ***Top of the Pops*** to mark an attempt on the Inter-City land speed record.

No mention of Howard is complete without reference to Jed, the mime artiste who stood behind him on the *Saturday Superstore* roadshow stage and interpreted his oeuvre through the medium of performance art.

If Jones's rivalry with Nik Kershaw –

another brooding artist with a penchant for hair gel and making albums with the word 'Human' in the title – never quite reached the intensity of the Cold War, Howard nevertheless briefly became an icon for the sort of adolescent who penned intense poetry about seals and Polaris missiles in their bedrooms.

RETROMETER: 7/10

Newspaper Bingo Wars

Tabloid tombola tumult

Peak year: 1984, when Murdoch and Maxwell wagered a million

It was Derek Jameson who unleashed the forces of housey-housey on an unsuspecting Fleet Street in the early 1980s when, as editor of the *Daily Star*, he launched a bingo game as the latest salvo in the soaraway circulation war.

Practically overnight, tabloid bingo became a national obsession, with both the *Daily Mirror* and the *Sun* piling in. New and ever vaster cards arrived through the letterbox and everyone found themselves breathlessly crossing off the numbers and declaring they only required one more ball to scoop that jackpot.

Elaborate variations on a theme materialised, like the Sam Fox-endorsed Twingo Bingo. And the ailing *TV-am* received a boost when Greg Dyke decreed that the station should broadcast the numbers from that morning's newspapers ('Moving on to the *Mirror*, game 55 day three . . . ') even if Nick Owen bristled at the suggestion he wear a boater and sound a bugle to call the digits.

The stakes were raised in 1984 with the introduction of million pound bingo. The *Daily Express* launched their Who Wants to be a Millionaire? game with a Fred and Ginger-style commercial, the *Mirror* inauspiciously anchored Robert Maxwell behind a desk and Leslie Crowther ran a live draw in full *The Price is Right* mode in a commercial for the *Sun*.

Even the Thunderer entered the fray, although *The Times* wasn't about to sully itself with something as common as bingo, instead presenting a game called Portfolio, based on stocks and shares.

RETROMETER: 6/10

Nimble Bread

'A lovely way to slim'

Peak year: 1975, Nimble shoot the last of their original girl in a balloon ads

Although still going strong today, *Nimble bread* is perhaps most strongly associated with the famous advertising campaign of the late 1960s and 1970s that featured Nimble girl Emily Jones precariously perched on a small chair secured to a red and white Nimble balloon. Accompanied by the memorable 'I Can't Let Maggie Go' by Honeybus, something about the ad caught the public's imagination in a way rival firm Slimcea's own balloon-based bread commercial singularly failed to do.

The product itself harks back to an age when the amateur ethos still prevailed in the sport of dieting. Phrases such as 'lean cuisine' and 'calorie controlled diet' were about as technically complex as things got. Nimble boasted it was only forty calories a slice (that's apparently 27 calories less than normal bread), although it probably helped that each loaf seemed tiny.

RETROMETER: 7/10

NME and Melody Maker

Quarrelsome fiefdoms of the music press firmament

Peak year: The ones you read when you were fifteen

'The *NME* – is that still going?' cracked Noel Edmonds when one of its scribes appeared as a contestant on the glorious *Telly Addicts*. One part creaky irritant, one part sixth-form common-room institution, the king of the inkies defied fashion by churning out the same bewitching brew of sage-like authority and immature whimsy on the same crappy-quality paper for decades.

Emerging butterfly-like from the *Musical Express* in 1952, the *New Musical Express* (do you see?) ran the first ever hit-parade based on sales of discs, eulogised skiffle, trailblazed the beat boom and hired Wembley to mount its Poll Winners Show (the Beatles, Stones, Who, Small Faces and Dusty Springfield on the same bill!). When Nick Kent, Charles Shaar Murray, Nick Logan and co were conscripted to make sense of glam and prog rock, Sir Cliff boasted he 'wouldn't have the *NME* in the house'.

Punk, however, was almost ignored until that ubiquitous 'gunslinger' ad washed up Julie Burchill, Tony Parsons and Paul Morley. All sorts of shenanigans threatened a calamitous 1980s (anti-rock rabblerousing, indigestible essays on the politics of noise, front covers with no pictures on) until the likes of Danny Kelly, James Brown, *Telly Addicts* moonlighter Andrew Collins and Stuart Maconie ushered in the 'smoking jacket' era of ace gags, stupid captions and an open door to everyone except The Levellers.

Famously never as good as you remembered it, the *NME* really wasn't very good after 1992 when all the above quit: the paper lost its sense of humour and proceeded to slag off every kind of music until only Northern Uproar remained.

At least *Melody Maker*'s decline wasn't so sudden. Launched in 1926 as a trade sheet for budding musos, *MM* boomed through the jazz years, slumped in the face of pop but fought back with diatribes on Jethro Tull time signatures. Its flagship feature was always the small ads section, supposedly responsible for the conception of a million bands, but in reality the begetter of Elton John and Bernie Taupin, Suede and, erm, little else. Over time half-arsed design (the worst logo ever) and lazy verbalese robbed it of a point, so much so that nobody wept for either publication when merger came in 2000.

The *NME*: remember it this way. *Melody Maker*: er, next!

RETROMETER: 10/10

Noah and Nelly in SkylArk

Double-headed biblical oddness

Peak year: 1974: all were aboard the typographically odd SkylArk

Less famed than its stablemate *Roobarb*, the other creation of DIY animator Bob Godfrey and writer Grange Calveley is just as enjoyably mad.

Nutty Noah and Niggling Nelly, a sou'wester-clad couple voiced by Richard Briers and children's-vocal veteran Peter 'Pugwash' Hawkins, oversaw an all-terrain ark populated by two-headed, constantly arguing animals – Humphrey the Pigs, Achmed the Camels, etc. They would travel to some odd 'themed' land with a problem – a world of umbrella people with no rain, a land of Toby jugs without handles – whereupon Nelly would knit an unlikely solution, and all ended happily.

It was more of an upbeat 'can do' affair than *Roobarb*'s philosophical nervousness, and the animation and theme tune were more jolly and less frenetic too (the straggly 'boiling' effect of *Roobarb* made way for a more straightforward, pneumatic look), but the spirit of green hound remained in the happy/depressed split personalities of the animals, and Calveley's unique touch lifted it way above most other cartoons of the time.

RETROMETER: 9/10

'Nobody Does it Better' by Carly Simon

The best Bond theme ever

Peak year: 1977

Hats off to John Barry for churning out 007 soundtracks on a seemingly annual basis, but when it came to the title song the man tumbled at every fence. *Dr No* didn't even have one, *Goldfinger* featured Shirley Bassey shrieking, Tom Jones charged like a bull through *Thunderball* and Nancy Sinatra got upstaged by a riff in *You Only Live Twice*.

No, the best results always came when the whole thing was turned over to a third party, like the looking-for-a-job-of-work Macca in 1973 (*Live and Let Die*) and Carly Simon in 1977, handed a peerless gem by Marvin Hamlisch and Carole Bayer Sager with 'Nobody Does it Better'.

From that instantly recognisable subdued piano intro, through the serene first verse, to the brilliant bit when the whole band came in (cue synth drums and chugging strings) and the effortless throwaway mention of the film's title ('Like heaven above me/the spy who loved me'), it was a masterclass in the perfect theme song. The end section, when Carly harmonised with herself, a ton of violins AND a battery of trumpets over and over, was simply as good as it got.

RETROMETER: 10/10

Novelty Socks

Non-conformity for the ankles

Peak year: 1981: Crazily coloured socks help Next take over the high street

Never was there a more nostalgia-inducing era than the 1950s. Not the original run of that decade, mind – that was rubbish. Nope, the 1970s revival (Showaddywaddy taking 'Moon of Love' to number one in 1976) was where the whole drainpipes and DAs thing got a bit more interesting thanks to its skilful fusion with glam.

However, even though that was great, the 1950s' best hurrah unarguably happened in the early 1980s. Shakin' Stevens, *Russ Abbott's Madhouse*, a winklepickered Joe Brown leaping about on demented big board-game show *Square One* – this was post-war austerity just as we liked it: in a grand meeting of minds with chrome wine bar stylings!

Of course, all this couldn't help but inform the fashions of the day, and as natty suits (albeit punctuated with speckles of colour in a manner that came to be known as 'flecked') and skinny ties hit the high street, that old Teddy Boy staple, the fluorescent sock, also enjoyed its Second Coming.

Most often seen in schools, where the discreet dab of bright colour was considered a smart V's-up to The Man, those garish greens and yellows were best offset with a snazzy pair of grey **slip-on shoes**.

Alas, the fluorescent sock's fall from grace was swift and ignominious. By the latter part of the decade, it had become as synonymous with 'wallies' as loud shirts and **big glasses**. Even Arthur

Daley's idiot son-in-law was sporting them in that **'laughing all the way to the Leeds'** ad.

RETROMETER: 7/10

Now Get Out of That 

The original 'reality' game show

Peak year: 1982, when the series went prime-time

In the last week of August 1981, BBC1's teatime slot played host to an odd little four-day experiment, brilliantly described by creator Derek Smith as an 'open-air action crossword'.

A team of four Oxfordians, thrown together with only perfunctory preparation in the art of outdoor survival, were dumped in remote British hillsides with the vaguest of instructions on retrieving an electronic device codenamed 'The BEAST' within one day. Using physical skill, ingenuity and blind guesswork, they made their way towards their goal, solving cryptic challenges (retrieving a petrol-less Land Rover from a mined swamp, building a raft etc.) along the way.

Failure to accomplish tasks or play along with the conceit incurred ten-minute time penalties. Then another team from Cambridge was put through exactly the same ordeal.

The two were edited together to enable comparison, courtesy of narrator-cum-heckler Bernard Falk who provided just the right sarcastic tone to offset the frantic arguments, which were plentiful – the teams having been hand-picked to include bolshy-but-wet students alongside haughty managerial types and no-nonsense farmers. An uneven mix of genders also added to the volatile fun.

It was so successful that a full weekly series the following year was given a prime-time slot. This time the McGuffin was an isotope from a crashed spy satellite, and hi-jinks included making supper from two dead rabbits, running through a stately home in fear of non-existent 'guards', and, er, dressing up as Arabs.

The third series played a team of Americans against the Brits, giving Falk full rein to lay into the Yanks' verbal inanities as well as the British propensity for sulky rows.

All subsequent game shows with a personality clash element owe this programme a great debt, but none of them have come close to the original's winning combination of genuinely entertaining tasks and knowing editorial cruelty.

RETROMETER: 9/10

Nutty 

The breeding ground of Eric Wimp

Peak year: 1980, before Bananaman sold out and went to the telly

You knew where you were with comics in the 1970s – Fleetway's publications tended to be sillier and more daring, while DC Thomson, publishers of the *Beano*, *Dandy* et al, were that little bit more staid and traditional. That was until 1980 and the launch of *Nutty*, which specialised in the sort of crazy comedy that until that point was the territory of, well, ***Krazy*** and the like.

Undoubtedly *Nutty*'s lasting legacy came with their superhero spoof, *Bananaman*, whose daft adventures became the number one reason to buy it. Pretty soon he'd taken over the cover, and the comic's profile was increased tenfold in 1983 when he span off into his own TV series, famously voiced by *The Goodies*. This was one of the only occasions when a TV show was based on a comic strip rather than, as was becoming the norm, vice versa.

Sadly none of *Bananaman*'s stablemates (Doodlebug, Peter Pest, The Wild Rovers) were quite as memorable and after five years the publication merged with the *Dandy*. Only *Bananaman* made the trip across safely, but within a few months he'd been relegated from the colour centrespread to a two-tone page round the back, where he was printed in red. They could at least have renamed him 'Beetrootman' to make more sense.

RETROMETER: 7/10

Oh No – It's Selwyn Froggitt

'Magic!'

Peak year: 1976, with Selwyn appointed concert secretary at the Scarsdale Working Men's Club and Institute

Municipal hole-digger Selwyn Froggitt, created by playwright Alan Plater and portrayed by Bill Maynard, was one of the great clown turns of sitcom. He was almost childlike in his relentless, hyperactive enthusiasm (life was one big double-thumbs-up), yet habitually accident-prone, a one-man whirlwind of ebullient destruction.

Living with his train-obsessed brother Maurice and absent-minded, pensionable mum in the Yorkshire town of Scarsdale, Selwyn enjoyed a simple life of digging holes, drinking beer and wrecking public property.

Despite avidly reading *The Times* ('It's great! On Sundays you get three and a book!') and bandying words like 'aesthetic' about with confidence, Maynard's stuttering, red-faced hero remained several steps behind everyone else, notably his compadres at the working men's club, including shifty, gimlet-eyed barman Ray (Ray Mort) and humourless club president Jack (Bill 'Harry Cross' Dean, who also penned the lyrics to the lilting male-voice choir theme tune, which winningly changed each week to document that episode's misadventures in between its immortal 'never mind' refrain).

Endless mucky holes, flyblown club interiors and pints of cookin' conspired to make this the brownest sitcom in history. A holiday camp sequel in 1978, *Selwyn*, backfired, but Yorkshire Television gave Maynard a worthy 1980s successor in *The Gaffer*, where his professional incompetence moved with the times into the private sector.

RETROMETER: 9/10

Oor Wullie 

'Jings! Crivens! Help Ma Boab!'

Peak year: 1982, When readers of the *Sunday Post* were presented with an exclusive Oor Wullie 'motif sweater in double knit' knitting pattern

With the honourable exception of 'The Jocks and the Geordies', there can be few British comic characters so obviously regional as DC Thomson's Oor Wullie.

First published back in 1936, the little Scottish tearaway (christened William McCallum) has long since confused readers south of the border. Who is he and what has he done to deserve his own annual every second year? What's his relationship to the similarly packaged Broons family? And, above all, what the crivens is a 'But 'n' Ben'?

Oor Wullie, and his close fictional neighbours the Broons, actually made their first appearance in the 'Fun Section' of the long-running *Sunday Post* newspaper. Since that time the fortunes of the two strips have been intertwined. Not only were both originally drawn by artist Dudley Watkins, but in the course of their various escapades (often involving Wullie baiting PC Murdoch or Granpaw Broon conning someone out of a juicy steak) the characters would turn up in the middle of each other's adventures.

While not widely appreciated in the rest of the United Kingdom, north of the border *Oor Wullie* has long since been associated with elderly relatives who still think the sparky wee lad's adventures are a braw laff.

RETROMETER: 8/10

'Other' Radio One DJs 

Not quite the Nation's Favourite

Peak year: 1985, when there was a new DJ seemingly every week

The big names at Radio One – Read, Wright, Bates – always moaned they could never go anywhere without being hassled by the public. This was never going to happen with the likes of Paul Jordan and Neale James, who spent much of their time at the station stuck in the unhallowed Sunday 6 a.m. slot, with a Gary Davies stand-in or a week on ***Top of the Pops*** about the peak of their achievements.

Most of them were certainly able to segue between two records and run a mediocre quiz, but could never quite make it as a daytime regular.

Perhaps the textbook 'other' Radio One also-ran was Graham Bannerman, who was clearly never going to be a star, as his name was too long to fit the jingles. He announced his style as 'not too serious, but not too jokey, either', and with this dynamic mission statement lasted less than six months on Saturday evenings in 1985.

Sometimes these DJs would try to better themselves. The most notable exponent was Mark 'Me, Mark Page' Page, who once claimed he was going to combine his radio work with playing professional football for Darlington FC. Sadly, Darlo's manager stymied this when he immediately announced he'd never heard of him.

RETROMETER: 7/10

Oversized Digital Watches

Fully functional at depths of up to 100 metres

Peak year: 1984: Transformers on a plastic strap

Cumbersome, pedantic, obsessive . . . yes, those people who didn't 'get' multi-furnished digital watches truly were, ho ho, out of time.

After all, what better way of passing a double lesson of Biology on Friday afternoon than pissing about with your own wrist? There was the stopwatch facility, for seeing how quickly you could start and then stop the timer again. There were **calculator** keys, because normal-sized electronic abacuses were for boring kids who couldn't handle buttons the size of pinheads. There were alarms, which announced to everyone when the bell should have gone. There were illuminations, from tiny bulbs to LED contraptions of vast red or green displays. And then there were the picks of true aficionados: a Casio game watch for alien-zapping jousting, or a customised Transformer watch that needed to be, yes, transformed through the sliding back of plastic outer casing before you could even peruse its contents.

Each and every one indispensable, indomitable, unsurpassable – until you fell over in the playground and the thing broke.

RETROMETER: 5/10

Oxo

The brown crumbly stuff that binds the family

Peak Year: 1983: Bellingham and brood tumbled onto the screen for the first time

First there was Katie, giving her grub 'man appeal' with an application of gravy granules. Then there was Dennis Waterman, who slouched about in a red T-shirt emblazoned with 'OXO' across the chest. Then cameth Lynda Bellingham.

From 1983 to 1999, the *General Hospital* refugee and her onscreen husband (jolly, moustachioed Michael Redfern) endured the growing pains of their three gawky kids, ladling out chilli con carne or Sunday roast to the accompaniment of arguments, misremembered directives ('don't forget to remind your father that he's picking me up!') and various rite-of-passage scenarios.

All of this was played out with mucho puff about how 'realistic' the family were, thereby ignoring the truth that by the mid-1980s, all evening meals in British homes were taken in absolute silence in front of *Coronation Street*.

RETROMETER: 5/10

Pages from Ceefax 

Text-based tittle-tattle over the tea and toast

Peak year: 1983, when it was virtually the only daytime telly around

Ceefax has been a part of the Beeb's output since 1974, when it was discovered almost by accident while trying to find ways of providing subtitles for the deaf. A couple of hundred text pages of news, sport and weather could be transmitted in the extra, unseen lines that made up the picture.

At first teletext TVs were hugely expensive, so the new service was shown off during the endless downtime on BBC1 and BBC2. With little money for proper programmes in daylight hours, it was an inexpensive way to keep broadcasting. The pages cycled round, and it didn't even seem odd when stories of murder, war and famine were backed by pleasant light music. Indeed, many people at home during the day enjoyed the tunes so much they kept the telly on constantly while doing their chores, occasionally glancing at the screen for the headlines.

Sometimes the *Ceefax* boffins could knock up special pages – when they were screened before kids' programmes on Bank Holidays, the imminent appearance of *The Pink Panther* was heralded by a blocky drawing of a pink cat drinking a bowl of milk. Sadly, the rise of **daytime TV** and the cheapness of teletext sets means *Ceefax* now rarely gets an outing on screen. But it was always more fun than *Kilroy*.

RETROMETER: 8/10

The Pan Book of Horror Stories

'Her last conscious experience was of two thick viscous streams edging their way down her burning face as her eyeballs melted'

Peak year: 1971, as the skull-adorned twelfth edition announced sales of two million

From 1958 onwards, paperback house Pan published a regular anthology of short stories of the macabre: spine-chilling tales of uncanny terror, subtle beastliness, eldritch nightmare, Grand Guignol and other adjectives only ever used to describe fruity horror of a certain vintage. For three generations of children, it was a grisly winner.

The stories, ranging from a couple of pages to several chapters, were selected by the perfectly named Herbert van Thal, who beckoned the reader in with foreboding entreaties on the back cover: 'We feel that the stories in this book are such that if your nerves are not of the strongest, then it is wise to read them in daylight.'

Many were disturbing indeed. Favourite subjects were grotesque creatures found in eerily empty Edwardian houses, brilliant surgeons taking revenge on unfaithful lovers as only they knew how, immobilised men being slowly devoured by swarms of rats and, best of all, lovingly described scenes of methodical dismemberment, preferably carried out by innocent young children. The writing was often of a high calibre – as well as genre stalwarts such as R Chetwynd-Hayes and Nigel Kneale, the likes of Patricia Highsmith, Muriel Spark, and even John Lennon contributed unholy offerings of nameless dread to leave sleep cowering in the halls of terror.

With their distinctive covers depicting the remains of some unfortunate victim, and their ghostly wobbly font, the books provided the ideal literary counterpart to spooky TV programmes like *Armchair Thriller* and *Hammer House of Horror*.

The quality started to wane, however, and after van Thal's death in 1983 the series limped on with derivative unpleasantness largely written by hacks (oh, and Stephen King), before finally resting in peace in 1988.

RETROMETER: 9/10

Panini Stickers

Ten Dave Beasants for one Ian Rush

Peak year: 1986: or 'Football '86', as we still call it

In previous decades, young children swapped cigarette cards with photos of Denis Compton on, but when fags went out of favour as an acceptable juvenile interest, it was an Italian company that filled the gap.

The Panini concept was simple – virtually everything of interest to kids would be turned into a sticker book, and for the next month you'd buy packs of six from the newsagent in the hope of filling it up. Of course, after a dozen or so you'd end up getting umpteen duplicates. This is where the iconic playground 'got . . . got . . . got . . . need!' ritual came in, as you tried to get as many as possible before admitting defeat and sending off for the rest.

The big hitter was the football album, published every season. The layout never changed – a double page for every team in the top flight, with spaces for all the players, a team shot and a flashy foil sticker for the badge. Lower division and Scottish sides got the latter two, and each received an exhaustive list of stats, which the more anal kid would memorise.

Other Panini classics include the regular ***Smash Hits*** collection and a tie-in for most films that hit the cinema, although some were more successful than others – we're not sure Disney also-ran *Basil the Great Mouse Detective* gripped the playground that much.

In the early 1990s, Panini had a rival in the shape of Merlin, who even nabbed the lucrative Premiership franchise. However, the company lives on, and has now diversified, even taking over the UK arm of Marvel Comics.

RETROMETER: 9/10

Paper Fortune Tellers 

Eight opportunities to be insulted for the price of one

Peak year: 1981, and in the last few lessons before every school holiday

They tried to get us interested in origami, but there was only one aspect of paper-folding we cared about. The paper fortune teller was a classroom staple, easily knocked up with a page out of your rough book and a set of coloured pencils.

The concept was simple – the paper was folded in such a way to create 'petals' that, when lifted, revealed either who you were going to marry, where you were going on your date or what you smelt like. There was some convoluted system to pick the result, either by spelling out your name or picking random numbers, or if you were feeling creative, a rhyme of the 'ip dip dog shit . . .' variety.

Whatever you picked, though, the result was the same – an utterly unfounded rumour about who you fancied that would come back to haunt you throughout the rest of your academic career.

RETROMETER: 5/10

Papier Mâché

Everyone's favourite wet-day-in-the-school-holidays timewaster

Peak year: 1985, before daytime *Neighbours* killed it off

Jack Hargreaves on *Out of Town* spent hours demonstrating traditional crafts but, among the brass rubbing and basket-weaving, never got round to the one pursuit that everyone in Britain tried at least once – normally when your mum couldn't be bothered taking old newspapers to the bin.

Papier mâché was such a familiar concept that most could still make it now from memory. You blew up a balloon and covered the exterior with newspaper stuck on with a stinky flour and water paste. When it was complete, it was stuffed in the airing cupboard for a bit until dry, at which point you popped the balloon and had, er, some dried paper in the shape of a balloon.

In fact many memorable icons were created via this cunning method. How many children would Frank Sidebottom have frightened if he hadn't worn a bulbous head created by back issues of the *Daily Star*? Elsewhere, Anthea Turner's Tracy Island make on *Blue Peter* was perhaps responsible for using up all of the nation's flour supplies in the early 1990s.

RETROMETER: 6/10

'Party Fears Two' by the Associates

'Awake me!'

Peak year: 1982

They didn't look out of place on ***Top of the Pops***. Another load of new-wave types who slinked behind guitars and synths, while a pale and interesting lead singer jigged about arhythmically behind the silver cigar mic in a Panama hat. The noise coming out of the telly, however, wasn't quite like anything else Peter Powell introduced at the time.

Billy Mackenzie's voice was a major factor. Sounding like David Bowie being physically assaulted by Kevin Rowland on the way to Bryan Ferry's wedding reception, it was impossible to ignore, whether you were enraptured by his exquisitely tortured operatics or joined parents up and down the land in a chorus of 'blimey, I can sing better than him!'

Main instrumentalist Alan Rankine duly backed the man with doom-laden synths, leavened by a relatively sprightly hook line which was bewilderingly chosen to introduce Radio Four's topical sketch programme *Weekending*.

Follow-ups included the wibbly effects-drenched 'Club Country' and the more superficially pleasant '18 Carat Love Affair', but 'Party Fears Two's number nine was as high as the Dundee duo got, and even that felt like a tenuous incursion into foreign territory for the band.

Despite personal rifts, the Associates continued in various incarnations until 1990. Mackenzie tragically killed himself in 1997.

RETROMETER: 10/10

Pebble Mill at One 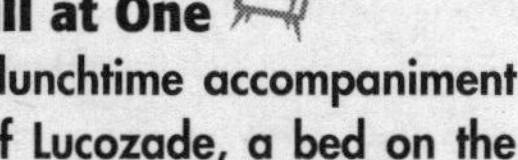

The perfect lunchtime accompaniment to a glass of Lucozade, a bed on the sofa and a fabricated sore tummy

Peak year: 1977: the show was in its pomp and the opening titles featured one bloke kicking another in the guts

Pebble Mill at One was a permanent fixture in the BBC1 daytime schedule from 1973–86, bringing us the full gamut of contemporary living in the form of mumsy interviews, the odd prerecorded item and inevitably some kind of display team running amok in the garden.

Music was always an important element and if it wasn't an up-and-coming band miming round the back of the building amidst the bins and piss, or a nameless cocktail-bar crooner adding unnecessary nobbly bits to a well-loved pop hit, then it had to be Gerard Kenny and the interminable 'New York, New York (So Good they Named it Twice)'.

However, the core of *Pebble Mill at One's* appeal was its crack presenting team. Many faces passed through, but best remembered are Bob Langley (the suave one with a cravat), Marian Foster (the strait-laced one with a line in dowdy blouses), Donnie MacLeod (cuddly, avuncular and Scottish) and Peter Seabrook (the waspish gardener with vocal chords seemingly up his nose). Between them they could easily surmount a segue from an item on the history of the much maligned traffic warden to an assault course for Alsatians before chatting amiably to Patti Boulaye.

RETROMETER: 10/10

Pencil Cases 

Indispensable ink-splattered treasure chests

Peak year: 1980, when clear polythene bags were finally usurped by ever more imaginative portfolios of packagings

As much a statement about who you were as hairstyle or shirt tails (tucked in or hanging loose?), buying a new pencil case was THE most important thing to get sorted before the start of the school year.

Metal tins were one dependable winner, especially as you could drill holes in the top using your compass to spell out swear-words. Fibrous pouches with shiny outer coverings, meanwhile, initially defied the concealment of particularly large weaponry until its titan of an older brother, massive enough to house an entire **shatterproof ruler**, burst onto the scene.

This was what you wanted. Stuffed full of crap it formed the perfect weapon (offensive and defensive), and announced occupation of 'your' desk with infinitely more menace than any paltry popperpoint pencil. All sorts of junk could amass inside, with excavations offering up tatty scribbled notes, the odd treasury tag, eraser shavings, and invariably, right at the bottom, a punctured cartridge slowly discharging its contents into the grimy intestines.

Even its one drawback, the boring outer design (a stationery set), was easily disposed of by turning the entire thing inside out, conveniently creating an ultra-absorbent alternative casing which, because it was fabric not plastic, was ideal for defacing with graffiti and ink blots.

Experience taught it was always better to opt for a plain cover. Suckers who went for one that spelled out PENCIL CASE had their wares dependably vandalised to remove the letters C, L, C, A and E.

An alternative, of course, was to ditch the case completely and go for a Helix novelty model, most typically the plastic calculator that, though cumbersome, boasted an excitingly titchy secret compartment up by that forever-confusing 'CE' key.

Regardless of your preference, however, WH Smith was always the place to make that crucial purchase. Brand leaders when it came to this top-rank merchandise, they were on to a winner with their perennial 'Back to School' campaigns every August: as much a sign the summer holidays were over as the coming of the 'New Season' in *Radio Times*.

RETROMETER: 8/10

Pencil Toppers 

Pointless pencil accoutrements

Peak year: 1983, the BA Baracus pencil topper hits the market, sucka!

Although most could see nothing wrong with simply chewing the end of your pencil (the red and black ones with the rounded coating over the base were the most satisfying), for some school kids (those who usually sported the most extensive and superfluous smelly pen collection), pencil toppers (and in particular those featuring anthropomorphic fruit) were an essential, albeit useless part of their stationery arsenal.

Aside from the rubbers that made smears on your exercise books, pencil toppers really had little bearing on either your academic prowess or your personal popularity. Even if you were given a really cool Star Wars set, there was very little you could do with it beyond affixing Yoda to the top of your HB and poking it up through the gaps between the double desks while teacher was trying to provoke a discussion on the Wars of the Roses.

Clearly a marketing man's dream, as almost any film or toy franchise was fit for transformation into something that could have a bit of wood shoved up its arse, and He-Man, Scooby Doo, the **Cabbage Patch Kids** and even loveable tyrant Henry VIII all found themselves astride a length of graphite at one time or another.

RETROMETER: 6/10

The Personal Stereo Cassette Player

Take 'The Kids from *Fame*' wherever you go!

Peak year: 1986, the year 'Walkman' entered the *Oxford English Dictionary*

It was one of those *Tomorrow's World* staples that came true – you could actually listen to your own choice of music on the move.

Sony's innovation of slapping a headphone into a tape player doesn't seem any great shakes from this remove, but it took the company until 1979 to come up with the idea.

The initial notion was to name the new creation 'Stereo Walky', but sanity prevailed and the Walkman became one of those brand names which slipped into common verbiage.

Hitting the UK at the start of the 1980s, suddenly everyone seemed to be BMX-ing, roller-skating or jogging while 'wired up' to their sixth-generation cassette copy of Hall and Oates.

However, by 1986, the first signs of the player's downfall were visible as Sony announced the oncoming of the D-50, a portable audio device which played a new digital medium that had also been remorselessly plugged by Judith Hann and company – the compact disc.

RETROMETER: 7/10

Pester Power

Mum! Mum! Mum! Mum! Mum!

Peak Year: 1985: Stinkor hit the shops

A whingeing child could be an advertiser's best friend. When caught unawares during the commercial break in *Number 73*, a juvenile was vulnerable to claims that 'there's lots of fun for everyone in **The Big Yellow ... TEAPOT**!' and would demand said item from mum and dad. Over and over.

A properly programmed kid would also turn on the tears during the traditional bathtime roundelay, declaring they were not getting wet unless someone made with the 'trillions of Matey bubbles' double-quick.

And then there was the sandpit hierarchy divined by the breadth of a child's Masters of the Universe collection, fuelled by exhortations from a demented-sounding Tom Baker to invest in the latest action figure: 'Stinkor! He really stinks!' Cue tears if mum didn't oblige during the weekend shopping trip to Big Town.

Other advertisers were more subtle. When Atari trumpeted their Video Computer System in 1982, they took time to big-up the 'educational games' that accompanied it. This was a coded message to all kids. Of course, *Super Breakout* and the like weren't remotely edifying, but hapless parents were none the wiser, making them easy prey for a browbeating about how said machine would 'help with the homework'.

RETROMETER: 7/10

PG Tips

'Coo-ee Mr Shifter! Light refreshments!'

Peak Year: 1971, and that record-breaking ad

Britain's longest-running TV ad campaign unleashed a group of hirsute hot beverage-obsessed simians onto the world. No, not Gareth Hunt and company in the **Nescafé** campaign (ho ho!), but the Brooke Bond PG Tips chimps.

The anthropomorphised apes were first pressed into service in 1956, and by the 1970s could be spotted in a range of scenarios, some involving sailing boats ('cap'n sir, I'm breaking out the teabags!'), plumbing ('pass the monkey-wrench') and espionage ('I'd like you to meet our man Bond, Brooke Bond').

However, their biggest success came in 1971 when they paid *homage* to Laurel and Hardy with a sublime thirty seconds featuring piano remover Mr Shifter and son attempting to transport said bulky instrument down a flight of stairs.

Ending in the immortal exchange: 'Dad, do you know the piano's on my foot?'/'you hum it son, I'll play it,' it became the most aired ad on British telly.

While the earliest efforts had boasted Peter Sellers on voice-over duty, it had taken a talent of Irene Handl's stature (who voiced the tea-serving homeowner) to secure lasting greatness.

RETROMETER: 7/10

'Pipes of Peace' by Paul McCartney

That piquant and puckish paean to peaceable pan-European relations

Peak year: 1984

It's hard to believe, but Macca's only ever had one chart-topping single on his own.

Yes, Paul regularly went toppermost with the Beatles, once with Wings and – best of all – that time with Stevie Wonder (when they were 'living in perfect harmony'). However, when left to his own devices he barely troubled the scorer.

That was until Christmas 1983, when someone had to say something. And that something was: come on, play the pipes of peace for goodness sake! A rather wonderful lilting melody fused a patented Macca call-and-response chorus with a kids' choir, a synth-flute wig-out and a 'we've got an orchestra' finale.

Inevitably the record found the top slot on 14 January 1984, ending the reign of Pop's Ugliest Band™, The Flying Pickets, who'd been at number one since Christmas.

Of course, the song is now better remembered for its ace video, which depicted that World War One Yuletide kickabout in No-Man's Land, and featured multiple roles for our man as both a moustachioed German in a porkpie hat and a plucky wide-eyed 'Tommy' who traded lockets in a sea of mud and barbed wire.

RETROMETER: 8/10

Pipkins

'Here come the Pipkins/there go the Pipkins . . .'

Peak year: 1974, when the puppets came to terms with the death of Inigo Pipkin in perhaps the most moving episode of any tots' programme ever

Pipkins was one of those programmes that could delight or terrify you – it depended entirely on your disposition. Certainly for a pre-schooler the aural and visual montage of clocks and chimes that accompanied the famous 'time . . .' sequence was enough to induce a panic attack. Some of the puppets were pretty terrifying too, particularly Topov the monkey (some sort of evil simian homunculus, we're saying) and the flea-bitten Hartley Hare (who appeared to be enduring a particularly serious dose of mange).

One of ITV's classic quartet of pre-school series (the other three being *Rainbow*, *Hickory House* and *Mister Trimble*), *Pipkins* and its motley collection of shabby animal puppets were each distinctively and cleverly realised, meaning every child had a favourite, be it the aforementioned Topov, the Brummy Pig or the show's star attraction Hartley.

The series began in 1973 under the name of *Inigo Pipkin*; however, this was truncated in 1974 after the death of the actor who played the titular puppet maker (George Woodbridge).

Pipkins ran until the end of 1981 when Hartley announced that 'next week there will be a new series with new people'. This turned out to be the forgettable *Let's Pretend*, whose sole concession to puppetry was a rather rubbish worm.

RETROMETER: 10/10

Pirate Reading Scheme 

'Acrooacree!'

Peak year: 1972, when the Dramatic Readers came out in child-resistant 'rag book' format

Of all the primary-school-reading scheme books (*Janet and John*, *Peter and Jane*, *Ant and Bee*) the best loved (and therefore, presumably, most effective) were EJ Arnold and Sons' Griffin and Dragon pirate stories.

Written by Sheila K McCullagh and illustrated with Mary Geraut's lush watercolours, the simple sentences detailed the maritime adventures of Benjamin the Blue (the blonde, dashing hero), Roderick the Red (hearty, slightly stout) and Gregory the Green (lanky, slightly devious), sailing away to sea in search of colour-coded gemstones, encountering merpeople and griffins along the way.

The threesome's uneasy coexistence often fell apart as Benjamin, initially, was the one with the ship, and the others, being pirates and all, kept trying to nick it. The later Dragon series took things a stage further, with black pirates, seahorses and *The Princess Who Wanted the Moon*.

It was all a delightful way to escape the confines of a rain-battered classroom on a Wednesday afternoon. With your fingers under the words, of course.

RETROMETER: 8/10

Play-Doh Barber Shop 

Let's face it, the 'dreadlocks' looked just like poos, didn't they?

Peak year: 1978, a combine harvester pipped the Barber Shop at the post to the title 'Toy of the Year'

The idea of the Play-Doh Barber Shop was to place a limbless plastic figure into a chair, turn a handle on the side of the seat, and gasp in awe as Play-Doh dreadlocks miraculously grew through the little holes in its head.

However, don't be mistaken. This toy was much more than just a chair and a handle; it also came with a pair of plastic scissors and other haircutting accessories, allowing the user to attempt all manner of weird and wonderful stylings – most of which admittedly ended up looking like Plasticine indiscriminately smeared over a bit of plastic. Alongside that, the use of different-coloured Play-Dohs theoretically offered the creative hairdresser further permutations, but inevitably all of the different hues would get mixed together, thus reducing your tinting options to one – a sludgy greyish blue.

RETROMETER: 7/10

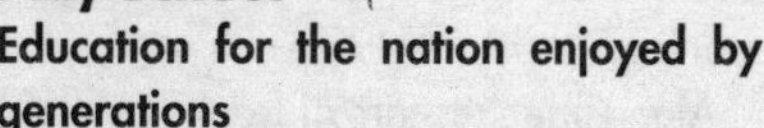

Play School

Education for the nation enjoyed by generations

Peak year: 1972, when it was one of the Beeb's biggest exports

We've got Battersea Power Station to thank for an otherwise unassuming pre-school programme becoming so well-known. An explosion there on 20 April 1964 meant the planned launch of BBC2 was cancelled, so the new channel was instead started the following morning with Gordon Rollings and Virginia Stride presenting fun for the youngest viewers.

From 1964 to 1988, *Play School* was an institution, helped perhaps by its never-changing format. Two presenters (drawn from the likes of Brian Cant, Fred Harris, Julie Stevens and Floella Benjamin) presided over songs, stories, dressing up, time-telling and makes. The hosts were often hired for their skills at improvisation – in Cant's audition he was simply handed a cardboard box and told to 'row out to sea'.

The stooges were the toys – Big and Little Ted, Humpty, Jemima and notoriously Hamble, the repulsive doll that annoyed viewers and presenters alike, prompting the production team to once draw pubic hair on her.

The biggest attraction was guessing whether the day's film would be screened through the round, square or arched window: the crew's favourite bit, as the budget was so tiny the show was normally recorded straight through, and this was the only chance for a break.

Editing was hugely expensive, as proven when Iain Lauchlan had to carry on with a scene despite Hamble's head having fallen off.

RETROMETER: 9/10

Please, Sir!

Stop holding hands at the back

Peak year: 1970: Hedges got hitched

The shouty classroom chicanery from a pre-*Good Life* John Esmonde and Bob Larbey was ITV's first all-colour hit and therefore ran forever.

Sheltering ludicrously under a giant power station was Fenn Street Secondary Modern, replete with dopey headteacher Mr Cromwell (Noel Howlett), bring-back-the-birch Miss Ewell (Joan Sanderson), sweary Welsh nutter Mr Price (Richard Davies) plus ex-Desert Rat caretaker Mr

Potter (Deryck Guyler). 'Privet' Hedges was an open-faced John Alderton in an oversized blazer, using a flutter on the horses to teach fractions, while the focus of all the capers, Class 5C, mustered twentysomething-looking teen oiks, including, erm, 'backward' Dennis (Peter Denyer), wide boy Eric (Peter Cleall) and Hedges-smitten Maureen (Liz Gebhardt).

The memorable titles featured titanic-sized captions and an ace harmonica-tootling theme with playground handbell accompaniment and singa-long middle bit not a million miles away from *Blankety Blank*.

Please Sir! mined the staff-as-bad-as-the-pupils seam shamelessly, but did it first and therefore not too badly.

RETROMETER: 6/10

Plug

'IT'S FUNI, IT'S POPI, IT'S SPORTI, IT'S TRENDI – IT'S TODAY'S COMIC' – it can't spell

Peak year: 1978, when Plug took a trouncing from Bjorn Borg

For reasons no one's sure of, in 1977 editors at the DC Thomson fun factory decreed that Bash Street Kid Plug should be awarded his own comic. And so the lanky loafter with the huge overbite turned into 'Percival Proudfoot Plugsley – known as Plug, world champion supergoon' in a luridly illustrated, genuinely off-the-wall sports-themed extravaganza.

While the supergoon himself festooned the centre pages with enticements for kids to join his 'Sports and Social Club', the likes of junior golfer Tony Jackpot, The Games Gang ('they're game for anything!') and Antchester United ('the insect football team with all the talent – and all the legs') let loose with PE-inspired funnies, often involving real celebs such as Pat Jennings and Mick Jagger.

Alongside the stars of track and field were a fleet of supporting characters far stupider than anything found in the ranks of the *Dandy* or *Topper*. 'Gnoo Faces' (best title ever!) detailed the efforts of three fame-seeking antelopes; 'Ava Banana' brought us the appallingly drawn exploits of the word's strongest girl; 'Sea Urchin' centred on the antics of a delinquent crustacean; and 'Violent Elizabeth' was standard naughty-girl stuff, but merits a mention here because it's another ace title.

Something for everyone, you'd think, but seventeen months after it launched, *Plug* was eaten up by the *Beezer*. So how did that work seeing as how Percival was also supposed to be keeping up his weekly attendance at Bash Street Comp in the pages of the *Beano*?

RETROMETER: 9/10

Pocket Libraries

Is that a Baby Face Finlayson in your pocket, or are you just pleased to see me?

Peak year: 1985, TV's Alan Wickerwork turns up in the pages of *Dandy Comic Library* to investigate the feuding 'The Jocks and the Geordies'

Pocket libraries occupy a niche area of the comics market. These monthly single story-based tomes never secured reader loyalty in the way the weekly titles did, but were always good for a read if you happened to have a spare 22p.

Although ***Commando*** remains the best known, in the late 1970s and early 1980s publisher DC Thomson somehow got to thinking the market was crying out for further such elongated adventures and, as such, launched *Starblazer* (which appealed only to the fans of stodgy 1930s-style science fiction), diminutive editions of *Beano* and *Dandy* and even a pocket-sized version of the comparatively dowdy *Mandy*.

The format was simple – take an already familiar character or genre and expand it to 64 pages, then print on the cheapest possible newsprint and publish. But although popular for a while, most of the titles failed to make it through to the 1990s.

Unlike the weeklies, the pocket libraries weren't well placed to reap the benefits of advancements in printing technology, and therefore looked exactly the same in 1992 as they had in 1982.

A brief word, though, for the *Sabre* library range of the 1970s which consisted of 'thriller stories in pictures' for the boys and 'romantic stories in pictures' for the girls. Although they are now hugely ubiquitous in charity shops up and down the land, at the time they only ever seemed to turn up in hospital newsagent kiosks – and to this day we're not sure why.

RETROMETER: 7/10

Polystyrene Gliders

Well, they could glide, that's for sure

Peak year: 1979: there was nothing else for it, all the telly was on strike

For some reason seemingly only sold in seaside newsagents, the polystyrene glider was a holiday staple for many years. The concept was simple – two thin sheets of polystyrene were slotted together and, er, you flung them in the air.

Along the way, there was clearly an attempt to turn this ultra-cheap plaything into an Airfix-style collectable, and manufacturers experimented with various liveries painted onto the glider. However, the success was slightly stymied by the fact that the craft only ever lasted about five seconds before being stood on, having its end broken off, or flying under your holiday caravan.

RETROMETER: 4/10

The Portable Television Set

Rubbish picture + rubbish sound = ace bedroom accoutrement

Peak year: 1983: your mother insisted she was having *the Treasures of the Burrell* on the big set, forcing you to watch *Doctor Who*: 'The Five Doctors' on crappy black and white upstairs

Classically cased in white plastic with a black dial for tuning in the picture and a hooped aerial that was maddeningly prone to losing the signal if anyone so much as looked at a power tool within a mile radius, the portable television set nevertheless opened up a new world of freedom for teens keen on sampling TV's forbidden fruits in the privacy of their bedrooms.

As a result, numerous episodes of *The Young Ones* were originally viewed in crackly black and white with the sound barely audible lest mum cottoned on to the unauthorised TV anarchy unfurling after lights-out.

The portable's other benefit was to provide most households with their first real choice in viewing. So, while the parents did the 5.40 p.m. current affairs courtesy of Nick Ross, Desmond Wilcox and the rest of the *Sixty Minutes* gang, the kids decamped upstairs with their beans on toast for some Peter Purves-endorsed bunny-hopping in *Kick Start*.

RETROMETER: 8/10

Prize Yoghurts

Muscle-bound dairy produce

Peak year: 1981, when a hazelnut tub was in every lunchbox

Yoghurts were dead exotic once upon a time. Though limited of flavour (strawberry, hazelnut, 'fruits of the forest' . . . er, that's it) there was something daringly European about the likes of Ski that made on-the-turn milk extremely popular.

For children the best yoghurts, undoubtedly, were Prize, and that was mainly down to the adverts, which were textbook 'so, how on Earth do we sell this?' anthropomorphised fun. Heroic animated tubs of the stuff – dubbed 'the Prize guys' – leaped into various melodramatic 'damsel in distress' situations to see off the thin and weedy villain yoghurts, before peeling off their lids to reveal temptingly chunky innards, and walking off with the rescued damsels, which were represented by, er, spoons.

There's something worryingly Freudian going on there that we can't quite figure out.

RETROMETER: 6/10

'Prog' Board Games 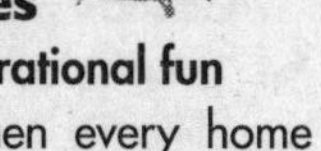

Over-complicated aspirational fun

Peak year: 1979, when every home seemingly had one

During the 1970s, a strain of board game emerged that was pitched well above the heads of your average Buckaroo devotee. They were often the product of shy Cambridge maths graduates who rolled up on *Nationwide* in regulation tank top, specs and mop of wayward curls to explain how their 'really very simple' game would make them millionaires by January.

The formula: take an abstract logic concept (preferably involving modish scientific references); render board and counters in fashionably minimalist design (preferably lots of black); slap on a portentous one-word title like 'Quantum', 'Vector' or 'Counterpoint'; illustrate the box with glamorous people in tuxedos pondering their next move while thoughtfully cradling whisky tumblers, and wait for the royalties to roll in.

But just how original were they? *Kensington*, for instance, was a suavely produced sort of octagonal *Ludo* that wouldn't look out of place on a coffee table in the titular borough. From the same people came *Skirrid*, a sort of letterless *Scrabble*/jigsaw hybrid. *September* was just the old pen 'n' paper game of *Squares* rendered in soft plastic, while *Mandala* used concentric spinning plastic rings to jazz up what was, again, basically Ludo.

The genre's apotheosis was *Black Box*, in which players uncovered the structure of a 'molecule' by firing 'lasers' through the titular darkened receptacle – all represented by counters and ball bearings, of course. Let's face it, it was just *Battleships* with an A level.

Perhaps the public caught on to this, as by 1986 the suave, complex board game had all but died out, and the shy millionaires instead gravitated towards computer games for their income.

RETROMETER: 5/10

Programmes for Schools and Colleges 

Son et lumière for the sick-note brigade

Peak year: 1981, when chicken-pox was in the ascendant

They were made to be watched in

school with rapt attention, but schools' programmes were best viewed from a sickbed, where a whole alternative TV schedule could be woozily lapped up with the Lucozade.

The day usually kicked off with something undemanding for the toddlers: *You and Me* (puppet dragon, crow and hamster find out what a library is), *Words and Pictures* (floating cartoon cockney Charlie introduces alliterative animal compadres), or *My World* (unthreatening adult reads sugar-coated moral lesson).

Then a swift gear change, as the higher realms of chemistry and mathematics were explored in no-nonsense programmes like *Experiment!* where pencils pointed at test tubes and a voice ordered, 'write that down!' or *Maths Topics*, a dizzyingly incomprehensible yet hypnotically soothing animated orange-and-brown guide to trigonometry.

Sanity was restored by the 'dramatised lesson': *Look and Read* (floating orange severed torso interrupts bowl-haircutted children's crimebusting adventures with songs about punctuation), or an oddity like *Maths-in-a-Box* (demented op-art-clad alien comes to Earth in inch-high cube to learn about numbers). History was brought to life by period soap *How We Used to Live*, dramatising the travails of an ordinary family who conveniently came into contact with almost every major event of the era. Of course, there was also *Scene*, the award-winning junior drama showcase, but we were ill, dammit, and wanted to see mad people jumping about.

Fred Harris and Sylvester McCoy duly obliged, conversing with marching squares in the spookily odd mathematical hotchpotch *Leapfrog*. Just as bizarrely, *Near and Far*'s producers thought geography could be made more palatable if prefixed by a vertigo-inducing shot of a skipping girl set to some terrifying scrapey music.

Mathshow parodied *Doctor Who* with the geometrical misadventures of the bumbling Dr Where, while *Blue Peter* was aped by the trio of cuddly investigative aunts and uncles in *Science Workshop*, and the plummy-but-chummy roster of smiling faces behind the Plasticine-titled miscellany *Watch*.

The schools' TV dress code – chunky pullovers for the men, floaty blouses and scarves for the ladies – applied to programmes like *Music Time*, where basic songs were trilled over and over again in strident falsetto while bored-looking kids bashed away at glockenspiels with all but two notes removed. *Good Health*, meanwhile, was made by kids for kids, detailing the perils of improper toothcare and nefarious fictional footwear block-a-boots.

By now time was getting on, and the last programme of the day was usually something unwelcomingly sobering about the adult world: *Starting Out*, in which school-leavers struggled with benefit forms, or *Maths Counts*, wherein Roy

Kinnear struggled with a builder's estimate – a bit of an anticlimax.

Fortunately children's programmes proper were just around the corner, and all thoughts of calculus and adverbs were swiftly forgotten.

RETROMETER: 8/10

Propelling Pencils

Just a small prick

Peak year: 1984, when you could even use them to scribble in **Ladybird Books**

Urbane **pencil case** practitioners were never seen without an army of these literally pointless pint-sized lead javelins, and they always made sure you knew about it.

The most useless and belligerent writing tool around, propelling pencils preferred to break, snap, splinter or simply disintegrate rather than see one double Geography lesson through to its end. The plastic outer casing was neither use nor ornament when, as often happened within five minutes of every pencil's appearance, its interior had been 'clicked' out so far by the class clown – using the push-button on the top – you were left wielding a giant hat pin.

In fact the only decent thing these insidious implements did was act as pretend syringes, allowing much comic business to be derived from appearing to uproariously inject yourself with a stream of toxic lead.

RETROMETER: 1/10

Public Information Films

Be smart – be safe

Peak year: 1970, and ever after

Celebrity-heavy shit-scary 'stop that!' dispatches, dropped into schedules without warning and scarred through repetition onto the minds of a generation, PIFs burst into unflinching ubiquity with the coming of colour and the TV personality.

Messrs Keegan, Stardust and Bugner led the charge, nonchalantly strolling through suburbia on the lookout for kids not following the Green Cross Code, before Jon Pertwee's attempt to make up his own incomprehensible set of rules – 'SPLINK!' – made road safety boring again.

The more extreme PIF carnage was always reserved for the most impressionable audiences: the young. Heaviest rotation went to pre-watershed depictions of a tousled-haired infant meeting their fate on pylons or electric substations then flopping to the ground to the sound of shrieking synthesisers and Brian Wilde ('never try to get toys back yourself – PLAY SAFE!'). Thankfully for every cloaked Reaper preaching about drowning ('sensible children – I have no power over them!') there was Rolf ('kids and water – they love it!') or an animated aquatic chorus ('breast stroke/back-stroke/butterfly and crawl!').

Celebrities frequented the second-league PIFs: all-purpose advice shops on everything from giving blood (a Glenda Jackson/Ernie Wise double act: 'You told me you'd take me to Hollywood!'/'No, Cricklewood!') to motorcyclists (Edward Judd: 'Think once, think twice, think bike'). There were calls-to-arms, typified by economy-down-the-pan 'SAVE IT' ads with Delia Smith cooking an entire meal in one oven, or 'Clunk-Click', debuted by Shaw Taylor ('people of the Tyne Tees area . . . your seatbelt is their security') then nicked by Sir Jim'll.

PIFs became so stamped in the memory because for ages they were simply never updated. Now they're virtually absent from screens completely, as if the country is somehow a less dangerous place. You can, however, occasionally catch a tribute to coastguards at 2 a.m.

RETROMETER: 10/10

Punch

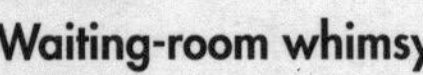

Waiting-room whimsy

Peak year: 1978, with Alan Coren at the helm

'*Punch*? But that started in 1841! Muggeridge, Betjeman, long-winded cartoon captions, the curate's egg and all that. Hardly relevant to the 1970s, surely?'

Well, no, but therein lay its charm: the old cliché of the lone patient idly leafing through a copy in the doctor's waiting room, staving off clinical boredom with a few Larry or Graham cartoons about bridge evenings, or a flight of agreeable whimsy by Paul Jennings or Basil Boothroyd on the subject of automated telephone switchboards or the demise of the eleven-plus.

Once the height of social satire, in its dotage it became a comfy bolster against the three-day week and the miners' strike, poking around in the minutiae of life in the manner of an after-dinner conversation at a gentleman's club. What better way to distract oneself from impending nuclear Armageddon than with Miles Kington's 'Let's Parler Franglais!', or Alan Coren's latest despatch from Cricklewood?

It couldn't last though, and after an increasingly rocky 1980s, *Punch* finally bit the bullet (half-arsed revivals notwithstanding) in 1992.

RETROMETER: 6/10

Quatro

Lilt-ing at windmills

Peak year: 1984: the Miracle cometh

An unlamented conglomeration of fruit

extracts (orange, lime, lemon and cherry, if you must know), packaged in oversized bottles stamped with a blocky Letraset-styled segmented 'Q', Quatro (working titles: Mondo and Boxer – fact) nonetheless had terrifically over-ambitious advertising: a grizzly-jacketed New Romantic obtaining the fluid from a *Blake's 7*-esque 21st-century dispenser to the boisterous slogan 'It's A Miracle, But We've Made It'.

Predictably, 'It' had all but vanished within a couple of years. Fellow contemporary beverage Squirt, hailing in a yellow can of fizzy nothingness, lasted no longer, but at least secured canonisation thanks to it being clutched by Paula Yates in the video for 'Do They Know it's Christmas?'

RETROMETER: 2/10

Radio Assemblies 

'Perhaps you'd like to share that joke with the rest of us?'

Peak year: 1985, when only a skive could save you from a surfeit of *Come and Praise* close harmonies

Whether you were slumped cross-legged on the floor or stood wilting in endless rows, the business of crooning (or, rather, mouthing) along with a school radio assembly couldn't help but leave you wondering why words that were full of virtuous things like love, peace and harmony left you so pissed off.

Standard-issue songbook was the BBC-produced *Come and Praise*, flaunting a lurid blue cover bedecked with huge grinning bowl-haired kids. Its rival, in a sort of ***Radio Times/TV Times*** manner, was the self-consciously more 'trendy' *Their Words My Thoughts*, which also boasted – eek – poetry and, in the middle, a terrifying black and white photo of a wrinkly pensioner, presumably to warn you of the ravages of old age.

Despite their unbending formality, however, these collective conventions were always a haven for japery ('stop holding hands at the back there'). Failing that there was always the easy way out; playing a soprano recorder in the school 'orchestra'.

RETROMETER: 1/10

Radio Luxembourg 

Pass the Duchy and fade to grey

Peak year: 1980, as Luxy became the 'Station of the Eighties'

The Great 208's location in the mysterious 'Grand Duchy of Luxembourg' added a touch of continental glamour and an almost illicit thrill to bedtime teenage listening. Luxy's after-dark British service provided the only real pop alternative to John Peel on Radio

One, in spite of its notoriously erratic Medium Wave transmissions from far-away Europe. For all its 1,300,000 watts of power, the station was guaranteed to fade out halfway through your favourite record before returning loud and clear in the middle of a commercial for Cuticura medicated soap.

In the aftermath of the pirate era, 'the biggest commercial radio station in the world' had become a sort of academy for a generation of DJs, including Noel Edmonds, Peter Powell, Kid Jensen, Mike Read and Timmy Mallett, while the roll-call of Luxy names also includes Mike Hollis, deep-voiced Bob Stewart, 'the royal ruler' Tony Price, and 'ma friend' Stuart Henry and his wife Ollie.

The 208 Powerplay single of the week was played every hour on the hour, while Luxy also broadcast *Next Week's Top 20*, an audacious attempt to trump Bruno Brookes.

By the late 1980s, more and more stations were broadcasting round the clock in FM stereo, rendering 208 a bit of a radio relic, and the station moved onto satellite, before closing down for good in 1992.

RETROMETER: 8/10

The Radio One Roadshow

'The fun starts at ten and we're live on air at eleven!'

Peak year: 1982, the year the Radio One caravan celebrated its tenth anniversary

Never mind solstices and Stonehenge, the first day of British summertime was officially signalled by the departure of the Radio One Roadshow on its annual circumnavigation of the British coast. John Peel once commented on the strange phenomenon of an event consisting of a man playing records, but ninety minutes of patented Wonderful 247 fun and games and that red, white and blue truck were enough to lure us to our local pleasure beach. And after the show there was the chance to grab the Hairy Monster's autograph, and bemoan the fact that it was your mate's card that Peter Powell picked from the Lucky Request Bin rather than your own.

The Roadshow began as the brainchild of executive Johnnie Beerling, as a means of promoting The Happy Sound and shedding its London-based image. Mike Read had less philanthropic motives for embracing the Roadshow ethos, as he admitted before his debut: 'I was very jealous last year. Every time I turned on the wireless I heard the other chaps raving about the willowy blondes and sultry brunettes.'

The generalissimo of the Roadshow was Smiley Miley, a genial West Country jester charged with transporting the BBC cavalcade from resort to resort, usually turning up on stage on a seaside donkey.

The Roadshow's high point was music

quiz 'Bits and Pieces' (cue Tommy Vance: 'One more record to "Bits and Pieces"!'), as audience members identified snippets of hits, interspersed with that 'bwoo-bwoo-bwoo' noise.

The Goodiemobile served up a bountiful array of 247/275 & 285/1053 & 1089/97-99 merchandise, including Mike Read Tea-Hee mugs, windscreen sunstrips, fluffy bugs ('don't bug me, I'm listening to Radio One') and even those quilted jackets the DJs wore while opening supermarkets and attending motor rallies.

RETROMETER: 7/10

Radio Times

First choice for all the family

Peak year: 1983, on the few occasions it was actually published

These days it's dead easy to find out what's on the telly – if you don't have an electronic guide via your remote then the schedules are in almost every magazine. Before 1991, though, it was very different, as the BBC ensured that the only company allowed to publish their listings were the Beeb themselves. Therefore buying *Radio Times* was more or less compulsory, and sales ran into the millions.

To allow accuracy in numerous regional editions, there were compromises made in the aesthetics. Bar a couple of colour pages, the rest was printed on horrible newsprint that was seemingly otherwise used for school toilet paper. Worse still the colour sections had to go to press weeks before the rest, leading to some embarrassments – in 1983 the cover looked forward to a long awaited race between Seb Coe and Steve Ovett, while the inside apologised that the latter had already pulled out. Many times, too, the magazine looked even more ragged due to printers' strikes, with pictures being replaced by big white spaces.

Still, other aspects made up for it. Unlike today's TV guides, that just stick press shots of the latest soap storyline on the cover, *RT* usually commissioned original artwork to illustrate the week's fare, while Roger Woddis provided poems. Furthermore, as a monopoly, it could print massively in-depth information, with full cast and crew for most programmes, which always fascinated the TV-obsessed kid. The likes of *Grandstand* got full, detailed timetables, and comedy shows had a whale of a time writing their own billings – whereas now you'd be lucky to get anything more than 'comedy sketch show', one *Not the Nine O'Clock News* blurb was written entirely in Gaelic.

By 1990 technology had improved enough to allow full colour printing, but the following year government deregulation compelled the BBC to give listings information to anyone who asked for it.

Hence while *RT* continued to sell well, it could never scale the heights some of the Christmas issues used to manage. As names of set designers gave way to more critical reviews and glossy photo-shoots, at least **Clive Doig**'s Trackword puzzle survived.

RETROMETER: 10/10

The Raising of the *Mary Rose*

'Babcock Power Construction Division'

Peak year: 1982, as the thing was raised from the bottom of the Solent – very, very slowly indeed

On 11 October 1982, sixty million people worldwide tuned in to watch the flagship of King Henry VIII's fleet being inched up from the ocean bed where it had been resting for 437 years. 60 million? Apparently so – doubtless in no small part due to Sarah Greene's numerous aquatic visits to the wreck in what seemed like a zillion short films on *Blue Peter*.

As a stack of sodden timbers finally rose out of the waves in a £4 million lifting operation, the majesty of recovering a 16th-century warship had been rather dimmed by hours of uneventful screen time devoted to a static bright-yellow winching arm emblazoned with 'Babcock Power Construction Division'.

Even for school pupils who were missing Monday lessons to numb their arses on the floor of the TV room watching the 'historic' events unfold, the whole thing quickly palled – with nary a laugh going up even when one of the pins holding the lifting frame sheared, causing a steel line to snap and send part of it smashing into the hull.

The vessel, which for a brief time had been a national talking-point, quickly passed into obscurity having rather outstayed its welcome. And *Blue Peter*? A few years later it was at it again, only this time going nuts over the prospect of designing new bosses for the ceiling of the fire-ravaged York Minster.

RETROMETER: 7/10

Raleigh Grifter

Reinforced king of the road

Peak year: 1982, the year of the Grifter XL

The Raleigh Chopper boasted real playground cachet thanks to its low-slung saddle and high-rise handlebars, while racing bikes sported a sort of authentic Milk Race prestige and enough gears to tackle Kilimanjaro, and BMXs had an irresistible American kudos attached to them in the tyre tracks of *ET*.

And then there was the Raleigh Grifter. Launched after the Chopper but before the BMX pedalled across the Atlantic, it straddled the two eras in a decidedly awkward fashion. It looked sporty enough, but with its solid chunky frame and padded handlebars, the Grifter was a distinctly cumbersome machine with all the manoeuvrability of a Sherman tank.

Perhaps the best thing about the bike was the nifty gear mechanism, incorporated in the handgrip of the handlebars, enabling the rider to switch between all three at the flick of the wrist.

Not even rebranding it as the Grifter XL with flash red and black livery could rescue matters, however, and thousands of leg-weary teens were left to reflect on the fact that it was lucky for ET Henry Thomas never owned one of them.

RETROMETER: 7/10

Reader's Digest

Amputation and amulet-obsessed lavatory installation

Peak year: Whenever you 'were entered' for the Prize Draw

Permanent fixture in your gran's bathroom and punch-line to a thousand sitcom gags ('Dinner with the mother-in-law? I'd have more fun with a year's subscription to *Reader's Digest*'), this irritatingly sized gossip sheet first plopped through the UK's letterbox in 1938 after sixteen years of soaraway success in the US.

Cooked up by the spectacularly named De Witt Wallace and his missus Lila Bell Acheson, *Reader's Digest* was initially concerned with gobbets of anecdotage culled from that enduringly catch-all topic, 'human interest'. But the mag didn't become a permanent guest in the world's smallest room until 1962 when the first 'Sweepstake' was launched.

Now the promise of enlightenment came hand in hand not just with chatter about the jet set but the chance to win everything from glass paperweights to a week on the Masai Mara game reserve. The twin pursuit of tittle-tattle and porcelain figurines became a national pastime, and entire shelving units were given over to ever-swelling piles of back issues, awaiting the day when there was time to finish that story about the man whose eye popped out in the desert or the woman who had to saw off her own toe in the middle of a monsoon.

RETROMETER: 5/10

Ready-mixed Booze

Beyond Tia Maria

Peak year: 1983, year of stomach-coating banana rum concoction Calypso

Cinzano and Campari began to look a tad retrograde in the brave new 1980s world of chrome barstools and rich men without moustaches, so distillers marketed a slew of ready-mixed drinks to capture that burgeoning female boozership.

Taboo and Mirage (white wine, vodka and spices/citrus fruit respectively) set the aspirational standard with chiffon-clad women dreamily sipping the beverages as they reclined against marble columns and gazed out over an airbrushed landscape. Elsewhere, globetrotting models enthused about Monterez, 'a delightfully bittersweet blend of white wine, brandy and a subtle tang of orange'.

Other ads sought to make provincial singles clubs look the epitome of urban swank. Lime-tinged Bacardi spin-off Bezique and fizzy infusion Volari were promoted as the one sure-fire way to turn a drab, empty nightspot into a vibrant hub of hand-to-mouth tittering rolled-up jacket-sleeve seduction.

But these drinks were largely consumed for one purpose only: to get smashed as quickly as possible. Small wonder the most popular was the sophistication-dodging blend of **British wine** and whiskey that was Clan Dew.

RETROMETER: 4/10

Record Mirror and Sounds

Coalface pretenders to the inky throne

Peak year: 1976, when *Sounds* stumbled on punk before anyone else

For almost two decades the guitar-addled teenager had the dilemma of splitting their pocket money between a quartet of equally poorly printed weeklies, each battling to outgun the others through ever more ghoulish headlines and bonkers cover photos. Somehow, though, the ***NME*** and ***Melody Maker*** always ended up on top, largely because the competition were forever conveniently frippering away their advantage at the last second.

Launched as a bible for prog loons, *Sounds* grabbed a lead on fellow inkies by being the first to champion punk, only for head writer Garry Bushell to throw in his lot with 'Oi' bands rife with dodgy National Front connotations. The paper's circulation tumbled.

Record Mirror, meanwhile, showed up in the late 1950s as a de facto DJs' handbook packed with the latest on new labels and US imports, but got festooned with a Mod following, a glossy relaunch, a million pop pedants and finally loads of joyless acid house apostles.

Both closed suddenly the same week in April 1991. At least they survived longer than *Streetlife* (European counterculture meets Deep Purple), *Superpop* ('Sex symbols of all shapes and sizes!') and *Pop Star Weekly* (Weakly more like).

RETROMETER: 7/10

Regional Adverts 

Local heroes

Peak year: 1980, ITV's local opt-out highpoint

Sadly, with ITV regions practically extinct, the humble local telly ad is becoming a rare species. The most basic was the still picture plus voice-over, exemplified by the Wigan Market campaign, which in its entirety consisted of a still of said location over which a voice implored 'come to Wigan Market!' Every region had these, be they for Yeovil Sheepskin or four-in-one Scottish electrical-goods merchants Glens, Hutchinsons, Robertson and Stepek.

Slightly more sophisticated ads employed a mascot: the animated lion who declared Don Amott 'king of caravans', the old lady who espoused the loveliness of Shackleton's high seat chairs, or the Superman clone with enormous packet who strode through a furniture store as the jingle proclaimed, 'when you walk through the door/your pound's worth more/at Williams . . . where else?'

Next step up was to rope in someone famous. Manchester's BOC Cars hired an ermine-clad Bernard Manning ('we're the Earls Court of the North!'), while Frank 'Captain Peacock' Thornton played a store manager for Welsh furniture shop Arthur Llewellyn Jenkins. Most glamorous of all was Midlands Yugo outlet Swithland Motors, who hired Sam Fox for a series of stilted skits with comical loser Wally, who fainted in awe of Sam's spoilers, sunroof and trendy white paint job.

If you couldn't afford a celeb, why not become one yourself? Many local entrepreneurs went before the cameras flogging their wares. In Ulster, it was Crazy Prices' perpetually terrified Jim Megaw. Colindale Volkswagen was plugged by parachuting proprietor Ray Thacker. The North West was treated to the spectacle of estate agent Owen Oyston falling backwards into a swimming pool. Most ubiquitous was the owner of Hackney telly showroom OTV, who took advantage of early Channel Four's cheap advertising rates to personally plug his very local business nationwide. Shoestring result!

RETROMETER: 8/10

'Rock Bottom' by Lynsey De Paul and Mike Moran 

Piano-led Eurovision nearly-hit

Peak year: 1977

The UK looked set for Eurovision victory in 1977 when ***Golden Shot*** theme composer Lynsey De Paul dusted down an old number she'd originally written for Blue Mink and teamed up with bouffant-haired session keyboardist and musical director of *Get It Together* Mike Moran.

Following Brotherhood of Man's famous victory the previous year, hopes were high at Wembley Conference Centre as the pair, clad in identical tuxedos with buttonholes, sat arse-to-arse at two baby grands and belted out their pluckily syncopated call-and-response anthem of despair: 'Tragedies?/We got 'em!'

Sadly, they had to settle for second place, a disappointing fifteen points behind France's Marie Myriam with 'L'Oiseau et L'Enfant', but comfortably ahead of 'It's Nice to be in Love Again' by Ireland's The Swarbriggs Plus Two.

The good folk of Royaume-Uni showed their sympathy by taking the song to number nineteen in the charts. Lynsey later returned to TV themes, knocking out the rousing opener to Esther Rantzen's *Hearts of Gold* in 1988.

RETROMETER: 6/10

Rockliffe's Babies

Blags, fags and council-estate slags with rookie coppers taming the concrete jungle. In a van.

Peak year: 1987, when Victor Tango Division screeched onto our screens. In a van.

'Rock-a-bye baby in the tower block/your mum's on the social, dad's in the dock!' declared the shouty stage-school kids providing the theme to BBC1's 'gritty' urban crime drama, as its trainee plain-clothes 'tecs glowered moodily under flashing blue lights in front of their van, the programme's name written on its side in the grime.

Under the tutelage of textbook sardonic copper Det Sgt Alan Rockcliffe, the Babies learned their stuff, attempting to maintain order on the Dragon Estate. In a van.

That roll-call of Babies and their handily chalk-and-cheese character traits in full, then. Gerry O'Dowd (hot-headed, Scouser, Joe McGann); David Adams (by-the-book); Steve Hood (smelt of pubs and too many right-wing meetings); Paul Georgiou (rotund, Welsh, asked colleagues to 'get us a pork pie and a sachet of brown sauce'); Keith Chitty (naïve country boy); Janice Hargreaves (feisty, ambitious); and Karen Walsh (brunette, demon driver).

Decent enough stuff to accompany a **Vesta** curry on a Friday night, before Ian Hogg took his maroon anorak after two series and headed for West Country spin-off *Rockliffe's Folly*.

RETROMETER: 7/10

Ronco

The *gruppenführers* of gadgetry

Peak year: 1978, when no home was complete without the Ronco Glass Froster

Poke around under the stairs or in the attic and it's a fairly safe bet that before long you'll stumble across a long-lost member of Ronco's family of gadgets abandoned beneath a thick coating of dust.

For most of the 1970s, Ronco produced a succession of indispensable labour-saving gadgets, like the Buttoneer, a nifty gizmo that enabled you to say goodbye to button-sewing misery, and the Ronco In-Egg Scrambler, a device that scrambled your Goldenlay inside their shell. Exactly how we'd endured eating eggs scrambled in the conventional out-of-shell form for so long remained a mystery.

The Ronco Record Cleaner scrubbed up your 33s by rotating them at an unnervingly high velocity, and grubby spark plugs became a thing of the past thanks to the Ronco Spark Plug Cleaner.

But perhaps the most extraordinary product from the House of Ronco was the Bottle Chopper, a miniaturised guillotine that allowed you to slice your empties in half to make attractive vases and drinking glasses.

Naturally all this relentless innovation was ripe for deft satire. Enter Jasper Carrott in 1983 and his hilarious 'Bonco' spoofs, featuring the Bonco Back-of-the-Head Viewer and the Bonco Knee Size Gauge.

Every Christmas, Ronco produce received lavish promotion, backed by a synthesised Deck the Halls jingle, as the mighty Tommy Vance intoned that their merchandise was available 'at Woolworths and most fine shops'.

RETROMETER: 5/10

Roy of the Rovers

Rocket man

Peak year: 1981, the year of Who Shot Roy Race?

It's become a cliché for commentators to refer to '*Roy of the Rovers* stuff', but real-life football has never quite lived up to Roy's world of gravity-defying overhead kicks, assassination attempts and New Romantic midfielders.

Roy's career at Melchester Rovers began in *Tiger* in the mid-1950s, and thanks to his legendary left-foot 'Rocket', Racey became so popular he was granted a testimonial match in 1975 (with Dickie Davies as MC) before spinning off into his own comic.

The publication featured a touch more realism, as Roy became player-manager and married his secretary Penny, and Melchester's red and yellow strip even embraced sponsorship ('What's that on the front? Gola? Shouldn't that be Goal?').

Roy's team-mates included 'Blackie' Gray, Charlie 'The Cat' Carter and 'Lofty' Peak. Indeed, you were forbidden from playing for Melchester unless you had a nickname that made you sound like a member of the cast of *It Ain't Half Hot, Mum*.

In 1981, the unthinkable happened as Rovers were relegated, and Roy was shot by an actor playing him in a TV soap. Both Roy and the team recovered, but in 1983 Racey quit to manage rivals Walford.

It seemed like the writers had started to run out of ideas, the nadir being the point Rovers signed Martin Kemp and Steve Norman from Spandau Ballet in 1985. No doubt chairman Geoffrey Boycott was delighted.

Meanwhile, the comic was home to a myriad of other strips, like 'The Hard Man', a tough-tackling defender forever in trouble with referees; 'Billy's Boots', a schoolboy who owned a pair of magical boots that had once belonged to a famous footballer ('Is this me or is this Dead Shot Keen?'); and 'Hot-Shot Hamish', a Herculean Hebridean blessed with a net-bursting striking action.

RETROMETER: 9/10

Rupert: The Daily Express Annual

A time capsule from another England

Peak year: 1984, the year Macca took Rupert to number three in the charts

Set in the quintessentially English environs of Nutwood, the titular bear's adventures with flying machines, mermaids and tinkers were – during the glory years – rendered in loving detail by Alfred Bestall, who became the definitive *Rupert* artist. Under his reign, the character pranced through a perfect storybook world, and appeared in numerous beautifully painted end-papers – one of which inspired Paul McCartney and The Frog Chorus's hit 'We All Stand Together'.

Despite Nutwood representing a rather 1940s version of the best of all possible Englands, there was the occasional controversy in that green and pleasant land. For one, Rupert's un-PC golliwog friend and his foray to 'Coon Island' were aspects of his life rarely talked about now. However, even those dubious dabbles with ethnicity palled in comparison to the great *Annual* dispute of 1973.

As was his wont, that year Bestall produced another fine front cover featuring a brown-faced Rupert, despite the bear always sporting ivory-hued features inside the book. Alas, Lord Beaverbrook's son took umbrage, apparently ordering an end to the disparity, and without Bestall's consent, Rupert was 'whitened up'.

At that point the great artist decided to call it a day, leaving a host of talented pretenders in his wake who continue to delineate the adventures of the furry chap in the *Doctor Who* scarf and golfing trousers.

RETROMETER: 7/10

S–Z: Sale of the Century to Yellow Pages

Sale of the Century

Before Alan Partridge, Norwich's lasting legacy

Peak year: 1978, when it was the most watched quiz show ever

A fortnight in Spain for two quid? A new sofa for 50p? There's no doubt *Sale of the Century* had a cracking concept – contestants played for cash to spend on goods at absurdly discounted prices. Yet this wasn't the reason you watched – you watched for the performance of host Nicholas Parsons, who dominated proceedings from beginning to end.

With his exquisite tailoring and florid turn of phrase ('one of these is not a blue cheese – I wonder, could you tell me which one?'), Nick brought a touch of class to the game show. He could talk up a prize like no other host, badgering the contestants into choosing a fur coat or dining table in which they clearly had no interest. Indeed, the IBA once censured the programme for 'gloating' over the prizes' value too much.

The unforgettable opening announcement from John Benson – 'From Norwich, it's the quiz of the week!' – was certainly true in December 1978 when it was watched by a staggering 21 million people, the highest ever quiz audience. Of course, this was helped by the fact the BBC was on strike, but the show was a smash hit throughout the 1970s.

Probably one of the few Anglia programmes anyone remembers, the series finally came to an end in 1983. The following year saw the start of a slightly different price-based quiz – *The Price is Right*, a world away from Nick's Tupperware.

RETROMETER: 7/10

Sapphire and Steel

Chilling sci-fi series featuring flying pillows and a man with no face.

Peak year: 1979, Sapphire and Steel's second adventure (set on a disused railway station) is a tour-de-force of directing, acting and whistling

Given that *Sapphire and Steel* was created by someone who had previously written for *The Sweeney* and starred an ex-*New Avenger* and the Russian bloke from *The Man from UNCLE*, the series' weighty sobriety must have been a shock for viewers tuning in for some high-kicking, Ford Cortina-themed fun.

The central concept was deliberately woolly, pitting two otherworldly investigators (David McCallum and Joanna Lumley) up against . . . well we're not quite sure, but we reckon it might have been time itself.

A hallmark of the series was the remarkably conceptual and, at times, prosaic weaponry employed by the titular protagonists. In addition to their telepathy and other not fully defined superpowers, their armoury consisted of nursery rhymes and the last few years of an old man's life. Although not the kind of arsenal you could menacingly stick up the hooter of a Dudley Sutton-type hard man, we somehow understood that, in the context of their adventures, Sapphire and Steel were well tooled up.

Of their six brief adventures, the best was perhaps the one set in a disused railway station. Lit and directed as if it were a stage play, the magnetic performance of the two leads plus Gerald James's carefully realised turn as fussy amateur ghost hunter Tully resulted in eight episodes of the scariest television ever made.

RETROMETER: 10/10

Saturday Morning Shows

Cartoons, phone-ins, pop stars and increasing amounts of gunge

Peak year: 1980, when Edmonds and Tarrant battled it out each week

The concept of Saturday morning TV owes a lot to its cinema counterparts in previous decades – simply a miscellany of items linked by a couple of presenters.

This was certainly the case in January 1974 when ATV launched *TISWAS* as simply a way to link cartoons and serials. Such was its low budget, they could only afford one chair and thus the two presenters – including one Chris Tarrant – never appeared on screen together. Originally it was Midlands-only, but as more running jokes and buckets of water were added to the mix, it started to spread around the country.

Meanwhile the BBC waited until October 1976 when Noel Edmonds presented the first *Multi-Coloured Swap Shop* – a marathon three-hour programme most notable for pioneering the idea of viewers interrogating celebrities over the phone. From this point you had two options before lunch – the slower, more involved 'nice' offering on the Beeb, or ITV's manic burst of rude jokes and custard pies. Which you chose was a hot topic in the playground.

The same ideas lasted, mainly, for 25 years. On the Beeb only the presenters – Mike Read, Phillip Schofield – and the names – *Saturday Superstore*, *Going Live* – really deviated from Noel's format. ITV were less adept after the '*WAS* ended in 1982 (a year after all, bar Sally James, quit for the ill-fated 'adult' version *OTT*) and normally relied on rather diminishing returns for the cartoons'n'pop'n'games formula (cf: *The Saturday Show* and the Tony Slattery-fronted *TX: Ready for Transmission*).

RETROMETER: 9/10

School Book Club Purchases

Educationally endorsed impulsive purchasing

Peak year: 1980, the year of the *Whizz Kid*

The school book club was a powerful way of teasing money out of tiny hands sent dizzy by a pamphlet featuring a toothy critter extolling the virtues of Gyles Brandreth's latest offering.

It was through these means the *Whizz Kids* series cascaded across playgrounds, advising juveniles on how to 'beat the experts at their own game' on subjects such as bikes, kites, chess and – ambitiously – 'how to be a detective'.

However, if that smacked too much of 'edutainment', there were plenty of good old-fashioned laughs on hand, thanks to the prolific work of Michael 'Cyberman Controller' Kilgarriff and his *1,000 Jokes* series, which included *1,000 Jokes for Kids of all Ages, 1,000 Knock Knock Jokes for Kids* and best of all, *Oh no! Not Another 1,000 Jokes for Kids*.

Children were also lured by the glamour of the film and TV tie-in. In 1981, who in their right mind could have resisted the high adventure of Schoolastic's Condorman novelisation or an extra portion of Irene Handl in Metal Mickey's Boogie Book?

The self-styled king of the book club publication was the aforementioned Gyles Daubeney Brandreth, who homed in on the joke racket with several volumes (including The Biggest Kids Joke Book Ever!) as well as trying his hand at the 'misc' category with such tomes as Super Heroes: The Facts Behind the Legends (James Bond can 'fly anything from a spacecraft to an umbrella', apparently), Quick and Easy Magic Tricks, The Hiccups at No.13 and many, many more.

RETROMETER: 9/10

School Crazes

From British Bulldogs to Cross Tig and other activities that descend into fighting

Peak year: 1987, an outbreak of mass classroom humming erupts nationwide thanks to an episode of *Grange Hill*

One of the immutable laws of school was that an activity or interest – no matter how benign – would get outlawed as soon as enough kids became interested in it. Indeed, the banning of the latest craze served an important function, establishing the playground black market as a going concern for the sale of yo-yos and Rubik's snakes.

The whole social life of the school yard was extremely complex. One week everyone was buying rubbish rub-on tattoos of non-copyright cartoon characters, the next they were constructing bombs out of 250ml bottles of Happy Shopper Cola and half a packet of Refreshers. And when they weren't doing that, kids were simply queuing en masse in front of the lunchtime ice-cream van to enquire how much a 10p mix-up cost.

It wasn't just outside in the playground where these important rituals were played out. One of the most popular was the inscribing of the commonly accepted symbol for the penis onto someone's exercise book. This was a simplistic three-line affair that was occasionally augmented with artfully drawn droplets emitting from the rounded end. The act was particularly important if the recipient of the symbol was just about to hand said book in to teacher for marking.

However, for the really bold school pupil the ultimate was to take a sex word and reverse the letters in it. They would then ask a particularly susceptible teacher whether or not they were a 'nigriv' or were into 'lana'. Surprisingly, in our experience not a single teacher ever cottoned on to what was happening – you would have thought the sniggers from the rest of the class would have given them half an idea, wouldn't you? What a bunch of Joey Deacons!

RETROMETER: 10/10

School Fun

The result of a particularly fruitless ideas session at Fleetway

Peak year: 1983 – actually, make that 'only year'

It must have been murder trying to think of concepts for comics in the days when new titles were coming out on more or less a weekly basis. However, few were quite as contrived as *School Fun*.

You can imagine the thinking behind it – kids relate to school, let's do a comic based on it. Presumably the staff failed to realise the last thing you wanted to think about in your spare time was more school.

Billed as 'The Happiest Read of Your Life!' the concept was at least implemented thoroughly – the contents page was headlined as, inevitably, the 'timetable', and strips were referred to as 'single period' and 'double period' depending on whether they were one or two pages long.

Perhaps the most notable aspect of *School Fun* was the heavy use of TV tie-ins. '*Grange Hill* Juniors' was a BBC-endorsed strip – the only 'triple period' in the comic – and managed to surf the zeitgeist somewhat. *'Coronation Street School'*, on the other hand, seemed entirely unofficial, and it's hard to imagine early-1980s kids getting much out of the antics of a mini-Mavis Riley. Still, the first issue did include an interview with Bruce Foxton.

Sadly the whole thing failed to last twelve months before merging with *Buster*. Meanwhile, Gripper and co headed off to greet the new term in the pages of ***Beeb***.

RETROMETER: 8/10

See-Saw

'Meet Nutty Noah and Niggly Nelly inside'

Peak year: 1976, when the *Barbapapas* gazed down from the newsagent's shelf

Full of fun and frivolity for the discerning toddler, the BBC's eightpenny compendium showcased in print the cavalcade of colourful animated characters who'd appear on screen after Donny and Marian had closed the ***Pebble Mill*** patio doors or before Richard Baker read the teatime news.

In between the educational puzzles and games, the escapades of subterranean furry recyclers *The Wombles*, sou'westered surrealists ***Noah and Nelly***, and the boho perm-and-canine combination of *Crystal Tipps and Alistair* were all present and correct, while Dutch hippie blobs *The Barbapapas* starred on the front page.

The majestically anarchic *Roobarb* translated effortlessly to the pages of *See-Saw*, meanwhile, given that the cartoon looked like it had been scribbled onto the TV set with the free 'lovely colouring pack' that had been given away with the first issue.

Mysteriously, the BBC didn't start using the *See-Saw* branding on screen for the lunchtime watch-with-mum slot until long after the comic disappeared, as after just 41 issues, in 1977 it merged with *Toby Comic*.

RETROMETER: 7/10

Shatterproof Rulers

Thirty centimetres of precision line-drawing power

Peak years: 1982, when indestructibility ruled OK

In the teeming jungle that is the **pencil case**, there is but one ruler. The shatterproof, of course, emperor of all he surveys. That trippy pop-art font declaring the Helix's indestructible qualities was an authentic hallmark of quality and distinction and reassured the owner it was not about to splinter into a thousand shards after two minutes. The shatterproof ruler was the Sir Peter de la Billiere of the measuring stakes. If Admiral Sandy Woodward wanted to plot a rainfall graph, he'd use a shatterproof ruler.

Besides measuring it had various other applications, the most important being to make a twangy noise. Few could resist the temptation to give it a bit of Hank Marvin when teach's back was turned, and the more skilled exponents could even accurately reproduce the noise from the animation that linked items on *Record Breakers* ('Woooosh! Pop! Doiiiiiiiiinnnnggg!').

But, as anyone who has attempted to recreate *The Three Musketeers* on the school bus has learned, not even shatterproof rulers are immortal. It might be an ad hoc common-room Test match or an unfortunate Bunsen burner incident, but for every shatterproof ruler, the time must come for its final line.

RETROMETER: 8/10

Shiver and Shake

Another fag break at Fleetway, another comic invented

Peak year: 1974, before the never-ending annuals

How to invent a comic in three easy steps. (1) Kids like comedy ghosts and monsters. (2) ***Whizzer and Chips*** has illustrated the clever gimmick of two comics in one. (3) Elephants are easy to draw. Hey presto, it's *Shiver and Shake*.

Perhaps not the most memorable comic to come out of Kings' Reach Tower, *Shiver and Shake* was split into two sections – the former, predictably, 'edited' by a ghost, while the latter came under the auspices of, bizarrely, an elephant. Wearing school uniform. While it's fairly easy to fill up the pages of a ghost-themed comic, it was pretty difficult to work out what the heffalump's bit was supposed to be about.

Inevitably it closed down fairly soon. Wisely, it was decided to merge it with *Whoopee!*, given that if it had joined ***Whizzer and Chips*** it would have required a gatefold cover.

RETROMETER: 6/10

Shoot!

It's like having *The Big Match* inside your holdall

Peak year: 1982, with Keegan in his pomp and *España* 82 mania

Shoot! was the periodical of choice for the playground football fanatic back in the era of the Milk Cup, the Adidas Tango and attempting to replicate Zico free kicks down the rec.

In the 1970s and 1980s, anybody who was anybody wrote a column for *Shoot!*, although whether the likes of Gordon McQueen ('My Soccer World') or Gary Shaw ('Soccer As I See It') actually sat down at the typewriter every week to impart their footballing wisdom remains unclear.

Everyone collected the League Ladders, the cardboard ready reckoner given away at the start of each season that enabled readers to keep track of their team with cut-out-and-keep tabs. And school roughbooks across the land found themselves covered in centrefold *Shoot!* team posters.

But the best bit of *Shoot!* was 'Super Focus', the questionnaire that gave readers an insight into the lager-and-lime lifestyle of their heroes. Footballers of the day revealed their favourite food ('steak and chips'), favourite music ('George Benson and Earth, Wind and Fire'), best friend ('I like to think I have many') and, of course, favourite actress ('Bo Derek or Jacqueline Bisset'), which was always a good excuse to sneak in a bit of crumpet.

RETROMETER: 7/10

Simon Bates 

What was the year? Every bloody year!

Peak year: 1989: Bates circumnavigated the globe at the Beeb's expense

Middle-aged, bespectacled and never giving the impression he was a serious music fan, Simon Bates was a Radio One institution, with his mid-morning show running for fifteen years between 1978 and 1993.

The programme became most notable (or notorious) for the dreadful syrupy dedication slot 'Our Tune', where he drawled his way through a turgid tale of lost love.

Simes always seemed to find the music an irritant, getting in the way of his plans to run Radio One, and perhaps the entire world. He was never happier then when he was single-handedly setting up a charity record or launching some government-backed youth initiative he'd invented. At least one show a week would come from Concorde en route to an exotic location.

Some Radio One staff claimed he spent most of his show on the phone running a gossip network, endlessly referring to management on air, and at least one applicant for the vacant controller's post discovered his CV had somehow landed on Bates's desk.

In 1989, he travelled the world in eighty days for Oxfam, and, ever the professional, still presented a live programme every morning from various deserts and jungles.

What did all this have to do with pop records? Well, nothing. He eventually left in 1993, by which time his extravagant jet-setting was out of kilter with Brit

Pop and the new incoming humour of Chris Evans et al.

RETROMETER: 6/10

Simulcasts

Surround sound on a shoestring

Peak year: 1988, when *'Pops* went multi-media

A giant white 'SB' in a black circle in ***Radio Times*** was the thing to look for: it meant it was time to start planning how best to rearrange your front room to appreciate a perennial of the pre-Nicam age.

The Old Grey Whistle Test was the first to try a simulcast, inviting viewers to defy common sense by switching on their radio at the same time as the TV. *Sight and Sound in Concert* followed, bringing many a ropey turn from a provincial corn exchange to serenade Radio One and BBC2 audiences simultaneously.

Each time, ***Radio Times*** painstakingly guided your bewildered dad through the business of properly arranging breezeblock-size speakers on the correct sides of the telly – or, in the case of *BBC in Quad* in 1974, asked viewers to sit with their TV inside a ring of four speakers, two each tuned to Radio Two AND Radio Three.

More conventional simulcasting found a home on *Top of the Pops*, which tested the water on its one-thousandth show in 1983 (a dinner-jacketed Richard Skinner greeting viewers from the Radio One studios) then from September 1988 did it every Thursday until 1991, when the Beeb went properly stereo and the age of the true simulcast was over.

They still exist, of course, though the advent of digital sound has meant the days of irking your mum by trailing speaker wires over 'her' chair are long gone.

RETROMETER: 5/10

Sky

I want my MTV. And Eurosport. And Dolly Parton Show

Peak year: 1989: Peter Marshall's *Sale of the Century*

In the 1980s, the imminent arrival of television from the skies seemed like the most thrillingly space-age innovation imaginable, narrowly outpointing jetpacks, hoverboards and those meals-in-pills we were all supposed to be eating by 1990. Breathless reports on *Tomorrow's World* promised hundreds of channels at the touch of a button, even if it seemed we'd need a dish the size of Jodrell Bank.

The reality, when it appeared in 1989, was somewhat different, in spite of Sky's reverse-psychology commercial: 'Four channels aren't good enough for her; she has to have ten or twelve!' When he postulated the concept of the geo-stationary orbit, access to complete reruns of David Hamilton's *All Clued Up* was probably not what Arthur C Clarke had in mind.

Sky One launched with a threadbare schedule of reruns of *Family Ties*, *The Young Doctors* and *The Dolly Parton Show*, while DJ Kat, a mangy feline puppet, linked hours and hours of cartoons and videos. It meant that a white Sky dish was not exactly a status symbol, while the dismal ratings provided tons of ammunition for deft satire ('Salman Rushdie's got a new job where nobody'll find him – he's got his own show on Sky!'), everyone from Smith and Jones to Clive James smirking at the non-stop appearances of Derek Jameson and Frank Bough.

But the **BSB** merger in 1990 brought in *The Teenage Mutant Hero Turtles*, while *The Simpsons* meant you spent more and more time round at your mate's who had Sky. Not, it must be said, to watch Keith Chegwin's dubious talent contest *Star Search*, featuring judges of the calibre of Jim Bowen and Rustie Lee.

Eventually, more and more channels appeared, from MTV, UK Gold and Paramount, with its legendary teletext pages, to more fleeting ventures like Granada Talk TV and Sky Scottish. But satellite's novelty had begun to wear off, and instead we returned to speculating whether steak and chips in tablet form was ever going to appear.

RETROMETER: 7/10

Slip-on Shoes

Oh-so-1980s easy-to-apply footwear

Peak year: 1987: *Grange Hill* ladies' man Freddie Mainwaring does the slip-on shoe shuffle to ace effect

For a time the slip-on shoe was the essential punctuation point to the generic 1980s 'skinny' wardrobe (from shoelace tie to pointy shirt collars) as popularised by your Freddie Mainwarings and Ant Joneses.

Always accompanied by rolled-up jacket sleeves and huge hair, the loafers classically came in grey, with flat undersoles that provided zero grip on any surface.

Nowadays only ever sported by Paul Calf-alike drunkards, the plastic winkle-pinker never really stood a chance once the more robust trainer became the fashion footwear of choice.

RETROMETER: 5/10

Smash Hits 

Quintuple bongzoi!!!!!!

Peak year: 1986, thanks to the comedic potential of Sigue 'Sigue' Sputnik

Before 1978 music journalism was split into two types – the 'what's your favourite colour'-style interviews beloved of teen magazines and the chin-stroking fare of the 'serious' music press. But then Nick Logan changed everything when he produced the first issue of *Smash Hits* from his kitchen.

Initially its attraction was including lyrics to latest singles, thereby adding a level of professionalism to your bedroom miming. As time went on, however, the quality of the writing became the major selling point. It knew that pop music was not to be taken seriously, but was canny enough not to concentrate on simply one genre – if it was in the charts, it was in *Smash Hits*, meaning you were just as likely to read about The Smiths as Duran Duran, and the two would be praised and parodied in equal measure.

The magazine didn't ask whether records said anything about the world, or if they were fashionable – it was only concerned about whether they were any good. By the mid-1980s *Smash Hits* was one of the most influential publications around, and had developed its own vocabulary, referring to itself as 'Ver Hits' while Rick Astley's forgettable nature led to him being permanently rechristened Dick Spatsley. The letters page, meanwhile, was helmed by Black Type, and home to demented missives about Una Stubbs' **Nescafé adverts** and the exploits of Reg 'Reg' Snipton.

But *Smash Hits* didn't do this to belittle pop, rather to celebrate it and glory in its excesses. Indeed it got more out of the stars thanks to its approach – if they were miserable and didn't join in, it was their loss. As Phillip Schofield once remarked in an interview, 'it's been a long time since I was asked if I've ever felt like a roundabout'.

Sadly, while the magazine is still going, pop is now a serious business and the acts are treated with the utmost respect. A shame as, in its pomp, *Smash Hits* was required reading long after you'd reached your teens.

RETROMETER: 10/10

SMP 

Crate expectations

Peak year: 1987: last chance to play the cards right

Inspiration for many a never-used-to-be-like-this rejoinder from your mum and dad, the arrival of SMP – the Schools' Maths Project – substituted multiplication tables for coloured plastic crates filled with numbered, wipe-kleen cards detailing various mathematical activities. Each colour corresponded to an ascending level of difficulty, and each crate with a school year. You were left to work upwards at your own pace, though the smart-arse kids on the top table always relished the chance to race onto the next level a few terms early.

Despite stationery-cupboard ubiquity and bumper acronym potential (Stupid Maths Project, Sums Mean Prats), SMP frippered away under the National Curriculum – as did its distant Welsh cousin, SRA (Stupid Reading Activity).

RETROMETER: 6/10

Soda Stream

'Get busy with the fizz-aahh!'

Peak year: 1978, when Soda Stream were perched to topple Coca Cola. What went wrong?!

'Wow! You've got a Soda Stream?!' Surely there was nothing quite like the do-it-yourself fizzy drink-maker (or 'dispenser' as they called it) to secure instant kudos with all your mates, and make school lunch-breaks round your house a dead cert.

Everything about the device screamed fun, from the distinctive whirly bottles, via the extraordinarily gloopy syrup (mmmm, Tizer!), to the fart sounds that emitted from the device when your drink was maxed-out with fizz – who would have thought carbonated water could be such fun?

First launched in 1903, the shaker-maker hit critical mass in the 1970s when that 'get busy' advertising campaign did the rounds, cajoling people – big or small – to 'create a fizzy flavour with water from the tap'. Soon own-brand coke, fizzy lime and non-copyright-baiting 'iron brew' flowed in abundance, demanding to be supped through one of those hilarious curly drinking-straws.

Still in production today, for some reason Soda Stream no longer seems to be quite the party-starter. Who's to say a later Tony Slattery-helmed advertising campaign wasn't wholly responsible?

RETROMETER: 8/10

Space Exploration Being Taken Seriously

Houston, we have a project lesson

Peak year: 1973, launch of the tin windmill that was Skylab

The manned exploration of space is the zenith of human technological endeavour, a stirring quest for knowledge and achievement that has the potential to reach beyond petty nationalist politics and unite the entire world. More importantly, it's a great way for weary primary school teachers to shut noisy classes up with an afternoon of 'project work'.

Looking back it's easy to view those mighty Saturn V launches as little more than elaborate entertainment, but back then such blasé derision for all things orbital was far from the norm. Hours of telly were devoted to serious discussions of plans for asteroid mines, doughnut-shaped space cities and the like. People truly believed a new era was just around the corner.

Some time towards the end of the 1970s, however, it became clear to even the most wide-eyed space cadet that a planet obsessed with cuts, strikes and of course 'prices' was not likely to be setting foot upon any new worlds in the foreseeable future, and Cape Canaveral reluctantly settled into its new, more humble role of enabling Adam Ant to bore half the western world with 'Vive Le Rock' at *Live Aid*.

RETROMETER: 8/10

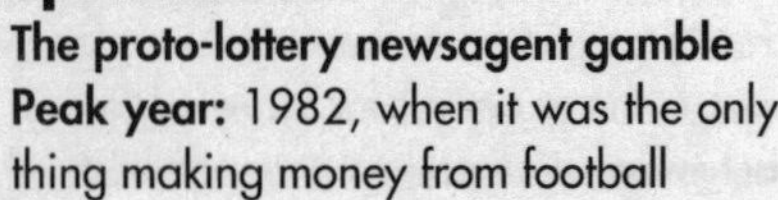

Spot the Ball

The proto-lottery newsagent gamble

Peak year: 1982, when it was the only thing making money from football

Here is a picture of a football match. The ball has been removed. Where is it? While Spot the Ball is probably one of the simplest games ever invented, in its glory days some people took it very seriously indeed.

Not for them simply scribbling a cross on the picture with a biro. Oh no, instead they invested in a stamp to mark the exact co-ordinates the ball had been hoofed to. Exactly where you bought the stamp from, or how you could be quite so sure, nobody knew. And similarly, nobody knew any of the winners, as when their names were printed in the papers they were always announced as 'Mr "X"' from a town you'd never heard of, like Snodland.

Spot the Ball does still exist, with ashen-faced pensioners handing over the coupon when they pick up their *Racing Post*. Still, in the days of Far Eastern betting syndicates apparently running the sport, we should be thankful for some innocent football fun when we can get it.

RETROMETER: 6/10

Stage School Showcases

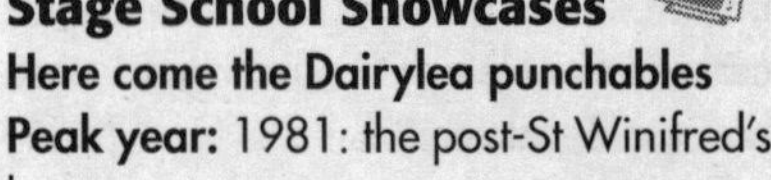

Here come the Dairylea punchables

Peak year: 1981: the post-St Winifred's boom

Captain Birdseye's 'crew' was the epitome of this advertising genre: the all-singing, all-dancing chorus of stage school children giving it full-on eyes-and-teeth enthusiasm in desperate hope of landing a starring role opposite Metal Mickey.

Problem was, while the captain capably delivered his lines in piratical baritone ('when I was a lad, this may seem odd/I dreamt of fish fingers, prime fillet of cod!') the kids were handicapped by that dreadful squawky timbre that results whenever a large number of children of varying ages try to sing together.

Yet advertisers persevered. Dungaree-clad imps pranced o'er hill and dale extolling the virtues of Dairylea ('straight from the tub/our mums have found/there's so much more to spread around!') or confidently proclaimed: 'we can tell it's Tizer/when our eyes're shut!'

Occasionally pop songs were rendered all shouty: Donovan for Bird's custard ('pour on mellow yellow!') and Madness' 'Baggy Trousers' for Colgate Blue Minty Gel ('mum and dad use it as well!')

Towards the end of the decade, however, the link between processed foodstuffs and children leaping around bellowing inanities at each other became more a matter for medical concern than celebration, and the genre slid quietly into remission.

RETROMETER: 5/10

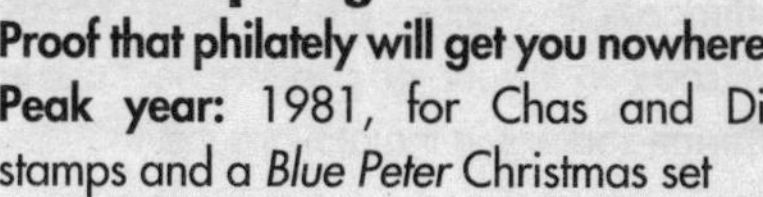

The Stamp Bug Club

Proof that philately will get you nowhere

Peak year: 1981, for Chas and Di stamps and a *Blue Peter* Christmas set

Led by a jaunty insect of indeterminate species in union jack dungarees, the Stamp Bug Club was set up by the Post Office in the early 1980s in a bid to lure school kids into the sinister realm of mint gutter pairs and first-day covers, his antenna ever-poised to alert collectors to the imminent arrival of the British Engineering Achievements presentation pack.

The philatelic industry had long waged a determined campaign to part kids from their pocket money. How many nascent collectors, tempted by the irresistible lure of the small ads in the back pages of ***Whizzer and Chips***, flouted the instruction to 'please tell your parents' and sent off for 150 'triangular' stamps 'on approval', a phrase that conjured up images of inspecting a priceless cache of rarities through a jeweller's eyepiece? Meanwhile, the philatelic godfather that was Stanley Gibbons held dominion over an army of collectors from his lair at the plush address of 399 The Strand.

The Stamp Bug Club existed to market new British commemorative issues, which sounded pretty exciting in theory, but in reality carried the damp whiff of the school project about them. Sets depicting 'textiles', 'folklore' and, most boring of all, 'cattle', hardly set the pulses racing.

Daydreams of stumbling across an immaculate Penny Black were hastily ditched in favour of a return to trading **Panini stickers** in the playground.

RETROMETER: 7/10

Starburst

The correct term is 'science fantasy', actually

Peak year: 1980, when the magazine went demented over the second coming – *The Empire Strikes Back*

Launched in 1978, *Starburst* tackled the sci-fi scene with a mixture of gosh-wow awe ('*Star Wars* literally is fantastic, incredible, unforgettable and glorious') and knowing sarkiness ('One sincerely hopes that Dino [De Laurentiis] makes a better job of *Flash* than he did *King Kong*').

The first few issues were packed full of '*Wars* and *Star Trek* miscellany, accompanied by photos scarily reproduced in negative (was this something to do with it all being sci-fi?).

Nowadays pictures of Nicholas Hammond got up as a wrinkly-suited Spider-Man, a moustachioed Lee Majors donning chain mail for fantasy flick *The Norseman*, or rotoscoped Hobbits from *The Lord of the Rings* cartoon seem like vacuum-packed artefacts from a past era. However, there really was lots to be excited about, with *Blake's 7* bringing snogging and stasers to the telly that year, while issue three broke the news that '20th Century Fox are backing "a thriller-horror film set in space" called *Alien*.'

Since those heady days, *Starburst* has passed through the hands of several publishing companies, and you can't deny it's lost some of its charm. Boiler-suited US no-marks in CGI'd spaceships on the front cover are no match for a clenching Lou Ferrigno in a litre of green body paint.

RETROMETER: 7/10

'Stars on 45' by Starsound

Medley intentions

Peak year: 1981, when virtually no original records were released

Let us hail Jaap Eggermont, the Dutch Svengali behind Starsound, the shadowy consortium that pumped out endless holiday 'medleys' of old hits, rerecorded by soundalikes and spliced together to a relentless hand-clap loop.

Essentially a device to enable Paul Le Roy-issue hotel DJs to stick on something for 'the mums and dads' and nip out for ten minutes for a fag, it was Starsound that kept on turning in our minds throughout 1981. 'Stars on 45 Part One' comprised an eclectic selection of old Beatles tracks – 'Nowhere Man', 'Drive My Car' etc. – along with, for some unexplained reason, 'Sugar Sugar' and 'Venus', all topped and tailed with that 'we can work it out/remember "Twist and Shout"!' bit. It reached number two in the charts, sparking a frenzy for lashing together medleys of any old hits.

In response, some Dutch bloke called Lobo assembled something called 'The Carribbean Disco Show' (technically a record, not a show) from bits of 'The Banana Boat Song' and 'Island in the Sun', among others.

Starsound struck back with a collection of Abba hits entitled 'Stars on 45 Part Two', including 'SOS', 'Money Money Money', 'Fernando' and 'Bang-a-Boomerang' ('Love is a tune you hummy-hummy-hum'), a record that nobody has ever heard in their lives outside of that medley.

Before long, everyone was at it. Even the Beatles flung together a 'Movie Medley', Tight Fit flounced their way through 'Back to the Sixties' parts 'One' and 'Two', and naturally, the Royal Philharmonic Orchestra got 'Hooked on Classics', welding together 'Rhapsody in Blue' and the *1812 Overture*.

RETROMETER: 9/10

Stork SB

Leslie Crowther goes tub thumping

Peak year: 1978, when nine out of ten housewives couldn't tell the difference

In between doling out the *Crackerjack* cabbages and soliciting estimates on a Mini Metro from *The Price is Right*'s baying mob, Leslie Crowther buttonholed housewives from behind his supermarket bunco booth, demanding to know if they 'could tell Stork SB from butter' in a blind taste test that involved scoffing scones in front of a horde of chattering pensioners. Fortunately, they could never tell the difference, and once Les had turned over the mystery plates and confirmed Stork's triumph, they vowed to spread the yellow gloop on their husband's meat paste sarnies forthwith.

Such was the fame of the Stork commercials at their height that Nookie Bear once responded to a scolding from Roger De Courcey for mumbling with the majestic line, 'can't you tell talk from mutter?'

RETROMETER: 7/10

Stretch Armstrong

The only action figure who actually bled

Peak year: 1976, Kenner Toys release the original incarnation of Stretch

At first glance Stretch Armstrong looked

like a gone-to-seed ***Action Man*** experimenting with a kind of Glen Campbell look, complete with kiss curl and sideburns. However, his unique attribute lay in his prodigious elasticity that – according to the packaging – allowed you to pull his limbs until he measured four feet in length.

Although innovative, there was something unwholesome about our pliable pal. Perhaps it was his immense weight, or his funny rubbery smell, or maybe it was just that over time he would develop tears in his flesh which revealed the glutinous substance lurking within and made him look as if he was suffering from severe radiation burns.

The rather eclectic Stretch range also consisted of Stretch Monster, (Stretch Armstrong's nemesis), Stretch X-Ray ('the see-thru invader') and Stretch Octopus. Few, if any, of these toys made it through the 1980s unscathed, and our man was given something of a makeover in the 1990s so that today he looks more like an 'out' Californian body builder who's let himself go a bit.

RETROMETER: 9/10

Sugar Puffs 

'Tell 'em about the honey, mummy!'

Peak year: 1985, when the whole family were collecting tokens

While adults stuck with their dull muesli and bran-based cereals in the morning, kids wanted something more interesting. For parents, the only way to stop them demanding chocolate bars at seven o'clock was to buy a sugar-based cereal.

Sugar Puffs emphasised their child appeal by an ad campaign starring the Honey Monster, a sucrose-addicted, hyperactive behemoth who seemed to be in a flat share with Benny Hill stooge and Puffs 'mummy' Henry McGee. Numerous slapstick antics prevailed, with collapsing shelves and the like leaving a gurning McGee permanently ruffled.

In 1988 the monster was paired with punk poet John Cooper Clarke to front a series of *TISWAS*-inspired adverts featuring plenty of gunging and shouting; something of a change from the nice kids who previously colonised these sorts of ads.

Even the duller cereals saw the potential of kid-friendly advertising, notably *Weetabix*, who employed a family of cartoon 'Bix skinheads (Dunk, Bixie and the rest) to bully and harass other 'titchy' cereals. So exciting were their exploits they even made it into their own 8-bit computer game, looking boxier than ever.

RETROMETER: 7/10

Summer Holiday Mornings

Why don't you just switch off your television set and go out and do something less boring instead? Yeah, right . . .

Peak year: 1983, thanks to the arrival of Roland Rat Superstar

The summer holidays meant six weeks in your pyjamas with the curtains shut, watching some of the most ramshackle television schedules ever devised, as BBC1 and ITV flung out anything they had on the shelves to entertain the kids.

Inevitably, this meant a mix of repeats, 1930s sci-fi serials and 26-part dubbed East European dramas. The pillar of the holiday schedules, *Why Don't You . . .?*, began with the Bristol gang, and some business involving invisible nemesis 'the Dorris' who could be repelled by stripy socks. *The Adventures of Huckleberry Finn and His Friends* also became a straw-hatted BBC holiday perennial, Mark Twain's tales of 'days that were slower/when living was easy and neighbours were friends' featured Mississippi riverboats, raft-building, tree-climbing, treasure hunts and whitewashing fences in abundance.

On ITV, you could tune into *Once Upon a Time . . . Man*, a majestically over-ambitious French animated history of mankind presented in unremitting detail ('Episode 17: The Golden Age of the Low Countries'). The title sequence, depicting man's evolution from the primordial soup to the space age, climaxing in an astronaut being pursued across a launchpad by a baying mob as he tried to flee the planet Earth seconds before it explodes, is the scariest thing ever screened in the name of children's television.

But the best holiday morning entertainment arrived in 1983, courtesy of TV-am's *Rat on the Road*, as the 'fast-talking rodent' and sidekick Kevin the Gerbil were despatched on tour in a pink 1957 Ford Anglia. Now, isn't it time you were getting dressed?

RETROMETER: 7/10

Swap Shop Books

Three hours of entertainment crammed into a hundred pages

Peak year: 1980, book three

With *Swap Shop* editor Rosemary Gill a graduate of the *Blue Peter* stable, it was obvious that the Saturday morning favourite would spin off into book form. In total four annuals were published in the late 1970s and early 1980s and, while never quite as eagerly awaited and collectable as the *BP* equivalent, still serve as a decent souvenir of one of the all-time great kids' shows.

In the pre-video times, of course, the books were more or less the only way to remember your favourite bits of the series, hence why much of the page count was filled with large pictures of the various bands and guests that had appeared, and notable features. There were 'signed' pin-ups of the team (though whoever wanted to put John Craven on their wall remains a mystery) and, as with *BP*, there were a number of articles 'written' by the presenters, including adventure stories apparently penned by Cheggers.

And when the inspiration flagged, there was always the chance to find out what the vision mixers did or what happened when you phoned in. The final page was always the chance to win a trip to the *Swap Shop* studio via some absurdly convoluted set of questions or brain teasers.

The first three books were conventional publications, albeit in paperback, but the fourth and final took on a new A5 format. This is the one you're most likely to see in charity shops, not least thanks to the iconic cover of Noel tittering into a trimphone.

RETROMETER: 8/10

Sweet Cigarettes

Non-carcinogenic mouth furniture

Peak year: 1975: despite the Earth's moon having been torn from its orbit, Commander John Koenig still finds time to endorse candy smokes

Apparently, the bad boys of the tuck-shop trolley have never actually been outlawed across the country (at least, if recent calls to ban them are anything to go by); however, those ice-sugar and gelatine cancer-rod replicas surely haven't been seen in shops for a good two decades or so now since they lost their red tip and suffered a rebranding to 'candy sticks'.

Originally marketed to resemble actual fags and resplendent in Lucky Strike lookalike packaging, the sweet cigarette became the quintessential spin-off standby as those white lengths of sucrose were packaged to promote a host of TV and film favourites.

Best of the bunch were the *Space 1999*-themed packs, which came with special cigarette cards depicting top moments from the sci-fi show (although card number 42, a portrait shot of a rather scarred Dr Mateo, had to be withdrawn thanks to its sheer gruesomeness). Then there were the *Dad's Army* faux-fags, marketed alongside the 1971 feature-film spin-off, and the *Moonraker* puffs – at last deriving from a fictional source where the main character was actually known to enjoy the odd drag.

As concerns began to bite about the logic of weaning kids onto the death tubes, there was still time for the most shameful excursion into the world of sweet smokes, when Superman draped himself all over a box of twenty. By way of penance, the Man of Steel spent the 1980s combating Rod Hull-lookalike and tobacco-endorsing baddy Nick O'Teen across surgery waiting-room walls the length and breadth of the UK.

RETROMETER: 9/10

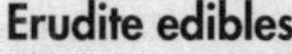

Swizzels-Matlow

Erudite edibles

Peak year: 1975, when Swizzels and Matlow formally shook hands

Sweets that did more than simply ask to be chewed were always going to be a good thing. The Swizzels-Matlow commonwealth embraced confectionery that had to be dissolved (Fruit Fizzers), excavated (Double Dip), succoured (Rainbow Drops), modelled (Dolly Beads), applied (Candy Lipstick), inhaled (Parma Violets), eroded (New Refreshers) and, most famously, read (Love Hearts).

The latter, masquerading as a contemporary equivalent of the 18th-century love token, commonly saw its 200-plus legends adopted for shameless muck-spreading (incriminatingly 'soppy' messages being planted on hapless victims by third-party malcontents).

Indeed, across most brands the intent was often more successful than the application, Dolly Beads rarely spending long around some nine-year-old's neck and Double Dips forever becoming separated from their 'Swizzel stick' applicator when someone hurled it across the playground.

RETROMETER: 7/10

Take Hart

Everyone knows someone who had something in the gallery

Peak year: 1977, *Vision On* may have finished but the boring art and crafts bit lived on in Tony Hart's new series *Take Hart*

Famed for his understated 'hullo's and overstated cravats, Tony Hart has racked up an incredible fifty years of salubrious, usually very quiet television, communicating by and large with an audience he seems to have no obvious connection with. Yet somehow his vague undercurrent of antipathy towards the young works for – rather than against – him.

Of all Tony's many series on art, the best remembered is *Take Hart*. Perhaps this is because it's the one that first introduced us to his two sidekicks: the claymation Morph and comedy caretaker Mr Bennett. This latter character never failed to elicit some eyeball rolling from Tone when he was distracted by the hapless janny while attempting to gently persuade us of the notion that creating a multi-layered landscape using only coloured paper was a more exciting way to while away a couple of hours than beating up your brother.

While Tony would dabble in all manner of picture-making processes (including blowing paint through a straw to try and make something that looks like a city at night, or wrecking a perfectly good football pitch by painting a giant picture on it), it was clear his first love was pen and ink. Indeed, he would routinely turn up on **Saturday morning kids' shows** for a picture-drawing phone-in session. Curiously, though, no matter what the caller asked for, Tony always ended up doing them a doodle of a giraffe eating some leaves from a tree.

RETROMETER: 6/10

TCR 

The 'other' racing set

Peak year: 1979, the end of the slot era

It was the squeeze-the-crackly-hairdryers Scalextric (always pronounced 'Scalectrix', as a strange slovenly-tongued point of childhood honour) that became synonymous with front-room-engulfing Formula One shenanigans, but Ideal's Total Control Racing was a fine 'upgrade' of the doughty original.

The problem with the old sets was that, powered tram-style as they were by electricity coming from a groove in the track, your John Player Special/Mini Cooper S/Escort Cosworth, however lovingly applied the stickers, was forbidden to change lanes while overtaking.

Not so with the slotless TCR, which liberated vehicles and led to more tactical play, and indeed fun. Further innovations included the snazzy-sounding Super Booster which gave cars a short-lived boost of speed at crucial moments, and the jam car, a slow-moving extra vehicle which dawdled round the track of its own volition to further complicate racing matters.

The slotless system was either nicked or improved upon, depending on which set of corporate lawyers you invite round to tea, by Matchbox with their Lanechanger set, which held the cars in a firmer grip, lanewise, as they shot round the bends.

Better yet was the outlaw pursuit-themed Matchbox Race 'n' Chase, in which a police car chased a stripy Corvette round a track with a tactically crucial tip-up bridge in the centre, and the ability to suddenly swerve the cars and skid round 180 degrees to head off in the opposite direction.

RETROMETER: 7/10

Telex

The future of technology – with an attractive wood effect

Peak year: 1984, when *Blue Peter* installed it on its appeal newsdesk

Of course, it's all e-mail nowadays, the average office worker sending around two dozen to the person at the adjacent desk every day, some of which aren't even about whose turn it is to make the coffee. In the past, though, the large company had to set up an entire room to co-ordinate its cross-country communication.

The thing about telex was that nobody ever seemed to know how it worked, but every business worth their salt would have a telex number in their letterheads. The equipment cost a fortune and hardly anyone was ever qualified to use it, but it was the medium of choice for anyone who needed something written down right now.

Now there are a million ways to ignore someone trying to get hold of you, so much so most companies' telex is gathering dust under a pile of paperwork in a back office somewhere. Had it still been going, of course, no doubt somebody would have worked out how to offer 'adult' content through it.

RETROMETER: 7/10

The Telly Cabinet

'Push from this end only'

Peak year: 1980: the year of Ferguson

They were mainly encountered at school: those seemingly gigantic tubular steel edifices which housed a clunky-buttoned Ferguson Videostar VCR and a huge TX telly (cue André Previn: 'I'd say it's the best picture of all time!') discreetly hidden behind two faux-teak laminated doors.

In retrospect there's something amazingly quaint about those doors intended to obscure the offending screen when it wasn't in use, but at the time the sheer size of this pioneering technology was awe-inspiring to many a child. The unit was ceremonially wheeled into class, the doors opened and light poured forth. Almost a religious experience.

RETROMETER: 7/10

Terry Wogan's On-Air Banter with Jimmy Young

Mobile commode and the DG's dentures

Peak year: 1979, when even Her Majesty was listening in

In one corner of Broadcasting House, a bonny-faced purveyor of whimsy, hailing the country with multiple spins of Kenny Rogers' 'Lucille', urges listeners to 'Fight the Flab' and tells of the 'Dance of the BBC Virgins'. In another, an erstwhile crooner grilling law-makers, keeping tabs on fish prices, and cueing in chipmunkesque Raymondo's salutation,' what's the recipe today, Jim?' Each orbited Portland Place in splendid isolation.

Then, one month in 1977, Terry Wogan and Jimmy Young suddenly found themselves side by side in the schedules and in adjacent studios, with Tel afforded a compelling view of the back of Jimbo's head. Ever one to capitalise on reduced circumstances for some on-air chicanery, Wogan decided to invite his colleague to pop in ahead of the 10 a.m. handover to trail his show. And in an instant, a radio institution was born.

Within days their discussions had turned to suspender belts. Within weeks the pair were receiving mailbags full of camiknickers. Nothing was planned, nothing was scripted, yet somehow the affable pointlessness and mock-abuse became one of the finest things on radio. They made the cover of *Radio Times*. They released a record, 'Two Heads are Better than One'. When Radio Two moved from Long Wave to Medium Wave in 1978, they loaned their pipes to an improvised harmonised rundown of the frequency changes – and still it worked!

'I quite like that little argument you have with Mr Wogan in the mornings,' the Queen confided when Jim picked up his OBE. A whole nation sat back in agreement.

RETROMETER: 7/10

Text Slides of Doom

Due to an industrial dispute, we are unable to bring you this entry

Peak year: 1979, when those slides were on more often than the programmes

Nowadays we know that whenever we turn on the telly we're virtually guaranteed the programme we want to see will be there. In the past, though, the number of industrial disputes and technical breakdowns meant there was always the chance it would be cancelled, and replaced with a fulsome apology, some light music, and a white-on-blue caption.

Anyone who watched telly during the summer of 1979 will remember that ITV's entire output for two months was simply a slide saying there would be no programmes until further notice, thanks to an enormous strike. Hence the BBC revelled in almost complete supremacy of the airwaves – although the caption and music enjoyed a regular audience of over one million, such was its soothing nature.

The only programme the third channel actually broadcast during this dispute was *Engineering Announcements*, the

IBA's regular Tuesday morning bulletin of transmitter information. Never billed in the listings, this low-tech series – often nothing more than a series of diagrams and charts – was shown every week for some thirty years, much to the surprise of any skiving schoolkid.

RETROMETER: 10/10

That's Life! 

Post-bathtime behemoth of crusading do-goodism, grainy vox poppery and mongrels

Peak year: 1980, the year a tent-sporting Esther was flanked by Cyril, Paul, Chris and Doc Cox

A terrifying juggernaut that roamed Sunday nights for a generation, *That's Life!* didn't really take off until 1976, three years after its birth, when a promotion to around nine o'clock on Sundays brought Esther Rantzen and her co-hosts – her 'Nancies' – monumental fame.

So began the feted, and fateful, cavalcade: the parpy brass band theme, originally blessed with lyrics sung live by, among others, Patricia Routledge ('that's your lot/it's all you've got/it's the naaaaaaame of the gaaaaaaaame/heeeeeeeeeeere's/*That's Life*!'); correspondence read out in insanely prolonged relay-style by the Nancies; OAPs eating snails or hedgehog crisps; OAPs playing their false teeth, or the top of their heads, or a garden hose whirled around their heads; Esther and the OAPs being arrested; dogs saying 'sausages', or driving a car, or pissing on rubber plants in the studio; Cyril Fletcher in a huge leather armchair reading bits out of the paper; Jobsworth of the week; the Get Britain Singing Campaign; and Adrian Mills trying to be Spanish.

Nestling forever awkwardly amidst this mayhem were the po-faced investigations and exposés, spinning off into *Hearts of Gold*, *Childwatch* and Marti Webb's 'Ben'. But while the Nancies came and went – including Glyn Worsnip, Kieran Prendiville, Chris Serle, Paul Heiney, Doc Cox and Gavin Campbell – the show was untouchable for aeons, Esther even managing to delay the news one week to show more dogs pissing.

The chop finally came in 1994. Never quite as cloying as you remember it, *That's Life!* was best enjoyed in small doses. Pity it was on for half the year, then.

RETROMETER: 8/10

Themed Savoury Snacks

Indeterminately shaped corn-pulp trinkets

Peak year: 1982, when cheese 'n' onion was no longer enough

There's only so much you can do with a crisp. New flavours, bigger bags, salt in a little sachet . . . that's about it. So when snack manufacturers fell upon the technology to injection-mould corn into a variety of zany shapes, a plethora of conceptually themed new snacks were released to stimulate kids' appetites. Problem was, emulsified cornstarch didn't exactly rival latex in its ability to be sculpted, so a little creative marketing was required.

KP got around the problem by basing **Monster Munch**, 'the biggest snack pennies can buy', on unidentified body parts of entirely fictional top-hatted furries, and for Space Raiders they were even cheekier, coming up with the odd shapes first and retro-fitting spaceship designs around them for the packets.

Other snacks had to work harder in the moulding department to achieve verisimilitude. Horror Bags aped bones, bats and fangs with a degree of pickled onion-tinged accuracy, but the unfortunate parachuting denizens of a packet of Sky Divers seemed to succumb to all manner of horrific injuries en route from Ashby-de-la-Zouch to Lunchbox-de-la-Tupperware.

Wickers were shaped, alas not like Alan, but little wicker baskets. Piglets had a fair crack at assuming porcine topology, but perhaps the most insanely ambitious entry in this category were Smith's Farmer Browns, a barnyard-themed snack that, far from delivering the promised 'bags of moo, neigh, woof, baa and cock-a-doodle-doo', were markedly pre-Cambrian in zoological shape. Recompense came from the marketing, which deftly reworded old Herman's Hermits song 'Mrs Brown, You've Got a Lovely Daughter' into 'Farmer Brown, you've got a crunchy snack there!'

Still, these technical shortcomings did impel children to exercise their imaginations at dinnertime, and, of course, your statutory rights were not affected.

RETROMETER: 7/10

'This Town Ain't Big Enough for Both of Us' by Sparks

Bizarre brothers' tales of tacky tigers
Peak year: 1974

The US duo formerly known as Half Nelson are a rare example of a pop band where no one was looking at the front man. While singer Russell Mael let out a camp falsetto, capering around with a Bolan/Jagger swagger, the attention of the young *Top of the Pops* viewer was fixed on his silent keyboardist brother Ron, who'd hit on a novel way of overcoming stage fright.

Sat immobile behind his synth, the moustachioed Ron maintained a steely gaze down the end of his nose at the camera, a cross between a reborn Hitler and Basil Fawlty checking your living room for hotel inspectors. The result scared a generation of kids witless. Thus Sparks made their mark.

All this wouldn't have mattered if the music wasn't great, of course. A heady mix of stabbing synths, circus fanfare guitars and Russell's anxious yelp, it stuck out like a sore thumb. This sort of pop can easily slide into studied novelty kitsch, but the Maels had sound-enough judgement to keep it on the right side of smart-arse. 'Town' was backed with 'Barbecutie', a cheery song about cannibalism.

When Sparks first rolled up at the *Pops* studio, they were denied a place on the show for work permit reasons, so unknown glam act The Rubettes were called in to replace them, boosting the dismal performance of their single 'Sugar Baby Love'. A few weeks later Sparks got the necessary documents, and their memorable appearance helped 'Town' reach number two, only held off the top spot by . . . 'Sugar Baby Love'.

RETROMETER: 9/10

Three of a Kind

It's quickfire comedy . . . with added Ceefax!

Peak year: 1983, when Tracey Ullman assailed the charts with 1950s pop pastiches and Neil Kinnock

Let's face it, you can't beat pacy sketch comedy performed against a white cyclorama, as Lenny Henry, Tracey Ullman and David Copperfield proved, even if gags about hostess trolleys, CB radio, Milton Keynes, *Crossroads*, snooker, Toyah, *Space Invaders* and *Guardian* readers eating muesli are now, truly, of another age.

The sketches were bookended by the no-frills three-way stand-up format: 'I arrested a librarian – and I booked him!'/'I arrested a car battery salesman – and I charged him!'/'I arrested an explosives expert – and I let him off!' And then there were the endless Quantel effects and 'Gagfax' ('THE HOME SECRETARY HAS CALLED FOR GREATER EFFORTS BY THE POLICE . . . HE DIDN'T LIKE THEIR LAST RECORD AT ALL!'), all of which looked hugely thrilling in 1981.

Len's playground comedy faves Trevor McDoughnut, Fred Dread and the Rev Nathaniel Westminster were all present and correct, along with David Bellamy, 'wummaging awound in the undergwowth'. Tracey was ace at doing comedy accents, even if her Sloane character Roz loomed a bit too large for the kids, while Dave wheeled out his Medallion Man schtick on a rather too frequent basis.

For Lenny and Tracey, bigger if not necessarily better things loomed. For Dave, it was juvenile comedy capers in *Lift-Off with Coppers and Co* . . .

RETROMETER: 8/10

Thriller 

Primark Hitchcock

Peak year: 1974, year of Nyree Dawn Porter and her malevolent butler in 'Ring Once for Death'

From 1973–76, *Thriller* was a textbook example of straightforward, unpretentious telly drama doing its job beautifully. *Avengers* mastermind Brian Clemens conceived and wrote most of the six series: separate, one-hour-plus stories of suspense and horror, often with supernatural overtones, always with plenty of plot twists.

The blood-tinged fish-eye title sequence with its jarring musical crashes set the tone for each week's dose of macabre happenings in, more often than not, a superficially cosy remote provincial setting.

Corny titles hid finely tooled drama, 'The Eyes Have It', the largely silent, almost unbearably suspenseful tale of blind medical students (including Dennis Waterman and Sinead Cusak) thwarting Peter Vaughan's gang of taciturn terrorists being a case in point.

The series toyed with clichés. Young married couple freshly moved into mysterious rural location, stranger turning up who may not be all he seems, unidentified killer on the loose etc. It was the masterly variations and wrong-footings wrought from these familiar scenarios that made the programmes riveting.

What would nowadays be dismissed as glacial pacing (the long, deliberate tracking shot across an empty room accompanied by sinister oboe cadence was something of a motif, for instance) was integral to the atmosphere. Rather than cut rapidly from shot to shot, the direction took its time, almost taunting the viewer with its creeping progress. A claustrophobic sense of place and foreboding was the result.

Lew Grade's ITC gave the scripts relatively lavish treatment, but, being mainly studio-bound, with a minimal amount of location filming, they look visually primitive these days. However, the technical limitations had an atmosphere all their own.

Various series followed in kind - the supernatural *Armchair Thriller* and *Hammer House of Horror*, and the twistcentric *Tales of the Unexpected*, but for sheer unadulterated suspense, nothing beats Clemens's original.

RETROMETER: 10/10

Tiny Tears 

It pisses! It blubs!

Peak year: 1976, when the doll could be purchased complete with a pink carry-cot (rubber bed sheet not included)

Play School's Hamble with an incontinence problem, Tiny Tears was marketed by Palitoy as a new member of the family, to be taken in and cared for by pre-schoolites for whom soiled bedding was still a recent memory.

Simply fill the thing up with water and within moments you had a pissing, weeping child on your hands. Not the best image with which to emulate the joys of parenting perhaps, but not the most inaccurate either.

First created in the 1950s, the toy hit UK shores in 1966, initially sporting a hard plastic head which doubled up as a useful cosh. By the 1970s, the vacant-eyed H20-leaking creation was sporting a realistic Elizabeth Montgomery-style coiffure which – due to a production error – poorly hid a misprinted 'POLITOY' branding along the hairline.

The Ken to Tiny Tears' Barbie came in the shape of Timmy Tears; however, the dungaree'd little mite didn't catch on quite so successfully. Let's face it, who wants to have anything to do with boy-piss?

RETROMETER: 7/10

Today Newspaper

Turns out they weren't ready

Peak year: 1986, the biggest year in newspaper history, apparently

After decades of relentless monochrome, we were told the desktop publishing revolution would allow the world and his wife to publish their own newspapers. Hence, the first issue of *Today* arrived on newsagents' shelves on Tuesday 12 March 1986 – but only just, as delays meant it went to press hours later than scheduled.

Eddie Shah was responsible for launching this new paper using untried technology, and warned that anyone who spilled coffee over the expensive new workstations would be instantly sacked.

The big deal was that this was the first daily newspaper to be printed in colour. So advanced was the process, though, that nobody in the office was able to see what the colour photos looked like until the paper had actually been produced. Hence the washed-out, blotchy picture of the Queen in the first issue. Still, there was much excitement about, the paper even sponsoring the Football League for a season.

After the novelty wore off, *Today* had trouble finding a niche – it was lively and liberal, but didn't have much of a personality. Shah flogged the thing to Tiny Rowland, who in turn sold it to Rupert Murdoch, but even hiring Anne Robinson as star columnist failed to garner much interest. As such, on Thursday 16 November 1995, he decided that it couldn't carry on, and the following day's issue was emblazoned 'GOODBYE - It's been great to know you'.

RETROMETER: 7/10

The Tomorrow People

Kids inhabit a world where psi-powers and dense policemen are a reality

Peak year: 1976, when minor pop sensation Mike Holoway joined the TPs

A title sequence in which a slice of green pepper rushes towards you is either very inspired or very wrong – but that's *The Tomorrow People* for you.

From its no-discernibly-real-instruments theme music to its treatise on prostitution (yes – really), terrorism, and underpants (yes – really too), *The Tomorrow People* was kids' sci-fi with the brakes off.

Some suggest *TP* creator Roger Price got the idea after a chat with David Bowie, but we're not sure that's true. What is fact, though, is that the notion of 'breaking out' and turning into a *Homo Superior* (basically someone who can do telepathy, telekinesis and other 'psi' things) is obviously meant to remind you a bit of puberty.

Over the course of its eight series (1973–79), *The Tomorrow People* got through loads of actors; however, Nicholas Young (who played John) and Philip Gilbert (who provided the voice for the *TP*'s supercomputer TIM) were ever-present. Week after week they would lead their motley gang into various adventures, including scrapes with scary shape-changing robots, the Third Reich and – believe it or not – Peter Davison in hot pants and a Shirley Temple wig.

However, was it just us, or did 'jaunting' sound more like some kind of rambling activity that you would partake in at a youth club rather than a term for teleportation?

RETROMETER: 10/10

Tony Blackburn – the Living Legend by Tony Blackburn

He's waiting for an important phone call

Peak year: 1985

Published when the man's career was in freefall – booted off Radio One, co-hosting a soul show on cable TV with Daphne the duck – this was as much an exercise in career management ('Once again I find there aren't enough hours in the day') as outrageous self-promotion.

Tone spent the chapters – 'as told to Cheryl Garnsey' – tackling every myth and smear imaginable, perhaps believing honesty would champion over such trifling matters as dignity and humility. The upshot was a glorious catalogue of indiscretion. Tone's stint on pirate radio is as much about foreplay – 'I didn't feel guilty about making love to the wife of one of my colleagues' – as airplay. He ignores invitations to 'sex orgies' but indulges in snooker with David

Hamilton to decide who should take which two women to bed.

There's the marriage to Tessa Wyatt – the sobbing down the microphone when it went wrong, the handfuls of sleeping pills while watching *Fawlty Towers* 'because if I did die I wanted to go out laughing'.

And there are cheery tales of life on **The Radio One Roadshow**: 'Noel locked some chickens in the bathroom to give Mike a shock when he opened the door. I packed my bags and returned to London in disgust.'

Modest to the end, as a parting gesture Tone promised to subject the citizens of Europe to 'the living legend. Now they will know there was at least one good reason to have Great Britain in the Common Market.'

RETROMETER: 8/10

The Top 40

Whatever you're doing tonight, have a great night!

Peak year: 1982, when Tony Blackburn was in the big chair

Of course release schedules and advertising campaigns now mean we more or less know what's going to be number one before the chart is compiled. In the past, though, you had to watch your favourite single make an agonising crawl up the listings, and wait with bated breath to see if it was ever going to make it to that top spot.

Up until 1987, compilation of the chart took a few days to sort out, with the final positions for the week not released until the following Tuesday. The first announcement was by Mike Smith or Gary Davies on Radio One that lunchtime, leading to much dawdling in common rooms to find out whether Duran Duran or The Smiths were highest new entry.

If you missed it then, you had to wait until Sunday teatime, when Tony Blackburn, Tommy Vance or Richard Skinner played the whole thing in full. For many, this was the ideal accompaniment to a pre-homework bath.

But finally, in that year, when Bruno Brookes was in charge, the process was speeded up. The supercomputer at Gallup started whirring the second the shops shut on Saturday and Bruno could reveal the new chart on Sunday evenings, which he did in the most frantic, breathless manner possible.

RETROMETER: 7/10

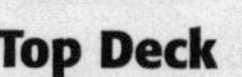

Top Deck

The hardest soft drink ever

Peak year: 1978, Top Deck's 'Meet *The Sweeney* on Location' competition makes it the most credible can of pop in the shop

Top Deck usually came in two flavours, the well-loved and ubiquitous lager shandy, and lager and lime – although this latter version was never quite as popular simply because it was always viewed as a bit of a girl's drink. Legend has it there was also a cider shandy version, but no one remembers much about that doubtless heady concoction now.

Apart from containing 'real beer', Top Deck's appeal lay in the fact it looked a bit like – well – actual grown-up booze. Unlike your normal can of fizzy pop, it didn't try to appeal with fancy logos or bright colours. Instead it had a pleasingly functional aesthetic that consisted of a no-nonsense logo and a flash of colour to denote the flavour, yellow for shandy, green for lime.

Before the arrival of Hooch and its alcopop cohorts, the mighty Top Deck was definitely the tough kids' tipple of choice. Granted, the amount of booze actually contained in one can was minuscule, but the stuff was indisputably present (there was an alcoholic content measurement on the side and everything) and therefore brilliant.

What's more it gave young Stan Ogdens the (false) impression the business of drinking proper lager was going to be a piece of piss. Only later would they learn the sweet flavour was several light years away from the bitter tang of a warm tin of Kestrel.

RETROMETER: 8/10

Top of the Pops 

The pop chart with pictures – nothing more, nothing less

Peak year: 1983, when the show used 95 per cent of the world's neon supplies

One of the longest-running programmes ever, for over forty years everyone has found something to moan about on *Top of the Pops*. This is thanks to its democratic formula – if you bought the records, they'd put them on, meaning you got a bizarre range of artists each week and nobody could possibly like all of them. But the 'three-minute rule' meant that if you didn't enjoy what was on now, there'd be something else along very soon.

For our money, the greatest era of '*Pops* was the early 1980s when producer Michael Hurll was in charge. He threw the kitchen sink at the series, forcing the audience to dance and jump about (rather than simply standing around staring as had been the norm), building enormous flashy sets and dazzling viewers with bright lights. Yet at the same time, he also hired John Peel as a regular presenter, whose links ('if this record doesn't get to number one, I'm going to break wind in your kitchen') showed it had its tongue firmly in its cheek. This was pop music, and not to be taken seriously.

Miming was the order of the day, and rightly so, as viewers wanted to hear the records they were buying. That was until 1991 when the practice was banned, leading to tuneless renditions of chart hits and the presence of people like Barbra Streisand and Neil Diamond who 'really could sing'. Ratings plummeted, and the first act of the new producer in 1994 was obvious – bringing back the miming.

RETROMETER: 9/10

Top Trumps

Perennial source of school-time debate as you and your mate try to work out what's better, a Sherman tank or Lotus Esprit, before realising you've got your decks mixed up

Peak year: 1977, the birth of Top Trumps

It was a sad day when you first learned noughts and crosses actually required no tactical acumen (you could simply play the same moves each time to force a stalemate) and, similarly, when the realisation dawned on you that a game of Top Trumps called upon no more skill than being able to identify the attribute with the highest number on the card you were looking at. Truly then, your childhood lay bleeding.

First produced in 1977 by the *House of Dübreq*, the original Top Trumps came in red plastic boxes with see-through covers that always got crushed by mum when she was doing the hoovering. Initially the series focused on ranking and rating various types of vehicles such as ships, planes and motor cars, but quickly diversified to cover subjects we were actually interested in, like *Star Wars*, Marvel Comics superheroes and 'Bobby Charlton's World Cup Aces'.

In 1982, Dübreq was taken over by Waddingtons and Top Trumps continued to proliferate however, the cost of licensing characters and images brought the classic-era range to a halt by the mid-1980s. Perhaps this wasn't a wholly bad thing, though. As much as Top Trumps stimulated debate, it also stifled it too, by providing inarguable, empirical proof that Dracula was indeed harder than Frankenstein.

RETROMETER: 8/10

Trade Test Transmission Films

Those weird short films wedged in the margins of the TV schedule

Peak Year: 1970, which brought us the unforgettable *Souvenirs from Sweden*

Algerian Pipeline, *Canadians Can Dance* and *Something Nice to Eat* were just a few of more than 160 hypnotic Trade Test Transmission films that crept onto daytime BBC2 at the start of the 1970s.

Shown in the run-up to nationwide

colour broadcasting, these oddities appeared at a time of day when there were no programmes scheduled. For those who chanced upon them, it was like accessing something forbidden. Here they were, hidden away, extra bits of telly!

Perhaps one of the best remembered was *Paint*, produced by Shell Films (who contributed a fair whack to this canon). Although it originated in 1968, it could be seen on our screens right up until TTT's last outing in 1973. Telling the evolution of paint, it was accompanied by that genre staple, a plush yet elegiac soundtrack.

Other highlights included a treatise on the *Prospect for Plastics*, a dispatch from *The Grass Growers* of New Zealand and a dizzying half hour on the assembly of a Bull-Nosed Morris in *The Home-Made Car*, much enlivened by TV tunesmith Ron Grainer's contribution, which echoed his own theme for *Steptoe and Son*.

RETROMETER: 6/10

Transfer Kits

Lead-fuelled instant diorama construction systems

Peak year: 1976, when Regan and Carter felt the power of your HB

Thanks to this pocket-money perennial of 1970s newsagent counters, you could create a thrill-packed tableau by simply rubbing transfers with a pencil on to the 'panoramic background picture' supplied.

Letraset's Action Transfer Kits ('Put Batman where you want him! Get your men well-positioned! Mastermind the whole operation with Letraset exciting rub-on transfer sheets!') boasted irresistible titles such as '*The Sweeney*: Hijack!', '*Kojak* vs the Manhattan Hit Mob' and '*Doctor Who*: Dalek Invasion of Earth', featuring Tom Baker battling to stop Buckingham Palace being exterminated.

Meanwhile rivals Kalkitos, of hazy Mediterranean origin and manufactured by Gillette of all people, featured the likes of Hong Kong Phooey and **Asterix**.

Despite the inescapable fear that one slip of the pencil or a hasty removal of the film sheet might decapitate Lee Majors or destroy the Battlestar Galactica, this was a concept that satisfyingly idled away many a rainy bank holiday afternoon at the dining table.

RETROMETER: 7/10

Trebor Booty Bags

The selection pack you can eat between Christmases

Peak year: 1980, when the Booty was the highlight of every 'big shop'

Like a sweet-toothed burglar's sack brimming with sugary swag, the Trebor Booty Bag held a multitude of delights inside its wrappings. Top of the wanted list, of course, were the chewy ha'penny sideshows, the Fruit Salad and its mouth-dyeing aniseed sibling, the Black Jack. The main course was a packet of Refreshers, the tongue-fizzling rainbow sweetshop favourites. Next up was invariably a lolly, of the sort largely stocked by chemists for some never adequately explained reason.

The feast was rounded off by a packet of Double Agents, hard-on-the-outside, sherbert-in-the-middle affairs (mmm, lime and chocolate) with useful espionage tips inside the wrapper. Bung in a free sticker and the Booty Bag became the perfect bribe to inveigle the kids into helping with the Thursday night trolley-pushing expedition.

RETROMETER: 7/10

Triangle

Felixstowe! Gothenburg! Amsterdam!

Peak year: 1981: the good ship *Dana Anglia* made its maiden TV voyage between *Nationwide* and reruns of *Star Trek*

An avowedly BBC take on glamour, the North Sea-faring soap was the brainchild of Bill Sellars, who had produced the successful 1970s business ball-buster *The Brothers*.

The programme may have broken new ground by filming everything on a working ferry, but the downside was an overall drabness. The necessity to shoot cabins with blinds drawn over portholes (to avoid continuity problems with external lighting) hardly helped matters.

Kate O'Mara was the big name here, playing hard-nosed Katherine Laker, who beguiled Chief Engineer Matt Taylor (a perspiring Larry Lamb) with such seductive doublespeak as: 'Think of me as your universal aunt . . . the crook of a little finger isn't always the promise of happy times' – whatever that meant.

From the off the critics were down on it, but the public were more forgiving, even if the show did translate Southfork-style disputes about oil wells into spats over the lack of Scandinavian dishes on the ship's menu.

All in all, the *Dana Anglia* wove its way between the dizzyingly glamorous locales of Felixstowe, Gothenburg and Amsterdam for three series – O'Mara jumping ship before it all came to an end in 1983.

RETROMETER: 9/10

Trio

Comedy advert that bizarrely caught the public imagination

Peak year: 1985, when **Betamax** owners waited for the commercial break with recording fingers poised

This memorable campaign consisted of an animated musical trio attempting to promote their brand to the tune of 'The Banana Boat Song'. Nothing strange in that, you might think. Yet all efforts at producing a melodic reading were undermined by the group's singer (Suzy) who continually bellowed the refrain 'Trio' at the top of her voice. This was hilarious.

Indeed back in the early-to-mid-1980s, dads all over the land could be found rewatching the half of the Trio ad they'd managed to get on tape while invoking that age-old parental mantra 'these days the adverts are better than the programmes!'

Quite why it should be considered such a watermark in comedy when similar work such as 'Blue Riband Blues' (in which Mike 'oh, thank you' Berry riffs on his guitar) is overlooked is something of a mystery. Perhaps the inclusion of a peacenik (voiced by Derek Griffiths) holds the key. After all, during the 1980s, the mere mention of the word 'hippy' was guaranteed to be greeted by knowing, raucous laughter.

RETROMETER: 8/10

TV Comic

Doctor Who **fan fiction in the days before the internet**

Peak year: 1976, before the broadcasters got wise to branding

For many years, if you wanted more adventures from your telly favourites, the place you'd turn to would be Polystyle Publications' *TV Comic*. Running for over thirty years, the bulk of the publication was devoted to licensed products – but not all of it, with the wholly original (well, as original as comic strips could get) 'Mighty Moth' lasting the duration.

For many, the great appeal of *TV Comic* was the official *Doctor Who* comic strip which ran for over a decade. Patrick Troughton, Jon Pertwee and Tom Baker all took a turn in the spotlight, but towards the end budgetary constraints saw the reprinting of Troughton stories with Baker's head glued over the top – thus ruining that vital continuity.

The final years of the publication also saw little else in the way of original material, with 'Ken Dodd's Diddymen' still starring by the closure in 1984, a decade or so after they'd disappeared from our screens.

For a while, their sister publication was *Countdown*, home to some of the more adult-orientated stories and not, as you may think, the comic-strip adventures of Richard Whiteley.

RETROMETER: 6/10

TV Times

So much more than . . .

Peak year: 1980, before it got sexed up

As with *Radio Times*, the ITV equivalent

was for many decades required reading, as it was the only way you could get advance details of what was on the commercial channels. Both publications fitted their broadcasters' profiles too. ***RT*** featured pages of solid text, with detailed viewers' letters on the issues raised in TV programmes and incisive essays into their construction. *TVT* was a picture-packed glossy, where readers offered their tips on opening pickle jars to Katie Boyle, and their idea of journalism was revealing an *Emmerdale Farm* actress was 'fed up to her navy blue knickers with playing schoolgirl parts'.

Radio Times, as a BBC publication, rarely featured any criticism of the programmes they billed, but they were the harshest critics compared to *TV Times*, who could happily hype up the latest effort from Mike and Bernie Winters as if the Second Coming was taking place on it. So reliant were they on hyperbole, pretty soon they had to invent new expressions for when something was genuinely exciting – no longer were ITV shows simply 'star-studded', they were now 'star-encrusted'.

It's perhaps fair to suggest that the households which chose not to watch ITV perhaps did so to avoid having to buy the magazine. However, for the juvenile telly fan there was plenty to enjoy, not least the careful denotation of the ITV company that produced each programme. Also notable were the small illustrations that were used to represent various programme genres – a goalkeeper was logical enough for football programmes, but the news was represented by people clapping, for some reason.

Sadly an era ended in 1981 when it was relaunched as the cumbersomely titled *TV Times Magazine*, emphasising the feature content in an effort to pretend anyone bought it for anything other than the listings. Then in 1991, deregulation meant it became one of umpteen listings magazines. At least now it wasn't quite so desperate to get us to watch *The Grumbleweeds*.

RETROMETER: 8/10

TV Tops

Poor man's *Look-In* on tracing paper

Peak year: 1981: another twelve-month wonder

From right down the back of the bottom drawer of the DC Thomson rainy-day filing cabinet came this flash-in-the-pan effort (originally titled just *Tops*) launched precisely one month after its rival, *Look-In*, had given itself a brand-enhancing makeover, conveniently ensuring it looked superfluous and a shameless rip-off before it'd even begun.

All the same, the publication dabbled in substances ***Look-In*** would've run a country mile from: unflinching violence for one, in the shape of comic-strip carry-ons from post-watershed fare ***Minder*** and *The Professionals*. But elsewhere somewhat over-ambitious sci-fi – the time-travelling escapades of Adam Ant – rubbed chiffon blouses with alternative comedy on 'Not the Pamela Stephenson Page', to instantly diminishing returns.

Very much not the sum of its parts, *TV Tops* failed to ever really catch on, and soon folded – which, given it'd been printed on paper the thickness of a one-ply tissue, proved very easy to do.

RETROMETER: 3/10

Twinkle 

Nursery delight for sandal-clad tots

Peak year: 1983, when it was one of the only glossy publications around

Back in the 1920s, the original pre-school comics were perhaps most notable for their policy of hyphenating long words to make it easier to read – though perhaps a better idea would have been not to use them in the first place. In any case, this practice had long been forgotten when *Twinkle* first arrived in the 1970s.

A DC Thomson publication, it was inevitably printed on notoriously thin paper (see above) – with the advantage that it could be used for tracing when you got bored. At least they were generous with their free gifts, which were always breathlessly plugged in their weekly adverts in the *Topper*.

Inside, the plaid-skirted Twinkle would partake in some wholesome activity, usually involving the essential girls'-comic props of a puppy and a toy pram, while Baby Brother ('He's small, he's sweet, he's seldom neat') tried everyone's patience, lambs and ponies frolicked in meadows, and a scantily clad infant invited you to clothe her in either a cut-out nursery school uniform or a fetching blouse and necktie.

Twinkle's stablemates on the bottom shelf during its golden age included its sister title *Pepper Street*, where all the strips were based around the residents of the titular road, the optimistically titled *Playhour*, and the quaintly monikered *Pippin*, which enjoyed the honour of the only *Super Ted* strip in comicdom. Plus there was also *Buttons*, the officially licensed BBC publication which had the added bonus of complete listings of all the week's pre-school output. The fact this amassed to basically just five episodes of *Play School* was neither here nor there.

RETROMETER: 6/10

The Two Ronnies

'And in a packed programme tonight . . .'

Peak year: 1976, when the Phantom Raspberry Blower of Old London Town made busy with the parping

The Two Ronnies were the comfy slippers of sketch-show comedy – little Ronnie on his Mastermind chair waffling on about his producer, the two Rons delivering 'some late items of news' and Barbara Dickson or Elaine Paige appearing (what seemed like) every single week for the obligatory straight musical number.

Yet scratch beneath the surface and the show was actually rather clever. Yes, they inhabited an old-fashioned world in which tramps wore raggy clothes and train compartments were stuffed full of bowler-hatted, repressed businessmen, but their sketches took single ideas to their very clever and illogical extreme. Alongside that, the big comedy musical numbers were always entertaining, employing the patented sing-lots-of-words-very-quickly approach that smacked of being very smart indeed without that necessarily being the case.

Besides if you missed the puns, malapropisms (Ronnie B 'pisspronouncing his turds') or occasional saucy innuendo, there were the evocative serials such as 'The Worm that Turned' or 'The Phantom Raspberry Blower of Old London Town'. Whether all of them or just 'Raspberry' were actually set during Victorian times we can't be sure, but they all had the smell of a less boring version of a BBC classic serial – which on balance was a good thing.

RETROMETER: 8/10

United Chocolate Bars

No-nonsense lunchbox support act

Peak year: 1987: zenith of the 'rogue' bar

Unashamedly ordinary on the outside, a United delivered the goods by layering its iffy-quality biscuity base with a mixture of deceptively thick chocolate and tiny pieces of honeycomb, making it feel and taste far more substantial than it actually was.

Like a Breakaway, the chocolate was also stencilled on top, allowing much patented brass rubbing-action using the foil wrapper. Crowning glory, though, was the segmented structure: three distinct pieces – one more than a Kit-Kat, importantly – which could be broken off with a pleasing snap and shared with mates. Your dad could dip them in his tea, making a United serve a dual purpose as both snack and father-and-child bonding tool.

Connoisseurs, meanwhile, kept a keen eye for rogue Uniteds: bars hilariously wrapped in TWO layers of foil, or, the holy grail, with the biscuity base mistakenly substituted by pure chocolate.

RETROMETER: 7/10

Usborne Books

Under-twelves' one-stop fact shop

Peak year: 1979, the dawn of The Future

From the 1970s onwards, Peter

Usborne's children's factual publishing empire was the Oxford University Press for the pre-secondary set. Their colourful info-packed tomes, liberally sprinkled with friendly, big-nosed cartoon characters, were the darlings of the school library (when *The Sorcerer's Apprentice* was on loan, at least).

The Usborne Book of Things to do on a Rainy Day was a self-explanatory favourite. Two friendly, big-nosed cartoon clowns guided the indoor-bound reader through a plethora of homely activities: growing washing-soda crystals, making paper hats, etc. The friendly, big-nosed, overcoated spies dotted throughout the *Usborne Spy's Guidebook* inhabited an exciting world where unbreakable codes could be written on a belt wrapped round an old stick, and oppressive Eastern Bloc governments thwarted with the cunning deployment of lemon juice as writing medium.

More heavyweight was the *Usborne Book of World Geography*, a comprehensive guide to the friendly, big-nosed peoples of the Earth, full of inoffensively rendered world facts. For instance, comparative gross national product was indicated by figures in national dress holding appropriately scaled money bags: while a sheikh from the United Arab Emirates rejoiced in his ten-foot sack, a peasant representing Bhutan put a bravely cheery face on his golf ball-sized pouch.

Best of all, however, was 1979's *Usborne Book of the Future: A Trip in Time to the Year 2000 and Beyond*: a mind-boggling grab-bag of never-going-to-happen wonders like lunar Olympics, nuclear-powered artificial super-hearts, domed underwater cities, and Jupiter being taken apart and rebuilt as a big shell around the sun, for some unfathomable reason. Its timeline of inventions from 1980 to the twenty-second century has, twenty-five years in, so far proved to be something of a disappointment to the legion of thirtysomethings still awaiting that robot butler.

RETROMETER: 9/10

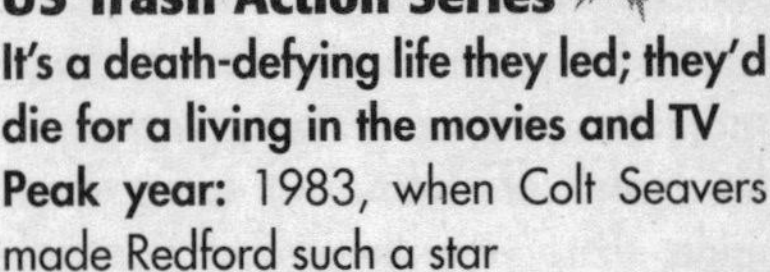

US Trash Action Series

It's a death-defying life they led; they'd die for a living in the movies and TV

Peak year: 1983, when Colt Seavers made Redford such a star

In an era before *The Sopranos* and *Six Feet Under*, the reputation of American television was not particularly high on this side of the Atlantic. Except among the kids that is, who lapped up everything that Glen A Larson and Stephen J Cannell could fling at them, re-enacting key scenes in the playground ('bags me Ponch!') and staking their claim on that crucial position in front of the Trinitron a good half hour before that action-packed title sequence.

The sultan of Hollywood action series was the peerless Lee Majors. The purists might argue that his finest hour was *The Six Million Dollar Man* ('gentlemen, we can rebuild him – we have the technology!'), but we'd opt every time for post-*Winner Takes All*, pre-*The Gaffer* trashfest *The Fall Guy*, starring Lee as 'unknown stuntman' Colt Seavers. He'd apparently been 'seen with Farrah' but, no, we didn't know who 'Cheryl Tiegs' was either. Colt was assisted by hapless sidekick Howie and bikini-clad saloon-door siren Heather Thomas (and not, as pub historians frequently insist, Heather Locklear).

Simon MacCorkindale starred in *Manimal* as a crime-fighting professor who had the power to turn into animals, although sadly the budget only stretched to sequences of his character Jonathan Chase transforming into a panther and a falcon, which they recycled every week, regardless of the plot.

In another shameless *Tron* knock-off (cf. *Captain Zep*), *Automan*, Chuck Wagner played a holographic policeman who battled criminals on the streets of LA in his nifty computer-generated car, which could make ninety-degree turns.

Matt Houston was a minor-league *Magnum PI*, right down to the luxuriant moustache, with sassy female assistant CJ played by Pamela Hensley, AKA Princess Ardala off of *Buck Rogers in the 25th Century*, and a crime-fighting supercomputer called Baby.

Two series have merged in everyone's memories, largely due to their shared uncanny resemblance to *Raiders of the Lost Ark*. *Bring 'em Back Alive* was the Bruce Boxleitner vehicle featuring the escapades of 1930s adventurer Frank Buck, based in Singapore's Raffles Hotel, while *Tales of the Gold Monkey* depicted the adventures of 1930s adventurer Jake Cutter, flying a biplane around the South Sea islands.

Then Bruce Boxleitner turned up in *Scarecrow and Mrs King*, and made us even more confused.

RETROMETER: 10/10

Velour Tracksuits

The tactile leisurewear

Peak year: 1986, the look gets a weekly outing courtesy of Ali Fraser's girlfriend in *Auf Wiedersehen, Pet*

Mostly seen in hues of lilac, lemon, peppermint and pink, the brushed velour tracksuit was the standard uniform for women who frequented Bermondsey solariums and festooned themselves with gold jewellery of Mr T proportions.

Contrived to look as though their wearer had just shuffled off the lounger in Marbella, the clobber's connoted signifier was that you were not-too-badly-off and somewhere in the background was the 'old man', bedecked in Farah trousers and a waffle jumper.

Club Sport was the prima label in this line, with Palm coming in a close second (that palm tree logo whispering of far-flung locales and bobbing ice cubes in A Slow Comfortable Screw), and both were ripped off in street markets everywhere. Fatally, the material was never quite as plush as the real thing.

RETROMETER: 8/10

Vesta

An exotic taste sensation on the shelves of Kwik Save

Peak year: 1980, when our palettes were slowly getting more sophisticated

At a time when curry is said to be the national dish of the UK, it's worth remembering the days when Indian restaurants were few and far between, and our Eastern taste experience almost always came in dried form via those masters of the convenience food, Vesta.

The Vesta range included an incredibly mild Chicken Curry and a Beef Risotto, all boxed in authentically Indian packaging (hem hem). Creating your gastronomic wonder involved a complicated sequence of numbered sachets that you would empty out into a pan of boiling water on the hob, and within minutes you had a gourmet meal in your lap. The extra advantage was that everyone knew how sophisticated you were as the smell tended to linger in the kitchen for the next week or so.

Vesta products still appear on supermarket shelves around the country, and any student who fancies a change from beans, toast or, on a special occasion, beans on toast can still find it a real godsend.

RETROMETER: 6/10

Victor

'A great new war story starts inside!'

Peak year: 1986, *Victor* gobbles up 'rival' DC Thomson title *Warlord*

When it began in 1961, *The Victor* (as it was then called) was something of a sensation, eschewing conventional text-based stories for picture strips. However, by the time the 1970s and 1980s rolled around, it was the most old-fashioned title on the newsstands. With its regular diet of war stories, football strips and the occasional science-fiction adventure, *Victor* was four-square entertainment for boys.

The comic's most memorable character was undoubtedly Alf 'Tough of the Track'

Tupper. This working-class athlete first appeared in the pages of *Wizard* and *Rover*, but it was in *Victor* he secured his most famous racing achievements. A typical cross-country for Alf would consist of being nobbled by a cheating toff from the Greystone Harriers' race club and then having to stop halfway through the race to rescue a bloke from drowning in icy water. However, inevitably the Tough would still manage to pip his arch-rival (whoever that was at the time) at the post and proclaim, 'I ran 'em all' in a manner that must have really infuriated the other competitors.

Other staples of *Victor* were 'Cadman' – a cowardly soldier in part based on George MacDonald Fraser's popular *Flashman* series – and 'Morgyn the Mighty', who seemed to be completely based on Tarzan (although with a Welsh lilt, presumably, going by the spelling of his name). Of course there was the perennial cover feature too, each week delighting the reader with another 'True Story of Men at War'.

Eventually, *Victor* tried to move with the times and in 1991 underwent a relaunch that saw it carry features on mountain bikes while trying to entice new readers with its offer of a free pair of 'zany laces'. It folded just a year later (although the annuals would continue for a time afterwards). Still, it had at least outlived all of its competitors.

RETROMETER: 9/10

Viewmaster

Plastic binoculars + cardboard discs = virtual reality

Peak year: 1980, when Herbie went bananas before your very eyes

Beloved of maiden aunts and kids alike, the GAF Viewmaster enabled the proud owner to step into a breathtaking three-dimensional re-creation of the Jersey Battle of Flowers or Hazzard County. It was just like being there . . . sort of.

The contraption itself resembled a 1950s NASA prototype of the kind of virtual reality goggles the boffins predicted we'd all be strapping to our heads any day now. To enjoy the show, simply insert a cardboard reel into a slot, look at the picture and click the lever to rotate to the next one. Repeat seven times or until bored.

The ingenious bit, however, was that each photo comprised a left and right image, merging to create a form of 3D 'stereoscopy'. Originally, the Viewmaster was marketed at adults, the discs featuring travel panoramas like 'Bullfight in Spain' and 'Niagara Falls', or momentous historical occasions such as 'Princess Margaret's Wedding'.

But in the 1970s the manufacturers cottoned on to the kids' market, producing a succession of reels starring the likes of The Muppets, Top Cat and, bizarrely, Keep Britain Tidy mascot Dusty. It might all seem a little primitive, but in an era before home video, and when you had to wait five years to see *Star Wars* on telly, the Viewmaster was the only way to enjoy C3PO and Chewie in lifelike action from the comfort of your living room.

RETROMETER: 9/10

Vosene

Serious shampooing

Peak year: 1989, ex-punk Captain Sensible dedicates a whole track on his *Revolution Now* LP to Vosene

In the 1980s, the only bath product kids had any interest in was Matey (and even then they were precociously cognisant of the fact there was very little you could do with him other than use him for the purpose he was intended for). However, parents had other ideas, and while you might have wished for a swarthy old seaman (or even Mrs Matey – up, women's lib!) with whom to share your bath, what you actually ended up with was something that was either carbolic or medicated.

Wella's Vosene shampoo (which has been around in one form or another since 1946) was a particular favourite. It came in a tear-shaped medicine-brown-coloured bottle (which was appropriate considering how much it would sting if you got any in your eyes) and after one serving would leave you with a head that smelt of TCP and felt as though it was corroding fast.

Yet despite all this, it was undoubtedly doing you some good, and at least you knew you would get a commendation from one of the school's nit nurses (who all seemed to be called Norah) during the next inspection.

RETROMETER: 5/10

Walters' Weekly

'Hi, fans!'

Peak year: 1988: Walters was on just before Peel

Fun Radio One always found it difficult shoehorning the charter-decreed token arts programme into their schedules. The awkward, patronising 'hey, kids! Abstract expressionism's a bit like The Cure!' approach wasn't fooling anyone.

Fortunately, to the rescue came John Peel and producer and wry humorist John Walters, who combined a genuine, infectious enthusiasm for everything from conceptual installations to graphic novels and acid jazz with a whimsical presentation style. For instance, each location report was segued into via 'The Magic Mingle Mangle Music': Walters singing the phrase 'mingle mangle' to the tune of the *Twilight Zone* theme. You're either rolling your eyes at this point or smiling delightedly, and either was fine with Walters.

Too many attempts to broach 'serious' areas with under-twenties lurch into self-conscious, ooh-mustn't-alienate embarrassment. Walters provided an unforced, carefree atmosphere that's eluded Wunneffem ever since.

RETROMETER: 7/10

Warrior 

'The magazine of jolly weird heroes'

Peak year: 1984, the year David J from Bauhaus released a 'V for Vendetta'-inspired EP

Created by UK comic legend Dez 'Sez Dez' Skinn (who'd previously launched *Doctor Who Weekly*, *House of Hammer* and *Starburst*), this black and white monthly arrived in 1982.

Featuring 'new stories from Britain's top comic creators', the first issue kicked off with the return of Axel Pressbutton, the 'psychotic cyborg!' Culled from the pages of *Sounds* magazine, the little-known slap-headed scythe-wielding nutter would prove something of an also-ran, alongside *Hammer* refugee Father Shandor 'Demon Stalker' and the sixth-century shenanigans of Prester John.

The real excitement lay in two strips, both written by Alan Moore (of 'knows the score' infamy).

'V for Vendetta' presented a grim depiction of a future Britain, ruled over by a fascist state following a nuclear war. Standing alone against The Man was V, in stovepipe hat, theatrical cape and Guy Fawkes mask. And the year when this totalitarian unpleasantness would come to pass? 1997.

Then there was 'Marvelman'. A smart update of a minor British superhero who'd briefly flourished in the 1950s, Moore managed to reconcile the dopiness of the original stories (MM's pubescent sidekick nursing the secret identity Dicky Dauntless) with the emerging 1980s appetite for 'grittiness' in comics.

Throughout its run – which stretched to 26 editions – *Warrior* was always a mixed bag, with the excellent (the aforementioned 'V for Vendetta') nestling alongside the mediocre ('Big Ben: The man with no time for crime'). Nevertheless, it allowed Britain's previously stymied comic creators the chance to stretch their muscles and jump-started the whole push to get the medium considered adult fare.

That, and there were a lot of nipples in it.

RETROMETER: 8/10

Watch It! 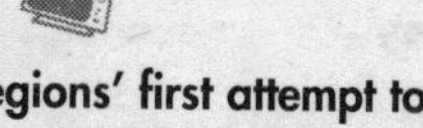

ITV in the regions' first attempt to bind together kids' programmes

Peak year: 1981, as the bejumpered announcers acted like surrogate dads

Although ITV has always produced its fair share of great children's programmes, come the start of the 1980s it seemed as if they were reaching the screen despite of, not thanks to, the scheduling – often kicked off for old films and rubbish imports. A concerned IBA told the ITV companies to produce a more coherent service for young people.

The result was *Watch It!*, invented by ATV and launched at Christmas 1980. For the first time, this was kids' TV as a self-contained whole, with its own branding, graphics and music. However, it was up to the regions to implement it as they saw fit, and most simply used their usual announcers to introduce the programmes, only now wearing a jumper and acting that little bit chummier.

This carried on for two years, before January 1983 saw the launch of *Children's ITV*, a more professional networked service with stars of kids' programmes linking the shows a month at a time. For the most part it worked, but thanks to the vagaries of ITV's regional structure and the hosts filming all their bits weeks in advance, one day Derek Griffiths just didn't know what he was going to be linking into and had to simply say, 'and now, a surprise!'

RETROMETER: 7/10

The Wheeltappers and Shunters Social Club

'This act really moves – I haven't seen speed like it since Enoch Powell walked through Bradford'

Peak year: 1974, and the 'Ms *TV Times* of Granadaland' episode

The basic premise of The Wheeltappers and Shunters Social Club was to recreate an authentic working-man's club on television. Central to this was the inclusion of an array of Northern comics. George Roper, Jim Bowen and Charlie Williams all featured, but the most popular by far was compere Bernard Manning.

He would introduce acts with withering lines like: 'This man can make a cat laugh – pity he can't do the same for people' and then interrupt performances or harangue members of the audience as he saw fit.

However, *The Wheeltappers* prided itself on featuring more than just comedians (after all that would have made the show *The Comedians*). Some weeks you would turn on and catch Lonnie Donegan, next time it would be the Ukrainians Cossack Brotherhood and the Royal Polynesian Revue. What either of those two acts did is anyone's guess but we're sure they entertained in a resolutely unpretentious way.

Indeed can a television programme ever have been aimed at a less aspirant section of the general public? We don't think so, and in this age of demographics and ABC1s we're certain we will never see its like again.

RETROMETER: 8/10

Where the Wild Things Are

'Let the wild rumpus start!'

Peak year: 1984 – when the monsters invaded the *Blue Peter* studio

First published in 1963, Maurice Sendak's sumptuous *Where the Wild Things Are* remains a perfect evocation of the daydreams of small children. The story concerns a lad called Max, sent to bed without any supper thanks to his bad behaviour. Once alone, however, his bedroom turns into a fantastical island in which large, scary monsters roam.

If this all sounds pretty conventional, then that's because it is, but Sendak's evocative illustrations and dreamlike pacing meant that *Where the Wild Things Are* managed to wheedle its way into the subconscious of the millions who read it. Although published back in the 1960s, for a period in the late 1970s and early 1980s it seemed as if you couldn't switch on your telly without catching a glimpse of Sendak's creations, or other monsters obviously inspired by his work (we're thinking here of *The Muppet Show*'s Sweetums and the *Monster Munch* bunch).

Perhaps the upsurge in interest can be attributed to Sendak himself, who in 1979 mounted an impressive opera based on the book, featuring fantastical larger-than-life costumes that four years later would provoke a fine bit of hackneyed 'scared' acting from *Blue Peter* presenter Simon Groom.

RETROMETER: 9/10

Whizzer and Chips

Possibly the best comic ever

Peak year: 1977, when it offered hundreds of characters for under 10p

Upon its launch in 1969, *Whizzer and Chips* was revolutionary. The slogan was 'two comics in one – double the fun' with its distinct sections (perhaps the inspiration for the *Sunday Times*), and the gimmick was that they were rival publications, sharing staples but hating each other with a passion.

As such, you were invited to pledge your allegiance to the Whizz-kids, led by Sid – an everyman with a pet snake – or the Chip-ites, under the auspices of Shiner, a hapless individual who couldn't help getting into scrapes. Make up your own arguments about class war if you want, we just followed *Whizzer* because we liked the colour red.

The main problem with selling them as rival comics, though, was that as they shared exactly the same editorial team, this was a rather half-arsed battle. No doubt hurt by the frequent letters from loyal Whizz-kids suggesting that *Chips'* strips were crap, and vice versa, the editorials regularly suggested that this was a loathing built very much on respect, and that the 'other' comic was quite good really.

Despite this gimmickry, for many years *Whizzer and Chips* was an excellent paper, with a level of anarchy and invention in the strips few could match. Sadly the last couple of years saw a marked decline with pages filled with reprints, and by its closure in 1990 they'd completely lost the plot and couldn't even be bothered with separate *Whizzer* and *Chips* sections. That was the entire selling point!

RETROMETER: 9/10

The Willard Price *Adventure* books

Hunting animals, patronising the natives and – best of all – never having to go to school

Peak year: 1970, Knight books reprint the whole Willard Price range with fully painted covers that look hugely exciting to boys

The big-game hunting adventures of brothers Hal (usually nineteen) and Roger (mostly fourteen) were a real treat for young lads, and were finely honed works in their own right. The books were written by prolific Canadian author Willard Price and, unlike lots of kids' novels, the action kicked off straight away with only a brief telegram from the boys' father (instructing them to go and capture some big scary animal) required to get things going.

Although the lads experienced many and varied creatures and locations (such as volcanoes, gorillas and tigers), the same Price formula would emerge time and again. For example, at least one Westerner per book would be disrespectful of the surroundings and as a direct result come a cropper. More annoyingly though, regardless of the extreme danger he found himself in, Hal somehow always found time to launch into a long and detailed lecture on some facet or other of the natural world.

Of course the *Adventure* titles were just one in a number of long-running book series that appealed to young adolescent boys. Some of the other notable entrants were *The Hardy Boys* (whose hundreds of books were all published under the pen name Franklin W Dixon) and *The Three Investigators*. This latter series proved very puzzling. Some of the stories featured Alfred Hitchcock, which begged the question: given he was a real-life person, did that mean Jupiter, Pete and Bob were too?

RETROMETER: 7/10

Willo the Wisp

Forest-bound messing about

Peak year: 1982, when even the nation's road diggers saluted Ken

To think that the sublime blending of the drawings and scripts of Nick Spargo and the vocal talents of Kenneth Williams almost didn't happen: 'The BBC people said it would be wrong to have your voice just before the news,' Spargo reportedly confided to Williams while taping the pilot episode.

The acerbic apparition was based on a spectre-like animated character Kenny had voiced in 1974 for an industry film about North Sea oil. For the series proper, however, Willo was transformed – via a blatant caricature of Kenny's own face – into the nosey narrator of Doyley Woods, an ordinary-looking copse peopled with a menagerie of the lovably lunatic.

Given that *Willo the Wisp*'s jumble of the surreal and the riotous was penned specifically to showcase Williams's trademark mannerisms, each of its 26 episodes was a joy. There was malevolent TV set Evil Edna falling in love with a BBC newsreader; the Moog, baleful pig-shaped mongrel who didn't have a brain, getting trapped inside his own thought 'cloud'; Mavis Cruet the hapless fairy (or 'interfering fat fairy person' according to Edna) refusing to direct a miniature fire-breathing dragon to a petrol station because 'there's a world shortage of fuel'; Carwash the erudite blue cat having his eyes stolen by Twit the bird; and Arthur the urbane caterpillar pretending to become a butterfly by hiring some fake wings from 'Moth Bros'.

The appeal was instant and enormous. 'I'd never have thought navvies would watch *Willo*,' Williams noted dispassionately after being hailed in the street. 'It's extraordinary the audience television attracts.'

RETROMETER: 10/10

Willy the Kid

Smashin' fun!

Peak year: 1977, when Willy presented his own reading of 'The Twelve Days of Christmas' complete with a tobacco-imbibing infant for 'eleven pipers piping'

On 21 October 1975, the man who'd created 'The Bash Street Kids', 'Little Plum', 'Minnie the Minx' and a host of other classic comic-strip characters jacked it in.

Instead, Leo Baxendale was off to join the world of 'proper' publishing, with the release of his first book, *Willy the Kid.* Published by Duckworth, this compendium of knockabout strips followed the bizarre adventures of the titular Kid. Many simply took the form of full-page illustrations, packed with incident and hidden gags – a particularly memorable example being Willy and company engaging in a 'roof-eating' contest. While one child declared: 'spreading Branston Pickle on the roof is CHEATING', another inevitably swore to 'eat the roof, the whole roof and nothing but the roof'. But – uh oh! – what was this? Jogging into the fray came the Loch Ness Monster who also fancied his chances.

Anarchy was the order of the day here, with Willy encountering a vampiric, Disney-baiting Snow White and the Seven Dwarfs, or travelling back in time via a 'time watch' to make merry with the dinosaurs.

Three *Willy* books were issued in all, but despite their quality, they always remained something of a curio in any kid's collection. Not obviously spun-off from any continuing comic book, they were treated with suspicion. Why exactly did they exist? And that, pals, was the most anarchic thing of all.

RETROMETER: 7/10

Women's Realm

The knit nurse

Peak year: 1973, when a nation stitched its way through the three-day week

Outside of a furtive browse in the dentist's waiting room, *Women's Realm* remained alien territory to 70 per cent of the population. A copy on your mum's bedside cabinet denoted the entire area was off-limits, while one resting atop an issue of *Reader's Digest* meant your gran had come to stay and you should retreat to your own bedroom without delay.

Launched in 1958, the magazine never wavered from its cautiously rationed diet of lifestyle tips, unfussy recipes and – the reliable big-hitter – serialised knitting patterns. Week by week your mum painstakingly pieced together a toddler's wardrobe until a heap of reassuringly ordinary-looking socks, mittens and that perennial sartorial staple, the over-sized woolly hat, lined your pushchair.

Grans with more time on their hands tackled an itchy babygrow or, for the more mature subject, your first very own sweater.

The title was abruptly axed in April 2001 for supposedly being out of touch with the modern female. It was merged with *Women's Weekly*, that well-known challenging contemporary journal founded in 1911.

RETROMETER: 5/10

Woolworths Christmas Adverts

Simply having a Wonder-ful Christmas time

Peak year: 1981, thanks to high-kicking fun from Anita Harris and the Goodies

The big massive all-singing all-dancing Woolworths spectacular was every bit as much part of the countdown to the festive season as calls to Dial-a-Santa and pencil-sucking deliberation over your Christmas list. Taking up – gasp! – an entire commercial break, the mighty Winfield empire recruited a cavalcade of stars to endorse their glittering array of yuletide delights. Like Anita Harris, Bill Oddie and Tim Brooke-Taylor, inviting us to 'have a cracker of a Christmas shopping spree' to the strains of a 'Super Trooper'-esque soundtrack, as a load of Cossack dancers and a Lady Di lookalike paraded round promoting bargains such as Matchbox Race and Chase (£29.99), John Bull Beer Kits (£1.99) and the Bontempi B225 organ (£199.95).

In 1982, the ads boasted an *Alice in Wonderland* theme, with John Inman as the March Hare, while Tweedledum and Tweedledee, AKA Clegg and Compo off of *Last of the Summer Wine*, duelled over *Galaxy Twinvader* (£24.99, batteries extra), King of Hearts Windsor Davies looked impressed at his Bostik Glue Gun (£9.95) and Kid Jensen dressed up as a giant playing card to endorse Sony blank tapes (£2.49).

The following year Joe Brown rolled up as the top-hatted ringmaster of 'the latest, greatest, ever more spectacular Woolworths Christmas show!' DLT parped a trombone and promoted Price Blitz records, although the rationale behind hiring Lennie Bennett to dress up as a strongman to extol the virtues of the Old Spice Gift Set remains unclear to this day. But that's the wonder of Woolies! And Woolco.

RETROMETER: 10/10

World of Sport

The ITV Seven, Monster Trucks and Shirley Crabtree – now that's sport!

Peak year: 1977, the year Dickie co-presented with Eric Morecambe

As much a part of Saturday lunchtimes as boring Westerns on BBC2 and cheese and pickle sandwiches, *World of Sport* was ITV's alternative to the other side's *Grandstand*. Kicking off with a fantastic rousing theme tune and thrilling footage of men jumping out of aeroplanes, *World of Sport* certainly beat its rival in the title sequence stakes. Unfortunately, that was about the only area in which the show proved superior.

The problem was *World of Sport* had no money and therefore couldn't afford access to any of the premier events. As such presenter Dickie Davies (he of the cravat and 'still haven't finished painting that ceiling' fame) would have to link straight out of log-rolling from Toronto into 'target clown diving'.

The hardy perennials of the schedule were speedway, stock car racing and – most famously – British Wrestling. None of these could be described as 'mainstream sport', but wrestling is probably still the only sport in which the majority of viewers are (or at least seem to be) women over the age of 65. Indeed during the 1970s over ten million of them would tune in to watch Giant Haystacks amble round the ring for a minute before stopping to catch his breath.

World of Sport was cancelled in 1985 for being 'too down-market' – a nation of pensioners wept.

RETROMETER: 8/10

Yellow Pages

It's just possible it could save your life

Peak year: 1989, when that bloke's parents were due back from the airport in three hours

JR Hartley's epic quest for a copy of *Fly Fishing* largely overshadowed the rest of Yellow Pages' bid to convince us they weren't just there for the nasty things in life.

But there were other ads, like the kid searching for the R186 signal box, the Hitchcockian twist being that it wasn't for him, but his model railway enthusiast dad, Colin 'Mr' Bennett. And then there was the impressively eyebrowed teenager (played by Simon Schatzberger, fact fans) groggily awakening in the aftermath of a massive party ('Who are you?'/'Who are you? And who's . . . she?') only to discover someone had scratched the coffee table, prompting him to thumb through Good Old Yellow Pages to locate a French polisher before his parents returned from holiday.

Meanwhile, David '*Science Workshop*' Hargreaves turned up as a bloke seemingly poised to heartlessly pension off faithful old gardener Ted, only to be leafing through the 'Pages to order a new ride-on lawnmower, while Kevin Webster's dad off of *Coronation Street* tracked down a racing bike ('I were right about that saddle!') for his teenage son.

RETROMETER: 8/10

B'Bye for Now!

And so some three hundred odd (a word we use advisedly) entries later, here we are at the end of the book. We're hoping we managed to provoke the occasional pang in you as you made your way to these back pages, particularly with some of the more insanely specific entries (did the 'Casual' font do it for you?).

But, as Denis Norden might muse, what of those items we didn't have room to include? We're talking about the likes of watching cricket scores change on *Ceefax*; Pierrot dolls; school trips to the local wildfowl centre; 01 811 8055; waiting for your TV set to warm up; The Barron Knights; those spidery octopus things that rolled down windows; *Chockablock* (and more specifically, 'Chock-a-bloke, checking out'); lacy fingerless gloves; Fine Fare supermarkets; the word 'cassingle'; *Ultra Quiz*; and – of course – TV newsreaders accidentally ducking their heads behind the little superimposed picture at the top right-hand corner of the screen.

How could we leave them out?

How indeed. Maybe Virgin Books will give us a future volume within which we'll be able to scratch those particular itches – although on sober reflection, maybe not. In the meantime you could do worse than get onto the World Wide Web and look in on our Internet home at www.tv.cream.org for more – lots more – of the sort of stuff that sets the retrometer's dials spinning crazily.

That's also the place where you can contact us with any of your own bygone pop-culture remembrances or queries – although, now this book's in the shops we should state for the record we no longer expect to be deluged by enquiries from people who want to know the name of 'the game show with the aspidistra in it'.

And on that note, it's time to put this tome away and face up to the present day. Come on! You've got to get back to concocting spurious reasons why you'd be better off staying home on Monday while everyone else trudges out to work or college or whatever. There you'll be, tucked up in bed with a bottle of clear, refreshing Dasani and a Kellogg's Pop Tart. But make sure you're downstairs and on the sofa come midday, because *Cash in the Attic* will nearly be ready to start and you don't want to miss that . . .